FIGHTING WORDS

FIGHTING WORDS

The War Correspondents of World War Two

Richard Collier

St. Martin's Press

New York

To
the Fourth
Estate

FIGHTING WORDS: THE WAR CORRESPONDENTS OF WORLD WAR TWO. Copyright © 1989 by Richard Collier. All rights reserved. Printed in the United States of America. No part of this book may be used or reproduced in any manner whatsoever without written permission except in the case of brief quotations embodied in critical articles or reviews. For information, address St. Martin's Press, 175 Fifth Avenue, New York, N.Y. 10010.

Library of Congress Cataloging-in-Publication Data

Collier, Richard.
        Fighting words / Richard Collier.
                p.   cm.
        "A Thomas Dunne book."
        ISBN 0-312-03828-3
            1. World War, 1939-1945.   2. World War, 1939-1945—Journalists.
        I. Title.
        D743.F534   1990
        940.53—dc20   89-24137
                                                                          CIP

First published in Great Britain by George Weidenfeld and Nicolson Limited under the title, *The Warcos: The War Correspondents of World War Two*.

First U.S. Edition

10 9 8 7 6 5 4 3 2 1

Contents

Alas, the days of newspaper enterprise in war are over. What can one do with a censor, a 48-hour delay and a 50-word limit on a wire?

– WINSTON S. CHURCHILL, 1900

[The war correspondent's] was a sporting life and a hard one. There was romance in it, and the hunter's instinct. It was the life of wandering men, true descendants of the troubadours . . .

– SIR PHILIP GIBBS, 1920

Somebody has to write up wars in the newspapers. It's an essential job of work, but not one of transcendental importance. And the men who do it aren't figures of romance. Just reporters in uniform.

– ALARIC JACOB, 1944

The jackal of our era is the war correspondent. His function is to describe in all its horror how men kill each other, in what manner they die and for what cause they imagine. His own and the censor's prejudice combine to see that this is done in glowing terms.

– CYRUS L. SULZBERGER, 1969

Illustrations

Acknowledgments

The men and women listed here helped me immeasurably in the writing of this book. Yet few of them realized it at the time; many were colleagues in the field during the two years that I was a war correspondent, more than forty years ago, when no such book was contemplated. Even so, I shall always be grateful for the insights they gave me into the ebb and flow of a warco's life. Both to them, and to those who helped me during my later researches, I extend my sincere thanks:

Stephen Barber (*News Chronicle*); Robert Barr (BBC); Eric Baume; Keith Beard (Chief Librarian, *Express Newspapers*); Edward Bishop (SEAC); Vincent Brome; Christopher Buckley (*Daily Telegraph*); Noel Buckley (*Reuters*); Hugo Charteris; John Clarke (*Globe News Agency*); Ian Coster (*Phoenix*); Reginald Cudlipp (*Phoenix*); Marquess of Donegall (*Sunday Dispatch*); Kenneth Downs (*INS*); Tom Driberg (*Daily Express*); George Edinger (*Reuters*); Robert T. Elson (*Time*); John G. Entwistle (Company Records Manager, *Reuters*); Jack Esten (*Illustrated*); Johan Fabricius (*The Times*/BBC); Sean Fielding; John Fisher (*Daily Mail*); Lael Wertenbaker Fletcher (*Life*); Ingrid Foan, with Wendy Boucher and Jill Nunn (*Copyprint*); O'Dowd Gallagher (*Daily Express*/*Globe News Agency*); Catherine Gathorne-Hardy; Martha Gellhorn (*Collier's*); Diana Gibson (*Daily Mail*); Clive Graham (*Daily Express*); Louis Hagen (*Phoenix*); Norman Hamilton; Arthur Helliwell (*Daily Herald*); Clare Hollingworth (*Daily Telegraph*/*Daily Express*); Len Jackson (SEAC); Robert Jackson (SEAC); George Johnson (Chief Librarian, *Mail*

Newspapers, PLC); Lindsay Kirk; Phillip Knightley; Steven Laird (*Time*); Adrian Lighter (Editorial Manager, *Daily Telegraph*); Robert Littell (*Reader's Digest*); Roger Machell; Anthony March (*Phoenix*); Hilde Marchant (*Daily Express*); Crosby Maynard (*Phoenix*); Joyce Meachem (Chief Librarian, *Daily Telegraph*); Ernie Miller (*Phoenix*); Alice Leone Moats (*Collier's*); Noel Monks (*Daily Mail*); Caroline Moorehead; Joe Alex Morris (UP); Ian Morrison (*The Times*); Leonard Mosley (Kemsley Newspapers); Carl and Shelley Mydans (*Life*); Ronnie Noble (*Universal News*); Rex North (*Sunday Pictorial*); Howard Norton (*Baltimore Sun*); Frank Owen (SEAC); Tom Pocock (*The Leader*); Hilary Raleigh (*Yorkshire Post*); Maggie Redfern (BBC); Quentin Reynolds (*Collier's*); Norman Riddiough (*Phoenix*); Erik Seidenfaden (*Politiken*); Richard Sharp (BBC); Harry Sions (*Yank*); Stafford Somerfield (*News of the World*); Martin Sommers (*Saturday Evening Post*); Graham Stanford (*Daily Mail*); Josepha Stuart (*Time*); Robert Strother (*Time*); Peter Stursberg (*Daily Herald*); J. Clyde Waddell (*Phoenix*); Ronald Walker (*News Chronicle*); William Walker (*Phoenix*); Sam White (*Evening Standard*); W. A. Wilcox (*Phoenix*); Colin P. Wilson (Chief Librarian, *The Times*).

My deepest debt is to those who worked closely alongside me throughout, most especially to Pat, my wife, who, besides keeping the home fires burning, typed the initial draft. Hildegard Anderson and Amy Forbert once again meticulously conducted most of my American research. The one sad note was the tragic death of Margaret Duff as the research was drawing to a close. For sixteen years she had tackled every book on which I worked with the same clear-sighted endeavour. Her contribution here, as always, was unsurpassed.

My agent, Michael Shaw, lent me his staunch support, as ever; my editor, Alex MacCormick, generously granted me an extension of time that made all the difference to the completed draft, as did the matchless editorial counsel of Allegra Huston and Amanda Harting. Elsie Couch and Ann Walker produced their usual impeccable typescript, and in the early stages I also owe a debt to Jill Beck and Enid Shaw. In addition I have to thank the staffs of the British Library, the London Library and the New York Public Library for their help and courtesy at all times.

I

Goodbye To Reason

(31 AUGUST 1939 – 13 MARCH 1940)

On Thursday, 31 August 1939, a silence that seemed to stretch to infinity hung like a hawk over all the nations of Western Europe. For the second time in twenty years the people awaited the advent of a world war.

None among them waited more eagerly than 735 men and women drafted in as an emergency measure to serve as war correspondents for the three great American news agencies: 500 for the United Press, 125 for William Randolph Hearst's International News Service, 110 for the Associated Press. Anticipating an iron clampdown of censorship if Great Britain and France declared war on Germany, they were currently cabling one million words a week, so jamming the telephone lines that messages to New York were arriving up to ten hours late. Within months their total number would swell to 10,000, for this was to be the most reported war – often boldly, at times hamstrung by military myopia, but almost always meticulously – in the history of the world.

To skilled observers of older crises it seemed that a state of war already existed in all but name. From the Park Lane Hotel on London's Piccadilly, the President of the United Press, Hugh Baillie, counted fully twenty-one barrage balloons, their steel cables designed to entrap enemy bombers, floating grey and motionless 4000 feet above Green Park. Stretching eastwards from the hotel towards Piccadilly Circus, Baillie noted that all the traffic stanchions had been painted yellow – warranted to turn pink at the first sign of a gas attack. Outside the American Express offices in the Haymarket, long lines of American refugees queuing for steamship space were taking no chances; those handsome Elizabeth Arden vanity bags sported by the women concealed the ugly new snout-shaped gas masks.

That night, in Piccadilly Circus itself, Oswald Garrison Villard, visiting correspondent for *The Nation*, groped his way among the 'little shaded crosses' that marked the traffic lights, marvelling that the Circus was 'as quiet as a hamlet in Kent'.

All through Thursday, as the temperature across Europe trembled in the high seventies, hopes for peace hung on one imponderable. Would Adolf Hitler, Führer and Chancellor of the German Third Reich, risk war to seize the Danzig Corridor (incorporated into Poland by the 1919 Treaty of Versailles) and thus provoke Poland's newfound allies, Britain and France?

Many new techniques now existed to relay the answer to that question. Since April, when Western Union had instituted cable photos, high-quality photographs of news stories could be sped across the Atlantic. Worldwide radio broadcasts had been pioneered in 1930. Long before television, the cameramen of five major newsreel companies were standing by. Yet despite these novelties, the war correspondents were essentially the archetypal breed of earlier conflicts – 'jocose and belligerent', in one estimate, 'sentimental and cynical, raffish at times, clannish and proud of their craft'. What counted, above all, was to be the man or woman on the spot.

At 5 am on 1 September, Hugh Carleton Greene, the lanky irrepressible Warsaw correspondent of the London *Daily Telegraph* – not yet as famous as his elder brother Graham – rang Pan Kulikowsky, head of the Press Department of the Polish Foreign Office on Pilsudski Square. 'It's begun,' were his opening words. 'Do you know that?'

Kulikowsky denied it categorically. 'Nonsense,' he expostulated, 'Negotiations are still going on. Absolute nonsense.'

But Greene could give him chapter and verse. From the industrial city of Katowice, 160 miles southwest, his number two, Clare Hollingworth, an energetic twenty-eight-year-old until recently a relief worker for the League of Nations Union, had reported 'a noise like doors banging' followed by 'planes riding high with the guns blowing smoke rings below them'. 'Oh, absolute nonsense,' Kulikowsky still maintained, but even as they spoke the cold high voice of the siren wavered and cried over the miles of Warsaw's rooftops. 'My God, you're right,' Kulikowsky said.

A war correspondent had been granted the dubious privilege of informing a government that they were at war.

Greene's next move was again altruistic: a phone call to awake his slumbering rival, Patrick Maitland of *The Times*. ('In time of war,' as their arch competitor, Sefton Delmer of the *Daily Express* put it, 'Fleet Street holds together.') Though still groggy from sleep Maitland now embarked on the first of twenty-five *appel éclair* or *blitz* calls to his paper at twenty dollars a time. The costs, he knew, would incur the wrath of 'editors sitting back at home in their padded chairs', yet his persistence paid off. Of all his calls and cables, only six got through.

From a strange gobbledygook of portmanteau words, known as 'cablese' and designed to save money on cable rates, *The Times* of Printing House Square, London, hard by Blackfriars Bridge, learned that war had begun:

PRESSE TIMES BLACKFRIARS LONDON EX MAITLAND
WARSAW FIRST HOSTILITIES BEGAN FIVETHIRTY
SMORNING GERMAN-POLISH FRONTIER CUMHEAVY
ETAPPARENTLY UNANNOUNCED BOMBARDMENT
KATOWICE AIRWISE.

At the heart of the combat zone two men had been alerted even earlier. In the lobby of a Danzig hotel, thirty-three-year-old Lynn Heinzerling of Associated Press heard a German officer place an urgent 3.15 am wakeup call for 1 September. Heinzerling was curious: in two months' residence he had hitherto known the German as a confirmed slugabed. As early as 2.15 am the United Press's George Kidd was equally vigilant; he aroused the British Acting Consul, F. M. Shepherd. His German colleagues, Kidd said, were already abroad on the streets and winding up their ciné-cameras.

At 4.47 am Heinzerling, who was standing by, heard the distant boom of firing. Doubling towards the River Vistula, a war correspondent whom history has forgotten was on time to record the war's first shots: the German warship, *Schleswig-Holstein*, her white sides blackened with gunpowder, was pumping shells into the Polish munitions depot at Westerplatte on Danzig Bay. (To the prescient editors of *Time* magazine, although only two nations were involved, this was already 'World War Two').

It was nonetheless war twentieth-century style: a merciless assault in which lives had been lost from 5 am did not become official until 10 am Berlin time. At that hour, the AP's Louis Lochner, the bespectacled fifty-two-year-old doyen of Berlin's correspondents, who had secured for himself and his colleagues exemption from the Nazi salute, was already stationed in the Kroll Opera House to hear Adolf Hitler's thirty-four-minute tirade against the Polish nation. It was humid that morning, noted young Wallace Deuel of the *Chicago Daily News* and as Hitler spoke the Opera House's dark red walls, maroon carpets and brightly lit eagle rampant on a silver backdrop seemed to breathe back stifling waves of heat.

Now the crucial question was: would Britain and France honour their pledge to Poland, a pledge that had only become a fully fledged treaty as recently as 25 August? All through the 1930s both countries had shown little more than a rare talent for appeasement, standing tamely on the sidelines as Germany swallowed up Austria and Czechoslovakia while Italy, their Fascist ally, ravaged first Abyssinia then Albania. During thirty-two months of the Spanish Civil War between General Francisco Franco's Nationalists and Communist-supported Republicans, Britain and France had again fought shy of entanglements. So could Poland depend on such past masters of equivocation as the British Premier Neville Chamberlain and France's Edouard Daladier?

In New York, as early as 6 am on Sunday, 3 September, it seemed that they could. Outside the fifteen-storey headquarters of Associated Press at Rockefeller Center the streets were grey and empty; only the straggling footfalls of worshippers en route to St Patrick's Cathedral broke total silence. But in the brilliantly lit fourth-floor newsroom, the tension was palpable; a bell had jangled on the pulsing cable machines and the men hovering round them watched the bulletin spelled out for 1400 US newspapers and countless foreign subscribers:

F-L-A-S-H
CHAMBERLAIN PROCLAIMED BRITAIN AT WAR WITH GERMANY

At this same hour in London – 11 am – British phlegm still reigned supreme. From Trafalgar Square, AP's Fred Vanderschmidt could report nothing more earthshaking than men dozing on benches in the sun and a small girl in a green coat arguing spiritedly with her nanny. At 11.15 am faces in Downing Street were strained towards the wide black door of Number Ten and ears were strained to hear the words of an old tired man, his voice edged with emotion: ' ... I have to tell you now that no such undertaking has been received and consequently this country is at war with Germany.'

At 11.32 am a siren wailed dolefully through the Sunday streets to be followed, eight minutes later, by the 'all clear': an unidentified French aircraft was ferrying two officers to join an Allied military mission. For the first time, but not the last, the British felt a total sense of let-down.

In those cities as yet untouched by war, other correspondents were remembering. Two at least had moments of total recall: episodes, temporarily forgotten, that now assumed a painful significance. At the Hangli Café, Budapest, the rendezvous for all the city's pressmen, Robert Parker, the gruff dark-haired AP chief, was recalling Warsaw in April of this same year, when Poland's fate already hung in the balance. One night Parker had dined at the fashionable Château de Sobanski, but as the evening wore on the Polish officers who had arrived with their best girls grew mean and drunken; champagne bottles became whizzing projectiles and furniture shattered. 'The priceless parquet floors looked as though a tractor had run over them,' Parker recorded in disgust; his parting memory was of the three-piece orchestra playing 'When All Is Finished' and paralytic Poles lying in heaps among the splintered furniture.

This was the week in which *The Times* of London summed up, 'Danzig is really not worth a war. It is essentially a question for skilful diplomacy.'

In the Mirror Room of Amsterdam's five-star Amstel Hotel overlooking the enamelled canal, Leonard Mosley, the dapper twenty-six-year-old correspondent of Kemsley Newspapers, lately arrived from Danzig with his wife Isa, listened in sceptical silence to Chamberlain's broadcast. What impinged on Mosley's mind more vividly was the memory of an encounter he had had earlier that summer; in the Bayreuth hotel suite of Dr Otto Dietrich, Press Chief for the Third Reich, he had met up for the first time with Adolf Hitler.

It had been the occasion for a classic curtain lecture. British journalists, the Führer grumbled, albeit good-humouredly, wrote entirely too much about the threat of war – 'There will be no war over Danzig.'

Mosley fought the British corner. 'We have had almost a year to get ready ... and this time we shall keep our pledge if Poland's rights are infringed.'

5

He remembered now Hitler's pale face 'growing ruddy with passion', the stubby forefinger with its bitten fingernail jabbing home his point. 'A year to prepare! What foolishness is that! ... For every man you have put in your army I have conscripted a thousand ... A year to prepare! You are worse off than you ever were! ... You will not go to war!'

As Chamberlain gave Hitler's prophecy the lie, twenty-five British and French correspondents in Warsaw were in a quandary. France, however reluctantly, had followed suit at 5 pm on the Sunday, so that now, although technically transformed from foreign correspondents to war correspondents, they were all, in event of a German victory, enemy aliens ripe for internment.

As a further complication Hitler's Foreign Minister, Joachim von Ribbentrop, had, on 23 August, signed a German–Soviet non-aggression pact in Moscow. When the time was ripe, Russian troops, too, would be moving into Polish territory, intent on a share-out.

Thus, only the Americans among the Warsaw-based newsmen were free to follow the German columns as they streamed across the Polish border, men like Otto Tolischus of the *New York Times*, whose sentiments were as impeccable as his logistics were faulty. 'Poland is being crushed like a soft-boiled egg,' he reported on 11 September, 'God has been with the bigger battalions,' although the 4000 German planes and seventy divisions he estimated in action in fact scaled down to 2000 planes and fifteen divisions. In a war where Polish cavalry squadrons were matched against German armour, no larger deployment was necessary.

But for the British the prudent course was to head away from the fighting, southeast towards neutral Romania – a course which their embassy had charted but kept strictly to themselves. It was Hugh Carleton Greene who by chance discovered their shameful exodus, one which the journalists were swift to emulate. By 7 September they had tracked the embassy down to Naleczow, a dreamy eighteenth-century spa eighty-five miles to the south. Oblivious to the diplomats' glares of hostility they set up their portable typewriters on the bandstand in the park and, in Maitland's words, 'banged merrily away'.

No man among them was then thinking in terms of ultimate retreat. 'People still believed that rivers were defensible,' Greene was to recall, and common to all was the belief that the Poles would hold fast all winter east of the river Vistula, among the Pripet

Marshes. No man embodied this tenet more sincerely than Patrick Maitland (now the Earl of Lauderdale). Despite the sweltering autumn heat he was even now accoutred in a fur-lined leather jacket, decked out with a pink blue-lettered brassard proclaiming THE TIMES LONDYN, high black jackboots and a fur hat. As Maitland saw it this was fitting equipment for *The Times* correspondent to report a winter stand.

Despite these illusions, it was retreat all the way. 'Things look grave. This is a private tip for you,' the British Ambassador, Sir Howard Kennard, warned Maitland on the quiet, and in a nightmare seventeen-hour journey diplomats and pressmen churned on a further 250 miles to the settlement of Stanislawow, 'like some dead city ruins turned up by an archaeologist's spade'. By any standards they were a motley cavalcade: Maitland and Greene in a battered old Standard flying the Union Jack, joined now by Ed Beattie, the moon-faced young UP man in Warsaw, the urbane Cedric Salter – 'Always a jump ahead of the Gestapo,' proclaimed the *Daily Mail* proudly – and the *Daily Express*'s Sefton Delmer, burly and ruthless, whose recent status as Lord Beaverbrook's man in Berlin had guaranteed him the luxury of both a butler and a chef.

All of them, whoever their employer, were by this time overwhelmingly conscious of one sin of omission. Behind them loomed two blank days in which no man had contrived to 'file' a story, as the despatch of a cable was known.

On the surface there was much to report. Clare Hollingworth, still touring the environs of Katowice in her reliable old Ford, functioned almost as a one-woman incident room: Hitler youth squads were being rounded up, twelve miles away a bonded cordite factory blazed against the skyline, at Trzelinia incendiary bombs had gutted much of the town. Yet not once did she see any evidence of a scorched earth policy. 'Many had relatives in Germany,' is her dry comment now.

For newcomers to the Fourth Estate this was a testing time for ingenuity and persistence. Twenty-seven-year-old Richard Mowrer, a tongue-tied, prematurely bald youngster, one of a family rooted in the *Chicago Daily News*, unexpectedly found himself caught up by a Russian spearhead and detained to await the arrival of a Commissar in the frontier town of Zaleszczyki. Two days later, with no Commissar in sight, Mowrer, once night had fallen, stripped down to bare essentials and waded across the River Dniester onto Romanian soil. Then, clad only in his sodden underwear, he headed for the nearest telegraph office – on the same mission as Ed Beattie, who had arrived from Warsaw with nothing but the clothes on his back.

'The luck of war's draw,' enthused *Time* magazine, bestowing their ultimate accolade, 'had given these youngsters the chance that every newsman covets, few achieve.'

Some, like Greene and Maitland, had above all coveted a respite; to Maitland, 'the peace of this neutral Balkan land was a balm.' Greene, who recalled walking through 'a tremendous triumphal arch saying "Welcome to Rumania"', carrying only a gas mask and a bottle of beer, felt the same. Yet no sooner had cables been filed from the cushioned santuary of the Athenée Palace Hotel, Bucharest, Romania's capital, than duty once again called. After sixteen days the Polish army was collapsing; it was mandatory to be there to record that collapse.

On Sunday, 17 September, Greene and Clare Hollingworth were 'some few miles on the Polish side of the frontier', when by degrees the 'great grey shapes' of Russian tanks became visible: the T–28s of Josef Stalin were moving in to claim their own. Like party guests who had long outstayed their welcome, both correspondents were suddenly of one mind: 'Well, it's time we were going, isn't it?'

And they went.

In the first weeks of October, thirty-two correspondents, quartered in the sombre French market town of Arras, were officially credited to an army that for twelve ludicrous days had not existed at all.

Although the bulk of Lord Gort's British Expeditionary Force had disembarked in Cherbourg on 10 September the War Office forbade all mention of this. Then on the evening of 12 September, the Ministry of Information, located in the six-storey Senate House of London University – 'Minny' to the newsmen – divulged a painful fact of life: Paris Radio had twice broadcast news of the landing. Accordingly, at 9 pm the War Office relented: the existence of the force could be acknowledged.

Then at 11.30 pm, when the main editions of Fleet Street's papers were already in trains en route to Scotland and the provinces, the War Office abruptly backtracked. The landing of the BEF was still top secret. Newspaper trains already under way must be halted. Posses of police hastened to Paddington, Euston and King's Cross stations to haul bales of later editions from railway vans. Long after midnight, phones all over London rang urgently as editors and proprietors, roused from their beds, lobbied their favourite Cabinet Ministers. At last, at 2.30 am on 13 September, the War Office accepted defeat. The landing – and existence – of the BEF was now official.

But not its size – which ultimately totalled 390,000 men – or indeed its equipment. A report from the *Daily Express* man in Paris, Geoffrey Cox, that 'heavy-tyred camouflaged guns and pontoons set the French people cheering madly' was censored out of hand. In vain, Cox's editor, the sometimes genial, most often irascible Arthur Christiansen, pointed out that any self-respecting spy could tally up formations that moved to the front in trucks marked '40 men, 8 horses'.

At first, hopes among the war correspondents on the spot – known always to the services as 'the warcos' – had run high. From Fleet Street, the crooked spine in east central London which was synonymous with journalism, they had trekked to Moss Bros or Austin Reed, to be outfitted as their forebears of World War One had been, in officers' uniforms complete with peaked caps, polished Sam Browne belts and green felt badges with the gold letter 'C' that denoted correspondent. But once in France, their role was as ambiguous as the war itself. If taken as POWs, the Geneva Convention ranked them as captains, though as non-combatants they were forbidden to carry arms. They rated no salutes from other ranks, but must acknowledge them when given. Moreover, they were geared for action – on a front where the entire war emerged as a gigantic stalemate.

In the shabby third-rate Hôtel du Commerce that became their press camp, long remembered for its execrable food and broken-down central heating, the warcos of necessity were forced back to 'think pieces' – speculation rather than 'hard news' – or to 'colour stories', which the Americans called 'situationers', which filled in the background. In his office on London's Bouverie Street the UP President, Hugh Baillie, once read with choleric disbelief an idyllic account of a batman on an autumn evening, washing his officer's socks. A go-go Nebraskan like the AP's William McGaffin was reduced to chronicling the life of an archetypal French housewife, Madame Jean Q. Frenchman. 'She knits for the soldiers ... but Madame has changed her pre-war favourite colours of blue and pink for khaki and beige.'

Some correspondents came, saw and as swiftly departed. Men like O'Dowd Gallagher of the *Daily Express*, a cynical South African

9

who had covered the Sino-Japanese War of 1937 with a money-belt stuffed with gold sovereigns and travelled by taxi to the Chinese and Japanese lines outside Shanghai, saw little future on a front where Tommies were digging trenches on the World War One pattern, six feet deep by four feet six inches wide. Others were longer in evidence, notably Harold 'Kim' Philby of *The Times*, who always flaunted the Red Cross of Military Merit, awarded him by Franco during the Spanish Civil War, to denote his right-wing sympathies. For reasons perhaps better known to the Kremlin than to Printing House Square, Philby was a fixture to the end; he had been a Soviet agent since 1934.

In essence, the damp fields round Arras, boxed in by low stone walls, were a fogbound facsimile of the England that the warcos had left behind, the England of the Phoney War, the Boer War, the Sitzkrieg. This was a world where Ministry of Information polltakers noted, though not for publication, that four million Britons wanted peace at any price, a world beset by twenty-five degrees of frost, where burst pipes, a chronic coal shortage and a blackout that had plunged the United Kingdom into the pitch darkness of the seventeenth century remained the contentious issues.

On the Western Front, to the very end, the canons of censorship remained a mystery. Even a McGaffin dispatch on a French housewife's knitting habits had to be submitted in quadruplicate to Gort's HQ, to French GHQ, to the French and British Ministries of Information – and this process might take forty-eight hours. No warco could move a step unless accompanied by a Conducting Officer – a tradition from World War One. Anonymity was a way of life. The RAF, one staff officer told the warcos, worked as a team, and there were no individuals; it would thus be wrong to glorify any one pilot or any one dogfight.

It was a briefing which prompted Walter Duranty, the spry wooden-legged little correspondent of the *New York Times*, to enquire innocently, 'But, sir, supposing the leader of a Hurricane squadron gets hit and has to bail out. Does the whole squadron bail out, too?'

Few warcos were more frustrated by the dead hand of officialdom than Richard Frederick Dimbleby of the British Broadcasting Corporation, which in this year was celebrating its thirteenth birthday. A fresh-faced assertive twenty-six-year-old, whose bustling manner earned him the nickname 'Bumblebee', Dimbleby felt with some justification that in Arras he *was* the BBC: the civilized

uncontroversial voice of objectivity which, according to taste, gratified or enraged its nine million-plus listeners.

Yet ironically Dimbleby and all that he stood for was anathema
to many among the BBC's staid hierarchy. To them he was the man
who, quietly, persistently – and unforgivably – had 'humanized' the
news with on-the-spot interviews, who had pioneered the first
mobile recording van, a converted laundry pantechnicon, and who
one year earlier had lobbied successfully for the BBC's first mobile
recording car. Yet already, despite his youth and his small-town
background – his family owned the local *Richmond and Twickenham
Times* – Dimbleby's sights were set on starrier horizons. A Rolls
Royce, to begin with, to share with his wife of two years, Dilys,
then thoroughbred horses and even, in the not too distant future,
a yacht.

But even the august BBC cut little ice with a High Command
obsessed with security to the point of paranoia. On one occasion,
after wangling a temporary attachment to the French Army,
Dimbleby and his recording team had driven 300 miles from Arras
to the Saar frontier, over roads so icy that their recording car seven
times skidded into a ditch. In Strasbourg, using the near-irresistible
Dimbleby charm, he had inveigled the French commander to guide
him to the Kehel Bridge, which divided the French from the
Germans. Moving out from behind the sandbags he had recorded a
commentary within sight of the German lines – overlooked stolidly
by a German officer at the bridge's far end. But all attempts to
localize the broadcast met with failure.

'You cannot say where we are,' the French censor insisted.

Dimbleby was blandly reassuring: 'I want only to say that we
are in France.'

'I am sorry, Monsieur, it is forbidden.'

'But everyone knows we are in France and everyone knows that
the French army is in France.' Again the censor was adamant. 'I am
sorry, it is forbidden.'

'For God's sake,' Dimbleby raged, 'what shall I say then? That
we are in the front line in the middle of Switzerland!'

Despite his normally sanguine nature Dimbleby was worried.
His broadcasts, brimming with optimism, owed nothing to truth;
among the French and British troops, who saw no point in this war,
morale was at lowest ebb and he knew it. If the German war machine
ground into motion, what was to stop them?

'Am I mad,' Dimbleby asked his sound recordist, David

Howarth, 'or are we going to witness the biggest shambles in history?'

In Paris, 200 miles from the Western Front, the correspondents assembled to cover the war knew the same unease as Richard Dimbleby. Few of them as yet had visited the trenches, but there was no need. The mood of the capital itself mirrored the mood of France.

'The French nation,' one compatriot had written, 'has gone to war looking over its shoulder, its eyes searching for peace.' The phrase of the day, decided Clare Boothe, newly arrived on behalf of her husband Henry Luce's *Life* magazine was '*Il faut en finir*' ('We've got to stop it'), a resolute motto embroidered on chiffon handkerchiefs or inscribed on gold charm bracelets, but the reality was a staggering unconcern. In this *drôle de guerre* (comic war) bored boulevardiers checked their watches by the air-raid sirens, tested punctually each Thursday at noon. The most chic gift of the day, reflected Alexander Werth, the moody Russian-born representative of the *Manchester Guardian*, reduced all war to mockery – terracotta Aberdeen terriers lifting their legs over terracotta copies of Adolf Hitler's *Mein Kampf*.

The root cause of this complacency was the 400-mile-long Maginot Line, whose sheer statistics in the twelve years of its construction had come to rival the Great Wall of China. Curving from the Alps to the Belgian frontier at Sedan, the Line, named after its creator, former War Minister André Maginot, was a veritable honeycomb of fortresses and casemates, 'like row upon row of sunken earthbound battleships', some of it housing formidable 75-mm guns, with ramparts manned by 1.8 million soldiers.

'You can't get out of the concrete,' the aging French Commander-in-Chief, General Maurice Gustave Gamelin, assured A. J. (Abbott Joseph) Liebling, in an exclusive interview for the *New Yorker*. 'There isn't enough heavy artillery in the world to get out of the concrete.' Liebling, although no military expert, still puzzled as to why the southern end of the Line, the Ardennes Forest, apparently considered 'equal to the best fortifications' remained undefended. Clare Boothe, likewise no strategist, came to the same conclusion after just one visit to the Line. 'I knew all of a sudden ... that the Maginot would one day break their hearts as it had almost bankrupted their exchequer.'

In truth, both correspondents were lucky. Few among their

number ever crossed Gamelin's office threshold at the École Militaire on the Place Maréchal-Joffre. Fewer still had seen the Maginot Line. 'You are going to describe only anonymous landscapes,' Gamelin had cautioned a group of warcos, among them Sefton Delmer, in October, but only the truly enterprising saw any landscape beyond the *grands boulevards*. It was the neutrals attached to the German camp who gained a truer yet more despondent perspective. The AP's Louis Lochner, touring the German side of the Line, glimpsed little beyond *poilus* peacefully fishing or openly bartering scrumped apples for German ham. On the Luxembourg frontier at Schengen, the Swedish warco Sven Auren painted an even more pastoral picture. 'Everyone has his lunch round here at twelve o'clock,' the Swedish consul explained, deftly unpacking a picnic basket. 'The Germans settle down for a rest and so do the French. It seems to be another of their secret agreements.'

To the devious Monsieur Pierre Comert, Chief of the Ministry of Information's Foreign Press Section, even random titbits such as Auren's would have been *absolument defendu*. At the Ministry's headquarters, the Hôtel Continental on the Rue Castiglione, two myths remained sacrosanct until the summer of 1940: the impregnability of the Maginot Line, and the steely determination of its defenders. Even French newspapers like *Gringoire* were not immune if they failed to radiate optimism; often whole columns were missing from its letterpress or replaced by the sinister emblem of a pair of scissors. Correspondents' dispatches were returned 'looking like a child's attempt to cut out a paper pattern'. As a result, Clare Boothe never submitted one line of copy during a three-month stay.

It took the guile of a warco like Quentin Reynolds to cut M. Comert down to size.

Not that Reynolds, like so many of his colleagues – Sefton Delmer, O'Dowd Gallagher – was a battlefield veteran. The Spanish Civil War, the Abyssinian conflict – these had passed him by. But at thirty-eight, older than most of his tribe, Reynolds's background, which he himself described as 'lace curtain Irish', had stood him in good stead. The son of a Brooklyn high school principal, one of a family seven strong, his childhood had been one long doorstep wrangle over unpaid bills. But this had only spurred him on to win his own place in the sun: the acclaimed sportswriter on the *Brooklyn Evening World* had in time become the Berlin representative of William Randolph Hearst's INS. Now, as a $12,000-a-year feature writer for *Collier's* magazine, the chunkily built (177 lbs.) red-haired

Reynolds had been assigned to Paris and was determined to visit the front.

It was this formidable mix of Irish blarney, Brooklyn savvy and repertorial low cunning – an undeniable armoury even for a war correspondent – that confronted Pierre Comert at the Hôtel Continental. Accompanying Reynolds were his old friends Kenneth Downs, quiet and implacable, the INS man in Paris, and Robert Cooper of the London *Times*, a pre-war lawn tennis correspondent, initially out of his depth in wartime France.

Comert was an old hand at what the French call *l'impressement*, translated by one embittered warco as Bullshit Baffles Brains. Before a visit to the front could be considered Reynolds must first submit a recommendation from the American ambassador, William Bullitt, together with six portrait photographs. He must also acquire a uniform. His application would in due time be passed to the *Deuxième Bureau*, who controlled internal security. If they approved it would be passed to the War Office. It was all, Reynolds would understand, a matter of channels.

Days later, with the formalities completed, Reynolds still suspected that those channels were clogged beyond redemption. In the Ritz bar on the Palace Vendôme – a cushier billet than his colleagues in Arras enjoyed – he first mulled it over with Downs and Cooper then, on an inspiration, called for a Cableform and blocked out a message. Both men, when they read the result, chuckled wryly. 'What the hell,' Downs said, 'all you can do is try it on him.'

Back at the Continental Reynolds was the picture of humility. He was cabling President Franklin D. Roosevelt to speed his accreditation with Daladier's successor, Premier Paul Reynaud. As a courtesy he wanted Comert to approve the cable.

The message was a masterpiece of mendacity:

DEAR UNCLE FRANKLIN, AM HAVING DIFFICULTY
GETTING ACCREDITED TO FRENCH ARMY, THIS IS
IMPORTANT. WOULD YOU PHONE OR CABLE PREMIER
REYNAUD AND ASK HIM TO HURRY THINGS UP? IT WAS
GRAND OF YOU TO PHONE ME LAST NIGHT. PLEASE GIVE
MY LOVE TO AUNT ELEANOR. QUENT.

'You,' Comert breathed finally with unfeigned awe, 'are a nephew of the President?' Reynolds said nothing, merely smiled enigmatically. 'Ah, but of course,' Comert reasoned. 'Quentin Reynolds, Quentin Roosevelt. A family name, *sans doute*.'

Reynolds was all modesty. He never talked about it. He would prefer that it was not mentioned. Now Comert too was humble. He himself would telephone for the accreditation.

In that case, Reynolds ventured, the cable was hardly necessary, but Comert would have none of it. With his imprimatur, it would reach the White House within hours – exactly what Reynolds feared most.

For twenty-four hours thereafter Reynolds was quaking at his own temerity. Would he receive a drumhead summons to Ambassador Bullitt? Would FBI agents descend precipitately on the Ritz? But although he checked that the cable had been sent the presidential reaction was precisely nil. Instead, the precious pink card permitting him to 'circulate in the zone of the French armies' was soon followed by a five-day travel pass.

Quentin Reynolds was now fully equipped to penetrate the mysteries of the French High Command.

Far to the north, like a muffled drumbeat offstage, the front-line action that Reynolds and Dimbleby craved was suddenly a painful reality. On Saturday, 30 November, Russian bombs were showering onto Finnish soil and Helsinki, Finland's capital, was all at once the dateline for every enterprising war correspondent.

Few of them had grasped the complexities of the quarrel, but few had bothered; such analysis could safely be handled by military experts like Britain's Captain Basil Liddell Hart or the *New York Times's* Hanson W. Baldwin. Here, for the first time since World War One, was a David versus Goliath situation, with Finland standing in for 'Brave Little Belgium'; the Finns, fighting against odds of fifty to one, were battling with a determination that the Poles had somehow never mustered. Before the war was a week old, 100 correspondents had flooded in to cover it.

In terms of power-politics, the assault was motivated by a Russian desire to seal off all access to the Gulf of Finland. What Josef Stalin and his Foreign Minister, Vyacheslav Molotov, had sought from the Finns since mid-October was a catalogue of major concessions: a thirty-year lease of the port of Hanko, on the Gulf of Finland, the cession of all islands in the gulf, the shifting of the Russo-Finnish border on the Karelian Isthmus, seventy miles away from the nearest Russian city, Leningrad. Although Stalin had only concluded his non-aggression pact with Germany two months earlier he explained ruefully, 'In this world anything can change.'

The reply of Juho Kusti Paasikivi, the leader of the Finnish delegation to Moscow, spoke for all those small nations still clinging doggedly to neutrality: 'We wish to remain at peace and outside all conflicts.' They were words that fell on deaf ears; as December dawned, the 'Winter War' began.

Five days after the first bombing, Martha Gellhorn arrived in Helsinki, to assume the yellow armband of all correspondents accredited to the Finnish High Command. Outside the Hotel Kämp, on the Pohjois Esplanade, she found herself moving through 'a frozen city inhabited by sleepwalkers shuffling among broken glass', a city where the freezing night began each day at 4 pm, yet a night that was still alive with silent people, carrying knapsacks or light suitcases, 'walking to the forest for safety'.

Not surprisingly, in this mortal century, war and Martha Gellhorn were old familiars. As far back as March 1937 she had arrived in Madrid to cover the Civil War for *Collier's* magazine, a tall twenty-eight-year-old blonde with shoulder-length hair and intense blue eyes, already known as a gifted short-story writer, who walked with a movie star's sway. And despite her Bryn Mawr College background, her Bryn Mawr accent – 'veddy Briddish,' some US colleagues scoffed – Martha Gellhorn was all war correspondent. Martha, as her lover of two years standing, Ernest Hemingway, would testify, treasured sleep, twelve hours a day whenever possible, yet in Finland, given four brief hours of daylight, she arose uncomplainingly at 6 am. Martha craved warmth as a kitten seeks a fireside; in Finland, moving in what her friend Virginia Cowles called 'the best Arctic circles', she endured a climate where the cold was rarely less than forty degrees below zero. Martha revelled in luxury, yet to report the war in Finland she had travelled more than 4000 miles, exchanging the solid comforts of Suite 206, Sun Valley Lodge, Sun Valley, Idaho, where she and Hemingway 'lived in contented sin', for the dubious nineteenth-century charms of the Hotel Kämp.

This was the unrivalled gift of the ace war correspondents, who could rise above all pride and prejudice, like a great actor submerging himself in a part, to achieve the ultimate fulfilment: the hazardous journey undertaken, the telling details noted under fire, the 'scoop' as exclusive stories were fondly known, secured.

From the first Martha Gellhorn and all her rivals were agreed on one thing: if there was justice in a dark world the Finns deserved to prevail. Even among civilians, subjected to air raids from as low as 3000 feet, discipline was rigid, impeccable; days after a bombing, recorded Geoffrey Cox, who had moved on from France for the *Daily Express*, the contents of smashed shop windows were still intact. His colleague Hilde Marchant, covering the war from the woman's angle, agreed; the Finns in temperament were 'very like the Highland Scots – quiet, humourless, hard ... I never once saw a Finnish woman or child in hysterics.' The closest approach to rancour was voiced to Martha Gellhorn by a plump nine-year-old boy on a Helsinki side street. 'Little by little,' he confided, as he watched the Russian bombers hovering overhead, 'I'm getting really angry.'

Others, like Leland Stowe of the *Chicago Daily News*, praised the Finns for what was termed their *sisu* (guts), a quality which took many forms. Infighting with Russian tanks in the strange false twilight of the forests, armed only with the wryly christened Molotov cocktails – bottles packed with potassium chloride, coal oil and sulphuric acid – took *sisu*. Above all, Stowe admitted, the *Lottas*, 100,000 women auxiliaries who served in the front line as nurses, fire wardens and cooks; some, spotting for Russian planes, lay for hours on top of water towers then, too numb with cold to climb to safety, crashed to their deaths. It took *sisu* for a Finnish bride to put a torch to her new home, with its hope chest and hand-embroidered linen, rather than yield it to the Russians.

To Webb Miller, the hard-drinking chief of the United Press in Europe, the toast that Finnish fighter pilots drank each time they boarded their Fokker single-seaters somehow embodied the whole suicidal stand in Finland and Poland besides: '*Tolkku Pois*' ('Goodbye to reason').

From justly crediting the Finns with courage it was but a step to credit them with victories-that-never-were. In Finland, claimed their C-in-C, Field Marshal Carl Gustav Mannerheim, 'A Thermopylae is fought out each day,' a boast which some warcos took at its face value. On the Lake Kianta front, the AP's Thomas Hawkins reported that the Finns had 'destroyed two of ... Josef Stalin's crack divisions and a third still faces annihilation ... vast quantities of supplies have fallen to the Finns'. Similarly the euphoric dispatches of the *New York Times*'s Harold Denny made euphoric headlines on the streets of Manhattan: FINNS VICTORS ON CENTRAL FRONT ... GAINS ON SOVIET SOIL REPORTED BY FINNS ... 3000 RUSSIANS DIE.

From Rovienemi, a mile and a half from the Arctic Circle, Virginia Cowles, the svelte Bostonian, filed a typical dispatch for the

London *Sunday Times* on a December sortie against the Russian 44th Division. Although accurate in itself, it was a report suggesting a decimation rather than a local victory. 'For four miles the roads and forests were strewn with the bodies of men and horses; with wrecked tanks, field kitchens, trucks, gun-carriages, maps, books and articles of clothing. The corpses were frozen as hard as petrified wood and the colour of the skin was mahogany.'

One survivor, Carl Mydans, then a twenty-eight-year-old *Time–Life* photographer, blames the Finns unreservedly. 'They were intent on keeping their losses secret even from their friends,' he says now. 'Even on a field of victory ... I was forbidden to photograph the Finnish dead.' Without equivocation, Mydans still labels the Finnish censorship, conducted by university professors behind barred doors at the Hotel Kämp, 'the most destructive war censorship I ever encountered'. Yet it was a censorship, he admits, in which many warcos shared an unwitting complicity.

For although the Finns were to astonish the world for 105 days, their army, pitting only nine divisions against a Red Army of more than a million men, lacked almost everything that a modern army needed. They had not one anti-tank gun and little more than 2000 Suomi machine pistols. To defend their main cities, Helsinki and Viipuri, from attack, they had barely 100 anti-aircraft guns. The much-vaunted Mannerheim Line, covering only eighty-eight miles, was scarcely more than an ordinary trench system dug by volunteers in the summer of 1939. At intervals concrete nests, two-thirds of them obsolete, stood in as tank barriers.

Although few among the first Russian troops, homespun villagers from Turkestan, were competent skiers and all lacked white camouflage clothing and frostproof equipment, these deficiencies were swiftly remedied once the strength of Finnish opposition became plain.

No such misconceptions marred the battlefield dispatches of Martha Gellhorn. 'Her pieces are always about people,' Ernest Hemingway explained at the time. 'The things that happened to her people really happened, and you feel as though it were you and you were there.' Thus the people that Martha pictured inhabited a world where it was almost always night: a world of blued headlamps and white-painted staff cars driven by wraiths in white overalls.

It was 'a night war in snow and ice with unending forest hiding the armies ... too fantastic to be true,' at least three hours' drive from Viipuri. It was a war where cars 'spun like coins' on the unmarked glassy roads, where one skid on a mined bridge spelt obliteration and 'gunflashes from the Finnish batteries burned like summer lightning against the sky.'

'It is safe to say,' Martha Gellhorn concluded carefully, 'that the Finns have a trained army, helped by knowledge of the terrain ... the army has that sound and comforting gaiety of good troops ... the determination of those who fight on their own soil.'

The flight lieutenant of an air regiment, she thought, crystallized the mood when he said: 'They will not get us as a present.'

The world was hungry for such news. Day by day, from Stockholm to Tokyo, an avid readership followed the fortunes of the Finns, although much as they would have done a hotly contested tennis doubles – a vicarious contest in a world selfish for peace. The enterprising Columbia Broadcasting System (CBS) through its correspondent, William L. White, had even brought the war into every American home: by telephone from the Mannerheim Line to Helsinki, thence by submarine cable under the Baltic to Stockholm, finally by Swedish landline and under-water transmission across Germany to the shortwave transmitter at Geneva. The 100 war correspondents at the Hotel Kämp still commanded their public.

It was a phenomenon they discussed nightly in the big first-floor Press Room, with its green baize tables and heavy blackout curtains, where no drinks, in the Puritan Finnish tradition, were ever served after 10 pm: a topic to return to time and again, after shrugging off their sheepskin jackets and stamping the snow from the boots, in the brief hour before the official communiqué. For despite the millions of curious adherents, the world was dragging its feet. The US Secretary of State, Cordell Hull, was understandably opposed to any aid to Finland. This was a year when President Franklin Roosevelt sought re-election for an unprecedented third term, in a neutral United States bitterly opposed to foreign entanglements. Any hints of Finnish aid would spark isolationist charges of projected aid to Britain and France. The American Youth Congress had staged a demonstration to this effect in Washington DC. A mooted Anglo-French expeditionary force could only reach Finland through Norway and Sweden, and both nations, obstinately neutral, were refusing right of way.

Plainly no help would be coming in time from any foreign power, but then no helping hand had been extended to the beleaguered Republicans in Spain, to the Emperor Haile Selassie in

Abyssinia, or to the hard-pressed Poles. The warcos were seeing no more than an old story played out against an unfamiliar backdrop.

Thus even the youngest among them were veterans in spirit, a new generation fast preparing to learn from the old. Three, against all precedent, were women: Martha Gellhorn herself, Virginia Cowles and Hilde Marchant who, mindful of the bombing of Madrid, had come with a store of chewing gum to stop her teeth chattering. (In World War One, only one woman, Peggy Hull, had ever been accredited to the American Expeditionary Force.) The acknowledged dean of this press corps was the UP's Webb Miller, a burnt-out case at forty-nine, taciturn, pallid, unsmiling, a smalltown boy from Pokagon, Michigan, with his classic profile and pencil-line moustache, a closet vegetarian still haunted by the wild pigs savaging the dead in the Spanish Civil War. All had listened respectfully when Miller pronounced on both the Finns – 'The damnedest fighters I've ever seen' – and the Maginot Line – 'The Germans will go through that line like crap through a little tin horn' – unaware that these were his last pronouncements. On 8 May, conceivably as far gone in drink as always, he was to topple to his death on the railway track at Clapham Junction, South London.

Like all those assembled here at the Kämp, Miller had vainly pursued a dream: the war correspondent as intrepid individualist, long on courage and short on introspection, a man upholding the traditions of William Howard Russell, a doughty Irishman and the first of the breed, who from 1854 on had covered the war in the Crimea, the Indian Mutiny and the American Civil War. Russell's had been the time-honoured way of Winston Churchill, who in the Boer War, in direct contravention of War Office orders, had served both as subaltern and correspondent for the *Morning Post*. In his wake had trodden Richard Harding Davis, the clean-cut high-minded all-American boy from Philadelphia, chronicler of every conflict from the Spanish-American War to the rape of Belgium, who claimed to say his prayers every night and to write to his mother every day. Such shining examples, along with hazy adolescent memories of Tennyson's *Charge of the Light Brigade* and Kipling's *Barrack Room Ballads*, had forged the war correspondent of 1939.

There was another side to this coin: the eternal and implacable enmity of the armies. If the Finnish High Command hated them, as suspect spies and troublemakers, the High Commands in all ages and on all fields of war had hated them. Outraged that William Howard Russell told the truth as he saw it, the Crimean C-in-C,

Lord Raglan, ostracized him, and junior officers slashed down his tent. In the American Civil War the Commander of the Tennessee Army, General William Tecumseh Sherman, would have no truck with them. In World War One the Secretary of War, Field Marshal Lord Kitchener, who had encountered them in the Sudan in 1897, decreed that 'the drunken swabs' should be arrested if they dared set foot in the field.

It was the new C-in-C from 1915, the then General Sir Douglas Haig, who had first struggled to come to terms with this relatively new phenomenon. 'I think I understand fairly well what you gentlemen want,' he essayed on his first meeting with them. 'You want to get hold of little stories of heroism, and so forth, and to write them up in a bright way to make good reading for Mary Ann in the kitchen, and the man in the street.'

At least it had been an attempt to pave the way to a better understanding.

That the Finns would collapse as surely as the Poles had always been a foregone conclusion. To a correspondent like the urbane Edward Ward (later Lord Bangor), then aside from Dimbleby the sole BBC man in the field, the only question was when, and under what circumstances.

The answer, unexpectedly, came not in Helsinki but in Stockholm. On 11 March, the day the Finns admitted that peace discussions were being held in Moscow with Sweden standing in as mediator, Ward arrived in the Swedish capital along with Virginia Cowles. By chance, both warcos sat in on post-dinner drinks at the Grand Hotel with the Reuters correspondent, Gordon Young. Young's host was the Finnish chargé d'affaires, Eljas Erkko.

Erkko, while lavish with the champagne, was sparing with information, although one gesture of goodwill was manifest. If Ward found difficulty in securing return plane seats to Helsinki, Erkko would fix them given an hour's notice.

Next day, taking Erkko at his word, Ward rang him at around 3.30 pm to check on reservations. On an impulse, he first asked, 'Is it true that an agreement has been reached in Moscow?' To his astonishment Erkko replied that it was. 'I hung up the receiver,' Ward recounted later, 'realizing that I had a world scoop in my pocket.'

As, indeed, he had. At 5 pm, through the medium of Press Wireless, Amsterdam, a Swiss-based organization which arranged priority hookups for correspondents, Ward had filed his message. One hour later it was the main feature of the BBC's 6 pm news bulletin – six hours before the Finn-in-the-street received any intimation. At 7 pm, as Ward and Virginia Cowles arrived for the Helsinki-bound plane at Stockholm-Bromma, a Finnish colonel, unaware of Ward's identity, accosted him angrily, 'Did you hear the report the BBC is putting out? Peace! We'll make peace when the Russians withdraw every last soldier from Finland.'

But it was peace for which the Finns had settled – a harsh peace which involved the cession of 25,000 square miles of land, including all the islands in the Gulf, the ports of Viipuri and Hanko and most of the Karelian Isthmus.

These were the terms which the Foreign Minister, Väinö Tanner, announced to the people at noon the next day, as the blue and white flags slipped slowly to half-mast all over the city. In the corridors of the Kämp the maids were weeping openly, but the Press Room was deserted now as the warcos hastily packed their bags, awaiting the next spin of the wheel.

The slate which had always announced the release time of communiqués had been wiped clean, but above it someone had tacked a slip of paper:

> BOMBING NEWS WILL BE GIVEN OUT
> AT TWENTY-THREE O'CLOCK.

It was the American political columnist, Dorothy Thompson, who summed up the lesson that the warcos were fast learning: 'The position of small nations in the world as it is at present is clarified. They have no position.'

II

No Defence, No Madrid, No Warsaw

(14 MARCH–17 JUNE 1940)

On New Year's Eve 1939, William L. Shirer, for three years the CBS man in Germany, noted a new phenomenon. On the two miles of the blacked-out Kurfürstendamm, Berlin's answer to Piccadilly or Fifth Avenue, he met up with more drunks than at any time in living memory – a stumbling cavalcade mainly intent on the phosphorescent-heart lapel brooches that picked out the street-walkers. But neither Shirer nor any of the 100 neutral correspondents left in Berlin were much surprised. After twenty years in the economic wringer, including seven of building the world's most stream-lined military machine, few civilians had reaped much personal benefit from Adolf Hitler's declaration of war.

The 70 million Germans outside the armed forces enjoyed red meat no more than twice a week. Butter was less in evidence than whale-oil margarine, with its distinctive greenish tinge. Because of fuel shortages they enjoyed hot water only at weekends, with one cake of rationed soap per month, and subsisted on a lacto-vegetarian diet of stuffed cabbage or boiled potatoes with onion sauce. To rule out hoarding, shopkeepers opened up canned goods, even sardines, in the customers' presence. Dining out was a nightmare of scissor-wielding waiters snipping blue rectangles from the meat card, purple from the fruit. At times loudspeakers barked peremptorily, '*Achtung!* This is the kitchen speaking. There is no more veal.'

On 9 October, spurred on by rumours that Britain had agreed to talk peace terms, hundreds of Berliners had flocked to Hitler's Chancellory, chanting '*Wir wollen unseren Führer*'. ('We want our leader'). But UP's Howard K. Smith reported this only circumspectly: Berlin civilians were expected to be as overtly martial as Maginot Line defenders. (In fact Britain had rejected the terms, and Hitler had fumed, 'They will be ready to talk only after a beating'.) Even so, Dr Josef Goebbels, the Führer's clubfooted Minister for Propaganda and Enlightenment, saw fit to confide in Lothrop Stoddard, of the North American Newspaper Alliance (NANA): 'The average German feels [about the war] like a man with a chronic toothache – the sooner it is out the better.'

Not that the correspondents who attended the 5 pm daily conference at the Propaganda Ministry on Wilhelmstrasse endured the privations of the average Berliner. In 1939, and for much of 1940, they were a prized and pampered breed: their presence round the long table draped with red felt, under gaudy crystal chandeliers, brought its undoubted rewards. After the faintly smiling Goebbels and his satraps had trotted out their daily parade of U-boat aces, Luftwaffe heroes and 'victims' of Polish persecution, none of the newsmen need go hungry; all of them were classified as 'heavy labourers' with double rations of meat, bread and butter. Two rival dining clubs vied to entertain them with real beefsteaks and real coffee: Goebbels's Ausland Club on Leipsigerplatz and Foreign Minister Joachim von Ribbentrop's Ausland Press Club off the Kurfürstendamm. Were Berliners forbidden to listen to the propaganda of the BBC? Not so Shirer and his colleagues; by courtesy of the RRG (the German state broadcasting company) radio sets were placed at their disposal.

This caring attitude had one end in view: a favourable press. Just as the British wooed neutral correspondents, arranging interviews with any Cabinet Minister they cared to name, Germany equally was wooing the United States: nothing prejudicial to Hitler's regime must ever reach their front pages. Millions of Americans still shared the isolationist view of their idol, the aviator Colonel Charles A. Lindbergh, of the America First Committee: 'The wars in Europe are not wars in which our civilization is defending itself against some Asiatic intruder.' This was thinking that Goebbels's Ministry both applauded and publicized.

Increasingly, warcos like Shirer found that there were strings attached. In Nazi Germany, as in Fascist Italy and Communist Russia, 'responsibility censorship' prevailed; a correspondent was free to phone or cable out a story but if it proved 'dangerous or antagonistic' he was in deep trouble. One recent casualty was twenty-seven-year-old Seymour Beach Conger of the *New York Herald Tribune*, who had charged that Hamburg U-boat crews refused to leave port unless they could torpedo commercial vessels without surfacing. Six weeks after it began, Conger's career as Berlin Bureau Chief abruptly ended.

And local bureaux were equally held responsible for gaffes committed by the foreign desk. When a Carl Mydans picture of Italy's Benito Mussolini reviewing his troops was captioned 'The elderly butcher-boy of Fascism struts out,' the entire Rome staff of *Life* magazine was escorted to Ciampino Airport – not to return for four years.

For those who stayed the course there were still stumbling blocks. Before Shirer's nightly broadcast from the RRG building on the edge of the Grünewald, timed at 12.45 am to coincide with 6.45 pm New York time, each script was vetted in advance. Any mention of RAF bombers over the city was forbidden. Later, lip microphones became mandatory, held so close to the mouth that the sound of anti-aircraft guns did not register. High Command communiqués must be treated as holy writ: 'asserted' or 'claimed', words suggesting a modicum of doubt, were both forbidden. 'National Socialist' was a permitted label; 'Nazi' was not. Later, even broadcasters' intonations would be monitored for irony or scepticism. Any infringement of these rules called for a *Kopfwaschen* (a mild rebuke, literally a 'headwashing') from a Goebbels minion over lunch at the Hotel Adlon.

A master of the half-truth and the snide innuendo, little Dr Goebbels rarely missed a trick. By his own lights, this was entirely legitimate. 'News policy,' he maintained, 'is a weapon of war. Its purpose is to wage war and not to give out information.' One such occasion was on 21 March 1940, when a British air raid on the island of Sylt was followed by a claim of serious damage. At once Goebbels put a plane at the correspondents' disposal so that they could judge for themselves. To visit the actual airbases would infringe security, but the few smashed houses they saw were assuredly the extent of the damage.

No man bothered to file a word, but next morning every German newspaper carried the headlines: BRITISH LIE EXPOSED. AMERICAN JOURNALISTS VISITED SYLT AND SAW NO DAMAGE.

Until now, though, Goebbels' propaganda had of necessity been low-key. Hitler's projected offensive against the west had allegedly been postponed fourteen times through the strenuous opposition of his generals, and for the soundest of reasons: the coldest European winter in forty-six years had bogged down both tanks and aircraft. On 8 April 1940, all this was to change.

That night, in Willy Lehmann's restaurant, La Taverne, on Courbièrestrasse, where the warcos foregathered, the excitement was intense. All those present – Shirer himself; the plump debonair Pierre Huss of INS; Sigrid Schultz of the *Chicago Tribune*, blonde and buoyant, whom the Luftwaffe chief, Herman Goering, dubbed 'that dragon from Chicago' – were keyed to fever pitch. In a belated attempt to halt the 10 million tons of Swedish iron ore that Germany imported each year, the British had mined Norwegian territorial waters, particularly in the region of the key port of Narvik.

'Germany will know how to react,' was the Foreign Ministry's prompt riposte, but the question buzzing in La Taverne that night was, how?

At 11 am on 9 April, they knew. In the Foreign Ministry building on Wilhelmstrasse, Joachim von Ribbentrop, formal in a field grey uniform, sprang up to justify the Third Reich's newest aggression: 'Gentlemen, yesterday's Allied invasion of Norwegian territorial waters represents the most flagrant violation of the rights of a neutral country ... However' – his teeth baring in a smug grin – 'it did not take Germany by surprise ...

'The Führer has given his answer ... Germany has occupied Danish and Norwegian soil in order to protect these countries from the Allies ... an honoured part of Europe has been saved from certain downfall ... '

Belatedly, the warcos on the Western Front were realizing their error: they were in the wrong place at the wrong time. This was not yet a war much concerned with Conducting Officers, censorship or filing in quadruplicate. It was a war for lone wolves.

In the second week of April, two of them, widely disparate personalities, were on the prowl in the northern latitudes. On the afternoon of 8 April Erik Seidenfaden, thirty-year-old correspondent for the Copenhagen daily *Politiken*, boarded the Norwegian national airline's afternoon flight from Copenhagen to Oslo. He thought himself fully briefed on the story he was to cover; the British had announced their intention of mining Norwegian waters and Seidenfaden aimed to see them in action.

A tall relaxed man who smiled a lot, Seidenfaden was due for a surprise. Among the passengers was a man he knew well, Captain Riiser-Larsen, Chief of Staff of the Norwegian Air Force. Suddenly a white-jacketed steward came hastening down the aisle: Riiser-Larsen was wanted in the cockpit.

Curious as to why, Seidenfaden craned from the window and beheld an astounding sight. Six thousand feet below, the grey waters of the Kattegat separating Demark from Sweden were black with German warships: the battleships *Scharnhorst* and *Gneisenau*, the cruisers *Blücher* and *Emden*, along with many torpedo boats, destroyers, E-boats and other craft. By pure chance Seidenfaden had netted a scoop – yet such was the mental climate of 1940 that he failed to recognize it.

His first instinct was to rationalize the scene: the German navy was reacting swiftly to Britain's defiant announcement. Thus, there seemed every chance that the two navies would do battle to the death in the Atlantic Ocean off the Norwegian coastline. The realization that he was witnessing a full-dress invasion of Norway never occurred to him.

All this was consistent with the mentality that Winston Churchill, then First Lord of the Admiralty, had deplored in a broadcast as recently as 20 January. Castigating the timorousness of the neutral nations, Churchill had summed up: ' ... their plight is lamentable, and it will become worse. They bow humbly and in fear to German threats of violence, comforting themselves meanwhile with the thoughts that the Allies will win ... each one hopes that if he feeds the crocodile enough, the crocodile will eat him last.'

Thus, when his plane touched down at Oslo's Fornebu airport, Seidenfaden hastened not to a phone booth but to the press gallery of the Storting, the rotunda-shaped parliament building on Karl Johansgate. The day's big story, he thought, would certainly be the formal protest that Foreign Minister Halvdan Koht would deliver to the British. But the debate dragged on so long that it was too late to file a cable for *Politiken's* morning edition. By midnight, Seidenfaden was in bed and asleep at Oslo's Grand Hotel.

Soon after 4 am on 9 April, a phone call brought him very wide awake. It was his colleague Sten Gudme calling from Copenhagen: German troops had crossed the Danish frontier. Seidenfaden, had, in fact, netted a scoop-that-never-was, for within the span of this Tuesday, *Politiken* and all Danish newspapers would pass under German supervision.

In another room at the Oslo Grand, Leland Stowe was also

wide awake. What had roused him was the eerie nonstop wail of the city's air raid sirens – an odd phenomenon, as no enemy aircraft were overhead. At first, though, Stowe failed to recognize this as such. 'It's a bunch of cars stuck behind a truck,' he insisted to his fellow warco, the *Christian Science Monitor*'s Edmund Stevens. In truth, both men, who had arrived on 4 April, had expected to cover nothing more dramatic than a diplomatic brouhaha between the Norwegians and the British. Neither could know that at this moment the German Minister to Norway, Dr Kurt Bräuer, was delivering an ultimatum to Foreign Minister Koht. Since a master switch had extinguished all lights in the city's centre, the text had to be read out by the wavering light of a candle.

Although his onetime employer, the *New York Herald Tribune*, deemed him 'too old to cover a war' at thirty-nine, Stowe, a self-styled Connecticut Yankee with prematurely white hair, was determined to justify the faith of a new boss, Colonel Frank Knox of the *Chicago Daily News*. Known as much for his hatred of British appeasers as for his noxious everpresent pipe, he had already repaid that faith in Finland. Now a new challenge awaited him.

His first intimation that an invasion was afoot came at 2.30 pm in the Grand's foyer, with the doorman's solicitous query, 'Aren't you going to see the Germans come in?' Along with Stevens and Warren Irvin of the National Broadcasting Corporation (NBC), Stowe first tried in vain for a place on the densely packed pavement then fought his way back into the hotel for a vantage point on the front balcony. There followed what he was to term 'the biggest bluff in modern history', as thousands of Norwegians, many of them of military age, watched unemotionally from the sidewalk cafes as 1500 goose-stepping German troops with gleaming bandoliers of bronzed bullets, escorted by six Norwegian mounted policemen, took over the city unopposed.

Although Stowe was slow to realize it, this was less acquiescence on the part of Oslo's 258,000 citizens than a kind of shellshock. As the Grand's doorman automatically snapped into the Nazi salute and citizens stared 'like children seeing a new kind of animal', a tall, untidily dressed man with bulging blue eyes was bluffing his way into Oslo's radio station to assume power on behalf of a nonexistent national government. Although supported by no more than 80,000 citizens, Major Vidkun Quisling was thereafter to symbolise a treachery from within of which the Norwegians had never been guilty.

Following a brief twenty-five-word message to his foreign editor

Carroll Binder, Stowe's mind was set on Sweden. He wanted freedom to file the full story, and from then until the war's end no country was to offer greater freedom: unless a dispatch affected her security interests, Sweden's objectivity remained total. Proof of this came when he arrived at Stockholm's Grand Hotel to find that two large salons, set aside by the Foreign Office, served as a Press Room. Of the 135 warcos representing sixteen nations, nineteen were German, who exchanged no more than a curt '*Bitte*' and stiff bows with their British and French counterparts.

In this chaotic climate, when much of Scandinavia was being 'saved from certain downfall', two British correspondents, just as in Poland, abruptly became civilians on the run. Both Desmond Tighe of Reuters and W. F. Hartin of the *Daily Mail*, after arriving on the noon train from Stockholm, had checked into Oslo's Grand before the Germans marched in. Both, too late, realized that they were dressed like caricatures of the Compleat Englishman: Tighe in a sports coat, canary yellow pullover and flat tweed cap, like a day tripper to Brighton, Hartin as an Anthony Eden lookalike, in a dark Savile Row overcoat and black homburg hat. Eight hours later – thanks to the hotel's friendly concierge, who routed their luggage back to the station, and the friendly Swiss Legation, which hid them in their cellar for the afternoon – Tighe and Hartin again boarded the Stockholm Express without ever filing a word.

In Oslo, by degrees, the picture became brighter. By 10 April, a great and stealthy migration was under way: young men toting rucksacks, armed with nothing more than sheath knives, were slipping into the forests in the wake of King Haakon VII, his Cabinet, and 150 parliamentarians, all of them bent ultimately on exile in England. On hand to cover their flight were Erik Seidenfaden, the Swede Sven Auren and the Australian James Aldridge of NANA – jubilant to record that the sixty-eight-year-old king, after surviving a low-level German bombing attack at Nybergsund, twenty miles from the Swedish frontier, salvaged a spent machine-gun bullet as a souvenir. 'This is a personal present,' he proclaimed dryly, 'from Hitler to me.'

Leland Stowe, meanwhile, was cast for a role more crucial than he realized in the sorry campaign that followed. On Monday, 15 April, some 20,000 British troops, aboard warships at anchor along the Norwegian coast, were preparing to go ashore, charged, in Churchill's words, 'to purge and cleanse the soil of the Vikings ... from the filthy pollution of Nazi tyranny'. Six days later, alerted to their

move, Stowe had reached Gäddede, 600 miles from Stockholm on
the Norwegian–Swedish border.

Along with a Swedish freelance cameraman, Paul Mylander,
Stowe had chosen this springboard with deliberation. The back-
door route over the mountain pass from Gäddede had been opened
only one day earlier and as yet was negligently guarded by the
Swedes. But a score of rival warcos on the border at Storlien, 100
miles south, were being denied transit. As Martha Gellhorn had
recently spelled out to her readers, the Swedes were excavating a
bomb shelter to protect 3000 Stockholmers and maintaining a standing army of 140,000, but their stance, for all that, was unavowedly
neutral.

As Stowe understood it, an Anglo-French force was fighting its
way from Namsos on the coast to capture the key Norwegian port
of Trondheim, 100 miles south. It was to meet up with these cru-
saders that he and Mylander now embarked on a fearsome journey
towards Steinkjer, fifty miles away, down one of the 'slushiest mudd-
iest roads in creation'. Neither had anticipated that at the end of
this road evidence awaited them of 'one of the costliest and most
inexplicable bungles in modern military history'.

Churning through ruts two feet deep, channels swimming with
water from the fast-melting April snows, Stowe and Mylander found
their Norwegian driver got stuck time and again. Finally, grabbing
his typewriter, Stowe slogged on with Mylander in tow, to hitch a
ride with a British ambulance half a mile ahead. At last, along the
tip of a wide fjord, 'tucked in the slanting palm of the spruce-covered
snowbound hills', they came to Steinkjer, yesterday a town of 4000
souls, now marked only by 'the scarred black fingers of scores of
chimneys'.

From the bruised and battered survivors of the Northwestern
Expeditionary Force, bivouacked in cottages outside the town, an
incredible story emerged. The veteran Stowe was, above all, astonished by their youth – 'beside those hardfaced machine-like pro-
fessional soldiers I had seen in field grey uniforms in Oslo ... these
fellows looked like boy scouts.' Hour after hour, the bitter tales
of recrimination were scribbled into his notebook. 'We've been
massacred – simply massacred. It's the planes – we've got no planes':
this from an agitated British lieutenant. A noncom, excited to the
point of feverishness, took up the story: 'We've got no anti-aircraft
guns and we have no field guns. We could hear our wounded crying
in the woods, but we couldn't get to them.' The lieutenant again:

'We've got no proper clothes for these mountains – we've got no white capes. The Jerries could see us everywhere in the snow.'

Stowe was appalled by his discoveries. All these men were raw Territorials, with barely more than one year's military service, lacking even entrenching tools; although all were armed with rifles some had no topcoats. They were equipped with mortars, but had only smoke bombs as ammunition. 'It's just like the Russians against the Finns, only worse,' the lieutenant blurted out, 'and we are the Finns.'

In a farmhouse near Steinkjer, waiting for a dairyman's wife to brew coffee, Stowe listened in silence as a BBC announcer delivered what was plainly an official handout: 'British expeditionary forces are pressing steadily forward from all points where they have landed in Norway ... In the Namsos sector German forces may soon be isolated.'

'Jesus Christ,' exploded Mylander, who had perfected his English in the Bronx, New York, 'What's the matter with these mugs? Are they crazy?'

Stowe was bitterly laconic. 'No, no, Paul. Not at all. You forget that this programme is sponsored by British Empire Soothing Syrup Limited.'

Back at the frontier, they found that a new Swedish safety measure forbade any foreigner to remain in Gäddede overnight. A hired car finally deposited them in Östersund at 3.30 am on 24 April. Out of ninety-six hours, Stowe had slept for just seven, in these four days he had gulped down two meals, but he had a war correspondent's dream: the story of how the men whom he called 'Mr Chamberlain's chickens' had been sacrificed.

It was 'a bitterly disillusioning and almost unbelievable story' that reached the front page of the *Chicago Daily News* and forty other subscriber papers on Thursday, 25 April, a story of how men had been 'dumped into Norway's deep snows and quagmires' to 'fight crack German regulars ... and face the most destructive of modern weapons'. It was also a story carried in the 6 May issue of *Time* magazine – more readily accessible on British newsstands than any United States papers.

This was only six days after the Royal Navy re-embarked the last of the battered British battalions from Andalsnes, 125 miles southwest of Trondheim, and one day before a bitter battle of recriminations fuelled by these disclosures began in the House of Commons. It was a battle that many officer MPs, who had served in Norway, were now emboldened to join, and the result was history. In a house traditionally Tory by a majority of 210, Neville Chamberlain scraped home by no more than 81 votes. Since no member of Labour's Shadow Cabinet would serve with him in a new coalition, he was forced to yield. On 10 May, after forty years of political frustration and vacillation, a former war correspondent, Winston Spencer Churchill, came into his own as Prime Minister.

About this time Leland Stowe, back at Stockholm's Grand, had a telephone call from a secretary in the British Legation. Whatever rebuke had been in store, Stowe decided to preempt it. 'I imagine some of your folks in London are pretty riled over my story about Steinkjer,' he volunteered, 'but, quite frankly, I believe I've done the British cause the greatest service I've ever had the opportunity of rendering.'

The secretary was equal to the occasion. 'Well, speaking with equal frankness, Mr Stowe, I'm inclined to believe that you are entirely correct.'

As early as 5 am on 10 May, the telephone wires were whispering in the night – 'René, René, René' – as the codeword passed from army post to army post along the Belgian frontier. Within the hour General Maurice Gamelin, at his Supreme Headquarters in the gloomy Château of Vincennes, was fully in the picture: with the suddenness of a coronary attack, Hitler had launched a concerted 136-division assault from the North Sea to the Moselle, striking simultaneously against Holland, Northern Belgium and tiny Luxembourg.

These, like Norway and Denmark, were non-aligned countries – observing a neutrality so strict that to all British queries as to his intentions if Holland were invaded, King Leopold III of the Belgians had maintained a stiff-necked silence.

To the King's subjects, secure in that neutrality, the first bombs, which struck the centre of Brussels at precisely 7 am, produced an emotion akin to trauma. From a window of the American Embassy on the Rue de la Science, Clare Boothe watched as the house opposite 'vomited glass and wood and stone into the little green square'; all at once the pavements were littered with 'a wanton mosaic of blue glass'. But within the Embassy all was tranquil; although the house-man pasted paper anti-blast strips across the windows, the butler changed into a frock coat with black silk stock to serve Ambassador John Cudahy and his guests lunch in the mirrored gallery. Three more alarms, Miss Boothe noted, sounded between the eggs mornay and the dessert.

On the streets of the city no such calm prevailed. The ravages of modern war were suddenly falling with totalitarian indifference on young and old, rich and poor alike; the all too human gut reaction was to flee. Caught up in 'a huge serpent of automobiles' 200 miles long, Marcel W. Fodor of the *Chicago Daily News* described it with pardonable exaggeration as 'the greatest mass exodus in modern history', although it did take him thirty hours to cover the 160 miles to Paris.

Ironically, the Phoney War had ended so abruptly that only one reporter – Arthur Mann, of Manhattan's Mutual Broadcasting System – was left holding the fort in Brussels. His colleagues, disgruntled to a man, had quit the Western Front weeks ago; as neutral Americans, Edward Angly of the *New York Herald Tribune* and Drew Middleton of AP were in London seeking passage to Norway. Walter Duranty had moved on to Bucharest. At the behest of his proprietor, Lord Camrose, Douglas Williams of the *Daily Telegraph* had also returned to London, en route to the United States to cover the political conventions in Chicago and Philadelphia. When the news broke Williams, without even bothering to inform his paper, sped to Croydon Airport, pelted onto the field in Hollywood's true hold-the-front-page tradition, waving a card that looked vaguely official, to pile aboard a plane full of astonished generals. By mid-afternoon he was filing dispatches from Brussels.

Most warcos saw Paris as the nerve centre of the action, but Ronnie Noble, the Universal News cameraman, had no such convictions; on leave in Paris, he found himself 200 miles from the war he had been waiting seven months to cover. Armed with the standard equipment of the time – a 20-pound Newman Sinclair camera, a tripod and 1000 feet of film – Noble hitched a ride from Le Bourget Airport to Arras, heading for the Belgian frontier and the long heartrending columns of refugees.

'They were old and young, fit and sick, yet one thing was common to them all,' Noble was to relate, 'the frightened stare in their eyes.' Worse was to follow. Minutes later, 'through the viewfinder I saw an incredible scene.' In a split second, the road was suddenly clear; the huge black shadows of German planes bulked above the estaminet roof where Noble was perched; 'the shadows swooped along the road pumping their noisy death into the ditches.' It was the first of a thousand archetypal views of World War Two, as the armies ebbed and flowed and the people paid the price.

Suddenly, it seemed, there were no more civilians, yet still the comforting concept of neutrality died hard. In Amsterdam, on 10 May, a new kind of fighting man was descending on the darkened tulip fields, the parachutist, neither aviator nor foot soldier but an amalgam of both. Yet the Amtrans teleprinter service of the United Press – relaying news of the invasion to New York in three minutes and equally keeping the British Ministry of Information up-to-date – was hastily severed by the Dutch at 10.25 am. The Reuters news agency link with their headquarters in London's Fleet Street was cut short at the same time. To transmit any news at all might imperil Dutch neutrality.

The priority rations that the Amsterdam warcos took aboard the steamer *Dotterel* en route to Harwich emphasized their disillusion. David Woodward of the London *News Chronicle*, like almost all his colleagues, had one small packet of sandwiches and a full bottle of Scotch. Another man came aboard with 1000 cigarettes and two bottles of gin – his sole sustenance for twenty-four hours.

All over Europe, as the cable machines pulsed, the German goal was emerging by degrees: skirting the northern end of the 'impregnable' Maginot Line and heading for the 'impenetrable' Ardennes forest, they were making for the Channel ports. The seizure of Belgium's Fort Eben Emael by nine gliders soon after dawn on 10 May was followed by the devastation of the ancient frontier fort of Sedan three days later. By 15 May Hitler's armies, sweeping through the forty-mile gap south and west of Sedan, were effectively cutting the Allies in half.

None of the Paris correspondents haunting the daily press conference at the Hôtel Continental could have charted that course so accurately – or been permitted to state it so baldly. In the world of M. Pierre Comert and the Chief Censor, Colonel Thomas of the Ministry of War, rumours, denials, evasions, then fresh rumours proliferated. 'If you wrote a truthful story with all the pros and cons, the cons were blue-pencilled and the pros alone remained,' remembered the *Manchester Guardian*'s Alexander Werth. 'The result was nothing but undiluted panegyrics.' After Sedan, recalled Eric Sevareid of CBS, in the hot spring days of what the doom-sayers called 'Hitler weather' 'German tanks by the thousand were pouring onto French soil – but nobody had got the news to the press and radio of the outside world, the censor was stopping everything.'

The name of the game was euphemism. 'The communiqués

never admitted that the Germans had pierced the French line,' noted A. J. Liebling, 'but invariably announced "motorized elements had made an infiltration" ... Two days later the "infiltration" became a salient from which new infiltrations radiated.' The UP's Ed Beattie, daily seeking the hard news that was the breath of life to an agency man, was equally bedevilled. 'For a day or two, it almost seemed that the French were doing better,' was his recollection. 'Then came more falling back, more "rectification of lines", more took up prepared positions.'

Around 26 May, a rumour which was barely credible reached Paris: that the British Secretary of State for War, Anthony Eden, had authorised Gort's BEF to deny the French High Command who were essentially their masters and effect a wholesale withdrawal to the 1000-year-old coastal port of Dunkirk. To heighten the crisis, on 27 May King Leopold, whose Belgians had taken the field in self-defence equipped only with rusty rifles and horse-drawn cannon, had sought an armistice from midnight. A mighty military débâcle was in the offing.

Lacking a modern air force and a modern tank army with which to react, the mass of the French forces, Ed Beattie summed up, 'became so many confused men, always falling back from a foe they seldom saw, without proper weapons, often without food, and above all without direction'.

On 16 May, and again on 22 May, Churchill flew to Paris to confer with Reynaud – himself a staunch enough premier, as the warcos had come to recognize. On 19 May General Maxime Weygand, overtly a spry seventy-three-year-old cavalryman, inwardly convinced that the French, like the British, were in superb shape to refight World War One, had replaced Gamelin. An ever-present spectre at these meetings was eighty-four-year-old Marshal Henri Philippe Pétain, the hero of Verdun, now serving as Minister of State, a man persuaded that the war was already lost.

Throughout the last week of May an uneasy calm prevailed in Paris. The report that the BEF as such had ceased to exist was thus far unconfirmed. The British evacuation of some 366,000 men from Dunkirk by more than 1000 vessels, ranging from sleek destroyers to Thames sailing barges, was one of World War Two's greatest scoops, yet one on which the warcos missed out.

There were valid reasons for this. The last of the reporters attached to the BEF, all of them sadly disillusioned men, had been evacuated via Boulogne on 24 May. At south coast ports like Dover, those newsmen who greeted the survivors – 'grimy, unshaven and tired ... but there is no dejection' – wrote with the censors frowning over their shoulders. In this hour of crisis, when the British now stood alone, they, too, were insistent on 'undiluted panegyrics'. The scenes of near-panic as boats were rushed and men deserted by their officers roamed the seaport in drunken mobs never reached the front pages. When the *New York Times*'s London bureau chief, Raymond Daniell, ventured that the lives of the BEF had been bought by abandoning almost 1000 heavy guns, the censor ruled it out of court. The *Daily Mirror*'s headline struck the right thumbs-up note: BLOODY MARVELLOUS.

Even the one newsreel cameraman on the spot, Charles Martin of Pathé News, secured only a few hundred feet of film. Boarding a destroyer at Harwich, he had found himself at first light off the Dunkirk beaches, filming long lines of British and French soldiers up to their necks in water as they waded out to his ship. Then, sensing the urgency of the moment, he put his camera aside to help the sodden soldiers clamber up the nets.

Back in Paris, on Sunday, 9 June, disquieting stories were abroad. The *Manchester Guardian*'s Alexander Werth put one of them point blank to Colonel Thomas of the War Office: Since German tanks were said to be fifteen miles north of Paris, was it true that the government was abandoning the capital? '*Je n'en sais rien*' ('I know nothing about it') the Colonel replied.

On this same day, A. J. Liebling of *The New Yorker* saw new grounds for optimism. At the Hotel Continental's 6 pm press conference, the AP's John Lloyd, as President of the Anglo-American Press Association, had invited the new Minister of Information, Jean Prouvost, to be the guest of honour at a luncheon on Wednesday, 12 June. He would be charmed, Prouvost answered, as he hurried away.

Toward noon on Monday, 10 June, Liebling was back at the Continental. It was always possible that M. Comert had some fresh news. At the foot of the staircase he ran into Waverley Root of the Mutual Broadcasting System. 'If you're going up to the Ministry,' Root greeted him, 'don't bother. The Government left Paris for Tours this morning.'

Suddenly Root began to chuckle. 'You remember when John Lloyd stopped Prouvost last night and invited him to the Wednesday luncheon?' Liebling did indeed remember. 'Well, Prouvost was in a hurry because he was leaving for Tours in a few minutes.'

★

At dusk on that day, Paris was a melancholy sight to all who loved her. Out through the Porte de Châtillon, in the fading light, groaned an endless line of trucks and private cars – Citroëns, Mercedes – heading for Tours, 150 miles southwest. After perfunctory heart-searching Reynaud's government, without a word of warning to the citizens, was abandoning the capital as an open city – leaving only the Prefect of Police and 25,000 gendarmes to represent authority in Paris.

From this moment, hope in France vanished as a dam gives way before an inexorable flood. On this hectic Monday night all the city – and soon all France – became obsessed by one single thought: to get away.

Inevitably the warcos were caught up in the flood. At the Gare d'Austerlitz, the terminal for all trains departing for the southwest, Virginia Cowles, arriving from London on the scent of a story, found 'the great iron gates in front of the station were bolted and in front of them was an enormous crowd of people, shouting and yelling . . . one vast sea of faces.' Everyone, she noted, 'was loaded with bags and bundles, even birdcages . . . a squad of gendarmes had climbed up on the iron railings and were shouting at them, "No more trains are leaving Paris! The last train has left! Go home, I tell you."'

None of this would come as any surprise to Clare Boothe, who had caught the London plane as early as 31 May. The sight of Louis Vuitton 'rigid' luggage piled outside the Ritz had suggested that, although the rich would be the first to go, thousands would soon follow the example of their betters.

Black smoke from burning fuel dumps cast a pall so dense over the city that at times no man could see across the Place de la Concorde, where lowing cattle now wandered untended. By now more than a million refugees had gone and Paris was dying by inches. 'No one had ever seen a Paris like this before,' reported Virginia Cowles, '. . . a Paris so quiet there was scarcely a cat stirring . . . gone were the noisy crowds, the rich smell of tobacco, the water splashing from the fountains.' Eric Sevareid of CBS was another who drove up the Champs Elysées to see that the cadres of wicker chairs on the cafe terraces were empty. 'The waiters had removed their aprons and were shutting the doors. One last client sat alone at his little round table, finishing a drink, while the waiter stood patiently beside him waiting for his glass.'

For many war correspondents still lingered, even now. Memories of heroic last stands were paramount in their rich lexicon of fantasy – the South Wales Borderers at Rorke's Drift, Custer above the Little Big Horn river – and in their own time, too, there had been memorable precedents. But, as Sefton Delmer finally decided, along with Robert Cooper of *The Times* and the BBC's Edward Ward, 'There was going to be no defence, no Madrid, no Warsaw,' so it was time for them, too, to trek southward.

Almost the last man to reach this decision was Quentin Reynolds. Ever since his consummate bluff that he could call Franklin Roosevelt his uncle, 'Red' Reynolds had circulated freely in the 'zone of the French Armies' – to register impressions that no French censor would ever have passed. At Nancy, the sight of ambulances packed with wounded Frenchmen had jarred oddly with French communiqués announcing heavy German losses. At Beauvais he had smelt war for the first time, 'smoke so thick that I felt I could chew it ... ashes and smoke bitter on my tongue'. On his return to Paris, learning of Sedan and Dunkirk only through BBC news bulletins, Reynolds was convinced that the French collapse was only a matter of time.

Even so, the occupation of Paris by Hitler's Wehrmacht would be a story to lighten the heart of Charley Colebaugh, *Collier's* foreign editor, and all the others in the Park Avenue office. It was one that Reynolds was determined not to miss, but on the morning of Thursday, 13 June, Colonel Horace Fuller, the American military attaché, quickly disillusioned him.

'The arrival of Hitler to accept the keys to the city will certainly make a great story,' Fuller agreed grimly. 'But you won't be able to report it. Only correspondents accompanying the German army will be allowed to use the cables and wireless. And as for your plea that you are a neutral correspondent, you are on their blacklist.' (And this was true; in his twelve months as INS man in Berlin, Reynolds had repeatedly fallen foul of Dr Goebbels and his acolytes.)

'They will be here tonight or early tomorrow,' Fuller concluded, 'and if you don't want to be interned somewhere or sent to Spain, I suggest you get out of here while you can.'

As so often happened through World War Two, luck was on Reynolds's side. At a table outside the Café de la Paix, the waiter who had served him coffee and brioches proved a heaven-sent go-between with the café's one other occupant: a doctor's wife in her early thirties, in a chic black suit and 'a pert little hat'. Above all, a lady who had a car for sale.

She was English, she explained, but married to a French neurosurgeon who could not leave his hospital; as of now he was operating eleven hours a day. It seemed better to have money in the bank rather than a car which the Germans might requisition, but as to its worth, she didn't know – 'I have never sold a car before.'

'I'll give you all the money I have,' Reynolds said feelingly, which on investigation proved to be $450 in travellers' cheques and $100 in French and American money. Without ceremony the keys to a Baby Austin two-seater, parked at the kerb nearby, changed hands. By midday, his car crammed with a kitbag full of clean linen, cans of boneless chicken, a steel helmet, a sleeping bag and a portable typewriter, Reynolds had checked out of the Ritz and was heading for Tours – intent on joining Kenneth Downs, who had pulled out three days earlier.

On the roads leading south, conditions were now at their worst. No correspondent who made this journey would ever forget the stripped silent villages, where not a crumb of bread or a thimbleful of milk remained. The main brasseries at Orléans and Le Mans resembled stage sets for a poorhouse, littered with orange peel, with refugees bedding on the banquettes. In Orléans, A. J. Liebling found even the brothels were jammed with earlier arrivals – 'They are so tired,' one madame assured him in a hushed whisper, 'that some of them are actually sleeping.'

By now almost 10 million were on the roads, mindless of a destination, coursing blindly on like lemmings, although to travel 200 yards an hour was now a rare achievement. Sefton Delmer, along with Edward Ward and Robert Cooper, found that in this 'frightened "I'm all right Jack" stampede', his high-powered Ford took nineteen hours to cover the 150 miles to Tours. Virginia Cowles, travelling with Tom Healy of the London *Daily Mirror* in Healy's Chrysler, openly resorted to bribery; two packets of cigarettes for a time secured them a privileged place in a convoy of tanks, roaring along at 40 miles an hour. Eric Sevareid, passing through Chartres, beheld an appalling spectacle that was yet the logical outcome of this hejira – 'many cars, casualties of the night, lying obscenely on their backs, their wheels still turning in the reactive motions of after-death'. Beside them, 'horses had been dragged to the edge of the road, their heads hanging limply in the ditches, little pools of blood drying up to their noses.' In these same ditches, 'whole families slept where they had fallen ... sprawled in careless heaps like bundles of rags tied with string.'

The panic was spreading from town to town, to the very foothills of the Pyrenees; few correspondents, however seasoned, had ever witnessed such a bizarre array of vehicles. Street-sweepers with revolving brushes jostled for road space with furniture vans, ice-cream carts and fire engines bearing firemen and their families. The Second Empire fiacres, thought A. J. Liebling, provided a welcome touch of class, although AP's Louis Lochner gave pride of place to a hearse drawn by ten men with a dozen children wedged in the space reserved for the coffin. Walter Kerr, of the *New York Herald Tribune*, was baffled by the glut of pushcarts – 'You cannot,' he reasoned, 'push a cart all the way to the Pyrenees or wherever they were going.' Most touching of all, thought Larry Lesueur of CBS, was the pram pushed by a young French girl, camouflaged with green branches like a truck bound for the front: a rudimentary attempt to save her baby from dive-bombing.

Quentin Reynolds, whose Baby Austin had caught up with the refugees as early as Versailles, was in a less compassionate mood. 'It is one thing to see thousands of weary refugees in the newsreels,' he grumbled. 'It is something quite different to be one of them.'

Even the veteran Reynolds now found himself part of a topsy-turvy world where past experience was of little help. No sooner had he reached Tours, midway through 15 June, to be reunited with Kenneth Downs, than a fresh shock awaited him: at 5 am on Sunday, 16 June, once more without warning, Reynaud's government again pulled out, this time for Bordeaux, 360 miles south of Paris. Within seven days, France had thus acquired three capitals, though every newsman now saw capitulation as inevitable.

As a magazine writer, Reynolds's need to file copy was less pressing than most, although as a pro he deplored the inflationary cable rates now in force. A 300-word message, complained Alexander Werth, at the rate of eightpence a word worked out at £7 for one cable, yet the cost must be borne; since his last cable that Paris 'is awaymelting', the *Guardian* had had no word. Virginia Cowles was in a similar quandary. A pre-luncheon chat in Bordeaux's Hotel Splendide with the new Foreign Secretary, Pierre Laval, had resulted in a scoop of sorts: Laval's contention that 'I don't think that France is Germany's primary object, I think her *real* aim is Soviet Russia.'

But Laval, whose drooping moustaches and white piqué ties were to become the delight of cartoonists, was still at this moment in history a relatively unknown figure. At eightpence a word via Press Wireless, the only remaining link with the outside world, it was, thought Miss Cowles, too expensive a luxury.

The one man standing aloof from the fray was Sefton Delmer; his last message to the *Daily Express* was no more than routine. Before leaving Paris, he had learned conclusively that 'the censor had killed all our dispatches ... the new ministers wanted nothing sent out of Paris or Tours that might give offence to the Germans or savour of defiance.'

The stage was thus set for the broadcast, soon after noon on Monday, 17 June, which Reynolds and Downs heard in the loft that had become Bordeaux's temporary press headquarters; the quavering voice of Marshal Pétain, broken by a dry cough, assuring the French people, 'It is futile to continue the struggle ... it is with heavy heart that I say we must cease the fight ...'.

Exactly thirty-six hours later, at Pointe de Grave, sixty miles from Bordeaux, Reynolds and Downs, their passports duly stamped by the US Envoy-Extraordinary, Anthony Drexel Biddle, boarded the Dutch freighter *Benekom* en route to Falmouth, four days distant on the Cornish coast. They still nourished hopes – by no means universal in this troubled year – that the English would be slow to throw in the towel.

In a suite at the Royal Duchy Hotel overlooking the shining waters of the Carrick Roads, the two men pondered all that they had seen to date: the smoke palls sluggish above the bloated bodies of men and horses, the refugees scavenging both for sustenance and sanctuary, the day-long screech of klaxon horns succeeded by the silence of fear. Yet here were snowy sheets, hangers in the closet, thick rugs on the floor and, unbelievably, a room-service waiter delivering Scotch, sandwiches, soda and ice.

From the depths of a hot and blissful bath, Reynolds called to Downs: 'I want to ask you an important question. What can heaven have that we haven't got here, right now?'

For a warco, Downs's reply was little short of subversive: 'No typewriters.'

The truth emerged in time, from Lisbon – mulled over in the weeks that followed by sundry correspondents in their natural watering-place, the Bar Americano of the Avenida Palace Hotel.

Three among them were staffers of *Life*, the magazine that Henry Luce, Clare Boothe's husband and founder of *Time*, had painstakingly launched in 1936. Of the Paris staff, most had left the capital on 11 June, joining the tidal wave of refugees southwards, but thirty-six-year-old Sherry Mangan had stayed until 8 August, preserving duplicates of all the cables which the Germans had quashed hitherto. Their entry into Paris, noted the much-censored Mangan, had seemed less like an invasion, 'more like a political convention with high spirited delegates arriving in force'. To date, anger against the occupying forces had been no more than 'a sub-terranean rumble'. The Germans were referred to as '*les invités*', the guests, or a phrase 'pronounced with elaborate cutting politeness', *ces messieurs*.

Another *Life* man, Frank Norris, had penetrated to the heart of the new regime, the spa town of Vichy, once just the name on a bottle of mineral water. Here one man, Pierre Laval, ran 'the barely viable' French state comprising the two-fifths of France unoccupied by Germany from Room 73 of the Hotel du Parc et Majestic, with Pétain serving as the state's 'ancient and lovable front man'. Winding up the Third French Republic with a new and inward-looking slogan, '*Travail, Famille, Patrie*', Pétain, the messiah of a new asce-ticism, had decreed three meatless days a week and three without alcohol. But, Norris reported, this, like much else, was a sham: although champagne was banned as 'decadent', a dining-room order for Vichy '28 brought a bottle of Cordon Rouge '28, 'emptied out of its lordly bottle' and served in an iced carafe.

The one crumb of comfort over France came from London. There a 'lanky gloomy brigadier', fifty-year-old General Charles André Marie de Gaulle, arriving in England on 17 June, had pro-claimed himself leader of the Free French forces, operating from two barren rooms in St Stephen's House, across the street from the House of Commons. But by early July, only a small cadre of 2000 Frenchmen had rallied to his cause. For the foreseeable future, de Gaulle would remain a mantra for the faithful rather than a political reality.

It was the chief of the European staff of *Life* and *Time*, Ralph Paine, who reported most trenchantly from Lisbon on the prospects for the French. 'France,' Paine stated with savage precision, 'was not conquered in forty-three days. France collapsed in forty-three days. The French defeated themselves and they know it.

'The basic sin for which the French are now punished was their long tolerance of stupid, bureaucratic, corrupt, slothful, hopelessly inefficient leadership.'

The tragedy was that millions of French citizens had known this all along. 'The reaction to the news of the peace was complete, bitter grief,' Paine would always remember, recording a soldier's comment that many of the British could have voiced up to 10 May, 'We've been led by men with the hearts of rabbits.'

III

You Must Understand That A World Is Dying

(18 JUNE–17 DECEMBER 1940)

In Cairo the place names were little more than a monotonous clatter on the ticker-tape: Dunkirk ... Bordeaux ... Vichy. They were not the reality. The reality was the Turf Club, swarming with officers newly arrived from England, and settling into flats in the modern blocks on green Gezira Island. The reality was the dozen open-air cinemas each night, polo 'in the roasting afternoon heat' though no offices functioned from 1 to 6 pm, the French wines, grapes, melons and steaks 'that belonged to rich idle peace'. The reality was Madame Badia's girls writhing through their belly-dance in the cabaret near the Pont des Anglais, the grey staff cars flashing back and forth across the Kasr-el-Nil bridge, the boatmen on the Nile feluccas cursing and chanting as they had always done.

There were troops in the Western Desert, it was said, but no one doing the rounds of the parties or the polo in Cairo or Alexandria 'ever seemed to see them'. Certainly not Alan McCrae Moorehead, an Australian recently arrived for the *Daily Express* via Rome and Athens, though he yearned 'to get to the centre of things', to plumb the secret of 'how to become a high-powered war correspondent'.

A trim alert bantamweight, Moorehead, then aged twenty-nine, had spent much of his life in this quest, thus far with qualified results. The son of a small-time Melbourne journalist, his childhood and teens had been one long battle to escape: from broken shoes, darned stockings and trousers whose patches were camouflaged with ink, from the eternal Micawberish changes of address, from 'the squalid pettiness of counting every penny'. Exactly four years earlier, after scrimping to save £500 as a *Melbourne Herald* reporter, Moorehead finally contrived that escape, to England and the *Daily Express*, as 'a very junior member of the foreign staff'.

Yet in these four years, Moorehead had remained mostly on the sidelines of history. For much of the Spanish Civil War he had been a 'stringer' – a journalist paid by results – in Gibraltar, earning a basic £5 a week with some expenses. 'I was used mainly as a courier,' he was to grumble later, for while *Express* paragons like Hilde Marchant and O'Dowd Gallagher saw the bombing and the fall of Madrid, Moorehead never even reached the capital. The summer of 1938 in Paris, when he contrived to lose a marked Cockney accent, was a quiet time for the *Express* bureau on the Rue de Rivoli, unlike the dramas that Sefton Delmer saw played out in Berlin. Throughout the autumn of 1939 and the spring of 1940 Moorehead, living in a Swiss pension near Rome's Piazza di Spagna, tried valiantly to keep The Desk posted on the vexed question of the hour: would Mussolini go to war? He could report 'the Fascist lads, wrought up to a fine fire of enthusiasm'; after 10 May he could report that 'war and glory marched through the capital . . . you didn't know the date, you didn't know how, but it was coming, boys, it was coming, and what the hell, it was going to be fine . . . Money, glory, medals, excitement, conquests . . .'

On 10 June, approximately one month after Moorehead had transferred to Cairo, Mussolini, who needed 'only a few thousand dead to sit at the conference table as a belligerent', *did* declare war against the Allies and it was AP's Richard Massock, not Moorehead, who reported *Il Duce* recalled seven times to the balcony in the Piazza Venezia and the bluing of the streetlight-bulbs that presaged the blackout – one of twenty-five neutral warcos battling for the three long-distance lines still connecting Italy with Switzerland.

It was a grievance that Moorehead had aired more than once to his friend Alexander Clifford of the *Daily Mail*, over the cold buffet lunch they shared on the balcony of the Gezira Sporting Club, a bargain meal much appreciated by GHQ secretaries. Contrary to the legend of the free-spending warco lashing out on champagne, both men, at this stage in their careers, were watching the pennies: although both were permitted two guineas a day expenses, Moorehead's basic salary was £12 a week while Clifford's, he suspected, ran closer to £20. Moreover, Moorehead had family responsibilities; in the winter of 1939, on Rome's Campidoglio, he had married Lucy Milner, the go-ahead young Woman's Page editor of the *Daily Express*. Soon, if a passage could be arranged, Lucy would join him in Cairo.

This in a sense was ironic, for in June 1940, as he later phrased it, Moorehead was 'mentally ... more married to Alex than ... to Lucy'. Yet to most on the Cairo scene the two men emerged as what a later generation would hail as 'the Odd Couple'. Moorehead stood five feet eight inches tall: he was, in his own estimation, 'aggressive, erratic and full of enthusiasms'. He was eager, gregarious, 'with the habit of making quick superficial friendships'. Clifford was topping six feet, podgy, testy and supercilious, with owl-like spectacles and a cold analytical approach to life. At five he had first played Bach on the piano, approximately the same age that he had mastered the atlas of the world. Intolerant of both his own and others' ignorance, he had travelled third class or by bicycle over most of Europe, absorbing everything from languages to cooking.

While Moorehead was generous to a fault, Clifford was downright mean. If someone ordered a round of drinks at Gezira, it was not Clifford. Both men roomed at the second-grade Carlton Hotel, where shower closets stood in for bathrooms, rather than at Shepheard's like the established warcos, but although it was Moorehead who kept the communal books, it was Clifford who carped over the bookkeeping. He never smoked, he would point out caustically, so if Moorehead laid on cigarettes for their guests, that was his affair. Unlike Moorehead, who relished expensive meat dishes, Clifford was a near vegetarian; it was for these dishes alone that he paid his share when they dined out.

Despite these fundamental differences they had much in common. As Moorehead put it, their friendship 'was based upon a web of recent experiences that could hardly be shared with anybody else'. During the long nights when the racket from the domino players in the café below combined with shootouts from the westerns at an open-air cinema to make sleep impossible, they were conscious of a slowly strengthening bond.

Both men knew that a crucial moment in this unlooked-for war was fast approaching. Preparations were afoot to establish a new front in Egypt's Western Desert, in the event of Mussolini's troops, under Marshal Rodolfo Graziani, staging an invasion from Italian-held Libya. In readiness for this Moorehead and Clifford spent one intriguing day kitting out at the Officers' Shop at the Kasr-el-Nil barracks. At their papers' expense, they bought suede desert boots fitting half-way up the ankle, knee-length khaki stockings, khaki drill shorts fastening with neat buckles at the midriff and regulation khaki sun helmets.

They bought mosquito nets, camp beds, sleeping bags and canvas washing buckets and to this incredible paraphernalia the army added, at their own expense, water bottles, gas masks, flat steel helmets and revolvers, although arms were normally forbidden. The revolvers, it was stressed, were for use not against the Italians but, if need be, against the Egyptians, who viewed British troops stationed on their soil, even by treaty, as a prickly provocation.

Now they could only wait. The gambit lay with Marshal Graziani.

If war came, they agreed fervently, the true enemy would be neither the Egyptians nor the Italians but GHQ. Although the officers of public relations battled loyally to achieve rapport, it was as if William Howard Russell and Winston Churchill had never plied their trade; the warcos' green-and-gold tabs were viewed by all senior ranks with puzzled loathing. 'The only time I want to see anything about my men in print is when the honours list comes out,' one brigade major told Moorehead sourly. Whether by accident or by design, the censorship offices of the three services were sited so far apart that to visit them all and obtain their stamps of approval a warco had to travel fifteen miles. One early concept was a Censorship Derby, in which correspondents mounted horse-drawn gharries outside Shepheards Hotel and set off to get a message stamped by all three censors.

Since the censors were often absent at golf or at parties, four hours was reckoned to be prime time for a course which ended at the cable office.

An early arrival on the Cairo scene had been Richard Dimbleby, who had moved on from Arras at his own request and was now bitterly regretting it. 'The outbreak of things on the Western Front – and tragic as they have been I shall never forgive myself for having missed them,' he wrote to a friend at the time, 'has put a different complexion on my work here, where the war has not yet begun.' But apart from friendly nods in Shepheards bar Dimbleby, Moorehead and Clifford found little common ground. Neither reporter considered themselves Lord Beaverbrook's or Lord Rothermere's Middle East representative; in Cairo, just as in France, Dimbleby *was* the BBC. Despite his modest £500-a-year salary, he was soon to boost his status with a houseboat on the Nile, complete with *safragi*, and a robed and turbanned chauffeur for his antique Auto-Union.

June dragged on and Moorehead and Dimbleby, both soon to emerge as Britain's foremost correspondents, yet had one thing in common: they had no war to cover. 'The war was not serious in Egypt at this time,' Moorehead was to remember. 'It was merely a noise on the radio.'

Across southern England, the war was abruptly a noise in the sky. Much of it, from a correspondent's view, was seen from what was, arguably, World War Two's smallest battle zone: Shakespeare's Cliff, reputed to feature in *King Lear*, one mile due west of Dover, Kent, looming 350 feet above the English Channel and dense with fluttering swarms of white chalk butterflies. Of the 150 warcos assembled there through August and September, squatting among ripening redcurrant bushes to cover the aerial tournament which Winston Churchill called the Battle of Britain, two-thirds, significantly, were Americans.

Some, to be sure, were old hands: Ed Beattie, Virginia Cowles, Quentin Reynolds. But each day more new faces were appearing on the scene: the red-haired argumentative Vincent Sheean of NANA, Ray Sprigle of the *Pittsburgh Post Gazette*, colourful with his corncob pipe and Stetson hat, Edward R. Murrow, for three years head of CBS in Europe but rarely seen outside London until now, a tall (six feet two inches) tormented figure, immaculate in a Savile Row houndstooth jacket, chainsmoking three packs of Camel cigarettes a day.

Destiny was in the air, and all of them were expectant: if the French had failed to produce a Historic Last Stand, perhaps the British could yet oblige. Ben Robertson, a likable fair-haired youngster from the New York daily *PM*, thought of Daniel Boone's Kentucky stockade – the Indians were coming and the settlers had manned the ramparts. Then the frontier had been the west; now England's frontier was the sky. Vincent Sheean recalled Dolores La Pasionara's exhortation at Madrid during the Civil War: '*Camaradas, no podremos perder más territorio*' ('My friends, we can lose no more territory'). Others, like AP's Robert Bunnelle, saw the cottagers of Dover as the ultimate in imperturbability. 'It's a bit public not having windows,' one householder admitted. 'But the fresh air is nice.'

They had brought along their typewriters, their cameras and their binoculars but somewhere back in their London hotel rooms they had left behind their objectivity. This had been a much discussed stance back in the Phoney War, and even earlier, but despite America's rampant isolationism much of the argument had been academic, even then. Although the *New York Times* was always scrupulous to print Axis as well as Allied communiqués, the London bureau chief, Raymond Daniell, was adamant on that point. 'Neutrality of thought was a luxury to which war correspondents in that first World War could afford to treat themselves,' he maintained. 'We, their successors, cannot.'

As early as September 1939, at a dinner for *Life*'s senior editors in the River Club on East 52nd Street, New York, Henry Luce had equally come down against neutrality, and thus against objectivity. 'This is not a backroom brawl,' he had emphasized, unashamedly quoting the words of Heywood Broun, a radical critic he detested. 'This is Armageddon.'

Thus the die was cast. Through August and September, the goodies, for whom it was permissible to root, were the Spitfire and Hurricane pilots of Fighter Command, defending a 250-mile front from thirteen south coast airfields. The baddies, by implication, were the Messerschmitt 109 and Messerschmitt 110 pilots, who weaved forth to invite battle from captured airstrips in the Pas de Calais – in an effort, it was hazarded, to neutralize the RAF prior to Hitler's seaborne invasion of Britain, Operation Sea-Lion.

Yet this was a campaign shrouded in mystery. Although the gung-ho young Whitelaw Reid, of the *New York Herald Tribune*, hailed the impending invasion as 'the biggest story since the coming of Christ', the Germans were evasive on this score. 'The censors won't let us mention the business,' Shirer noted in his diary on 5 August, and, one month later, 'The word "invasion" is still taboo.'

For the most part, what the warcos witnessed, on these blue and breathless autumn days, was a clawing stalling mass of fighters bent on destruction, battling within a cube 80 miles long by 30 miles broad, more than five miles high: a battle that within thirty minutes might number above 200 individual dogfights. Yet the spectacle, as often as not, produced poetic rather than warlike images. To Hilde Marchant, the planes at all times 'seemed to make an aluminium ceiling to the sky'. For Ben Robertson, the silver wheeling shapes were 'like the white birds you see in far off parts of the Pacific Ocean, like the white birds you see off Pitcairn'.

Despite their overtly partisan stand the Americans still faced censorship problems. In one mid-Channel battle betwen a squadron of Spitfires and a squadron of Messerschmitts, seven German fighters retired smoking from the fray and three British planes hit the water. It was, both Robertson and Reynolds agreed, 'a grand story, and a fine tribute to the RAF', but one censor on the Ministry of Information staff, now monstrously swollen to 999, failed to see it. Robertson could mention the loss of seven Messerschmitts but the three British losses were inadmissible.

Robertson, a tenacious youngster from South Carolina, elected to fight this. From the censor himself, he went to a higher level, and finally, three levels higher to the then Minister of Information, Alfred Duff Cooper. The Minister passed it without question, but it had taken Robertson thirteen hours of impassioned argument to reverse the verdict.

As Reynolds saw it, the main trouble was always with 'the censor himself, the little civil servant, badly paid, who had been given a set of rules, and who would never allow himself to digress from them'. At the outset of the battle, the Ministry's passion for anonymity quite overrode the British public's need for heroes with whom they could identify. A chance meeting between Noel Monks, the *Daily Mail*'s cherubic pewter-haired air correspondent, and the columnist Dorothy Thompson at Lisbon airport revealed the names of aces suppressed until now: Squadron Leader Douglas Bader, whose tin legs, the result of a pre-war crash, were a legend in the RAF; Robert Stanford Tuck, who favoured monogrammed silk handkerchiefs and long cigarette-holders; the South African, Adolph 'Sailor' Malan, one time Third Officer of the Union Castle line.

Once these names had appeared in her column, across the United States, they became, by courtesy of Miss Thompson, equally a part of British folklore.

Yet to one incident which profoundly shocked the Americans, a broadcast by the BBC's Charles Gardner, the Ministry turned a blind eye: a distinctly unneutral description of a dogfight over Dover's white cliffs, charged with as much adrenalin as a racetrack commentary. 'Somebody's hit a German ... and he's coming down ... he's coming down completely out of control,' Gardner was heard to enthuse. 'The pilot's bailed out by parachute ... he's going to slap into the sea and there he goes ... SMASH. Oh boy, I've never seen anything so good as this ...'

Committed as they were to the British cause, the Americans could not yet share this strident approach to battle. For them, the outcome was by no means certain; the fate of the United Kingdom hung in the balance; it was a time of waiting. As Ed Murrow was to recall much later: 'Those were the days and nights and even weeks when time seemed to stand still.'

In the Balkans, too, it was a time of waiting. The five capital cities where time had forever seemed to stand still – Athens, Belgrade, Bucharest, Sofia, Budapest – were just as Oslo and Stockholm had been, a fertile field for loners.

Essentially, these correspondents were a breed apart, wandering cosmopolitans only truly at home at a café table somewhere in Europe. In the Grande Bretagne, Athens, 'with its Prisoner of Zenda atmosphere', the front page of *Messager d'Athènes* absorbed them while the ouzo turned milky in its glass. In the ornate Srpski Kralj Hotel, Belgrade, the equivalent would be the *Balkan Herald* and a slivovitz with iced water chaser. The Britons among them felt few pangs for the trappings of their Fleet Street days, for the sprawling page proofs just down from the stone, the curling photographs fresh from the hypo, the eight-by-six chicken coops that passed for offices or the high stools at the Old Bell, where no reporter nursing a pint could ever be counted off-duty since every newspaper switchboard held its number. They were long since voluntary exiles from that world.

Whatever the hotel or the city, the same cast of characters loomed large at centre stage. There was the suave Cedric Salter of the *Daily Mail*, rarely seen without his ancient but devoted sheepdog and his lovely blonde fiancée Nelly Ciorascu. There was the red headed Irishman Terence Atherton, another *Mail* stalwart, whose Serbo-Croat was fluent. Often David Walker, broad-shouldered and bullet-headed, would be there, juggling his roles as London *Daily Mirror* correspondent, Reuters standby and British intelligence agent. The redoubtable Clare Hollingworth, now covering for the *Daily Express*, shuttled from city to city, dutifully obeying her resolve to sleep on the floor once a week to harden herself for the field, proud that she could strip and reassemble a machine gun as fast as any man. The wooden-legged Walter Duranty, now the *New York Times* man in the Balkans, was usually on hand in Bucharest, to lure them all to what he called 'a whore's breakfast' – caviare and champagne – at his favourite bodega, Fanica Luca.

To join these exalted ranks, two men at least had undergone real hardship. Ray Brock, the hefty and courageous young Texan, accompanied always by his wire-haired fox terrier Slatko and his long-suffering wife Mary, was at last established as the *New York*

Times man in Belgrade. But for nine months all three Brocks had lived on the breadline, filing dispatches to any source that would bankroll their overnight lodgings. It was the same with Robert St John and his wife Eda, who had actively sought war across five countries, standing in train corridors for most of the way. But at thirty-eight, with no foreign languages at his command, the burly, bearded St John, who most resembled an English monk, was thought, like Leland Stowe, to be 'too old for war'. Even now, with the Balkans poised on the threshold between life and death, St John had landed nothing more substantial than a temporary job with AP, drawing $150 a month in any city where action seemed imminent.

Yet St John, like any correspondent worth his salt, had now built up his own retinue of agency stringers and tip-off men, informers who despite the anonymity of crowded hotel lounges spoke mostly in whispers. In five capitals, their sights were set on five men and the looming question mark of the day was: which, if any of them, would capitulate to Adolf Hitler?

A case in point was Admiral Nicholas Horthy, the Regent of Hungary since August 1919. The buzz in Budapest, the capital, was that most senior officers saw Hungary's true future as a German model protectorate, supplying raw materials to the Third Reich with parliament, trade unions and political parties abolished. Certainly no influential Hungarian could say as positively as Ioannis 'Little John' Metaxas, the plump little 'carpet-slippers dictator' of Greece, when cornered by AP's Robert Parker on the Foreign Office steps: 'Greece is neutral, absolutely neutral. We are determined to stay out of this war.'

But all the Balkan rulers were equally in a quandary. In his Sofia study, as cluttered as a storeroom, King Boris III of Bulgaria, an amiable lepidopterist who also collected mountain flower petals, might insist to Parker that he saw Hitler as 'no threat'. Yet Clare Hollingworth coolly adjudged him as 'shrewd, selfish and self-seeking ... able enough to act a double part, politically speaking'. King Boris, like Prince Paul, Regent of Yugoslavia, whom Miss Hollingworth wrote off as 'that sad specimen of Oxford-educated humanity', really sought to immure himself inside a wall of privacy, with few commitments to either side.

Inside the great hotels – the Carlton, Budapest, the Athenée Palace, Bucharest – the wastebasket trade was by now in full swing. Sizable sums in Romanian *lei* and Hungarian *pengoes* were doled out to chambermaids who in turn delivered the entire contents of a wastebasket from any specific room, wrapped in a pillowcase. This precious expertise, with distinct undertones of Ian Fleming and John le Carré, was, as Robert St John said, 'as much of a gamble as a grab-bag'; the pillow might contain confidential letters but equally it might yield only chewing-gum wrappers and torn-up laundry bills. Yet the traffic continued unabated; British warcos bought up German wastebaskets, the Germans bought up British, while the Greeks and Turks, with cheerful abandon, bought up everybody's.

It was by no means all cloak-and-dagger histrionics. What a ruler said might be one thing; how he might secretly yield under pressure was quite another. 'National Socialism may be good for Germany, Fascism for Italy and Bolshevism for Russia but ... none of these is wanted by Bulgaria,' was the stance of King Boris III, as reported to the State Department by the US Minister George Earle. None of this entirely jibed with what the warcos were soon to discover for themselves. In Sofia, Cyrus L. Sulzburger of the *New York Times* was conscious of 'hundreds of Germans dressed in civilian clothes and carrying light baggage, with smooth soapstone faces and cornflower blue eyes'. Michael Padev, the London *Times* man on the spot, got a priority tip-off from a local: signposts in German were being erected at great speed on all the roads round the capital. At Ruschuk on the Danube, Clare Hollingworth chanced on the first of the German technicians arriving to construct fourteen airfields for later use by the Luftwaffe.

In the high summer of 1940 the eyes of the Balkan-watchers were primarily focused on King Carol II of Romania, a flabby green-eyed descendant of Queen Victoria, who was currently giving a discreditable imitation of Bunyan's Mr Facing-Both-Ways.

Ever since the outbreak of war King Carol had been in the hot seat. 'Germany has no hold whatsoever on this country and never will have,' he told the ubiquitous Robert Parker, but this was for public consumption. In an endeavour to stay Hitler's aggressive hand, Romania was currently shipping $10 million worth of wheat each year to Germany and 300 tank cars of oil a day. To ensure that the wheat sprouted on time, Carol had even mobilized the four million boys and girls of the National Youth Movement behind the plough – to forestall the despatch of 6000 German 'agricultural experts'.

It was a drama played out from first to last against backdrops of stupendous bad taste. The Royal Palace on the main square, Piata Athenelui, had been built to rival Buckingham Palace; the interior,

Parker noted, which included a 1000-seat theatre, 'would have made even a Hollywood film director gasp'. Marble staircases soared to right and left, with a flunkey in blue and gold livery stationed motionless on each step; the entire first floor was an unabashed reproduction of the Hall of Mirrors at Versailles. Huge portraits of Carol, twenty feet high, loomed at intervals along corridors bristling with suits of armour and china cuspidors.

Across the square, the warcos were ensconced in the Hotel Athenée Palace, a white blue-shuttered pile approached across a vast expanse of asphalt, flanked in summer by blood-red gladioli. In the main lobby, walls of rust-coloured marble were crowded with narrow gold-framed mirrors, and these in turn were offset by heavy marble pillars and raspberry-coloured plush sofas. It was a lobby, reported David Walker to all three of his employers, currently teeming with spies, notably Edith von Koehler, a plump and dressy blonde who, incredibly, passed herself off as Agricultural Correspondent for the *Deutsche Allgemeine Zeitung*. Security was so tight that when Margaret Bourke-White, a red-haired Valkyrie, arrived on a photographic assignment for *Life* she was escorted everywhere by the Prefect of Police, a Propaganda Ministry official, an army officer and the city architect.

Elaborate codes had been dreamed up to fox both censors and telephone-tappers. Thus, in the secret vocabulary of AP, whose headquarters in southeastern Europe was Budapest, Hitler was 'Oscar', Mussolini was 'Armstrong', King Carol was 'The Boy Scout', from his passion for designing their uniforms, and his mistress, the red-haired Magda Lupescu, was 'Glamour Girl'. Just before midnight on 26 June, the telephone rang unexpectedly in Robert Parker's Budapest office. On the line was St John from Bucharest. 'Here it is,' he shouted, his voice high with excitement, 'Uncle Joe has sent the Boy Scout a letter about Bessie.' Then he hung up.

Translated, this meant that Joseph Stalin – 'Uncle Joe' – had demanded from King Carol the cession of 17,000 square miles of Bessarabia, eastern Romania, formerly a Russian domain. Within minutes, this coded message had been passed to New York by radio.

At first, in desperation, King Carol had sought help from Hitler, but the Führer was unresponsive; above all, to ensure his oil supplies, he wanted peace in the Balkans. He advised Carol to yield to the Russians. Now the King saw for the first time that all his conciliatory gestures had gone for nothing. He had actively sought a German military mission in Bucharest. He had restored freedom to the pro-Nazi Jew-baiting Iron Guard under its chief, General Ion 'Red Dog' Antonescu, a personal friend of Hitler's. On 21 June, with one decree, he had made Romania totalitarian, with a single new Party of the Nation.

Although Carol had it within his power to call Hitler's bluff, threatening to destroy the oil wells around Ploesti, he feared for his personal fortune and did not dare. Personal fortune was an intimate concern of both the King and Magda Lupescu; in his nine-year reign they had treated the country as a cash register, to be milked at will, with regal rakeoffs from both the state railways and the state textile mills. To keep the state looms humming the Boy Scouts' uniforms had been changed three times.

As Romania approached crisis point passions, not surprisingly, ran high. Views as to whether Carol would or would not yield grew acerbic. When the *Chicago Tribune*'s Edmund Taylor ventured that Romania was ripe for a Russo-German attack his proprietor, the choleric Colonel Robert McCormick, cabled angrily: 'Suggest you join Foreign Legion or else take rest cure in sanitarium in neutral country until you regain control of your nerves.' Clare Hollingworth, mindful that any exclusive story might be denied, always protected herself a few hours after phoning it to Geneva by passing it on to AP. Their duplication of her story, she thought, would give the solid imprimatur of accuracy. When the Romanians, galled by her honest truths, tried to summarily expel her, Miss Hollingworth promptly stripped to the buff, refusing to slip on more than a dressing gown until the police agents left her apartment.

As September dawned, King Carol, under mounting pressure from Hitler, finally cracked. Intent on maintaining absolute peace within the Balkans, the Führer was conscious that Romania was still pockmarked with islands of foreigners, whose parent states coveted their return. The prospect of a local fracas that might cut off the Reich from its main source of crude oil was unthinkable, and on 30 August Carol was ordered to restore the province of Dobruja to Bulgaria and 16,000 square miles of Transylvania to Hungary.

When nationalist riots erupted in Bucharest in protest at this sellout, Hitler's reaction was prompt: unless order was restored, Germany would occupy all Romania with troops.

The King saw the red light. He offered to abdicate in favour of his son, eighteen-year-old Prince Michael. The reins of power now passed to General Antonescu. Within six weeks the rule of his Iron

Guard saw even neutral correspondents seeking safer frontiers.

At least they remained long enough to piece together the details of Carol's departure. Travelling with Lupescu by night under the aliases of 'Mr and Mrs Carol Caraiman', the King fled in suitably Ruritanian style, in a nine-coach train with three bulletproof automobiles, the royal stamp collection, four Rembrandts, sixteen poodles, six pet white turkeys, $2.5 million worth of jewels, a flock of peacocks and a million-dollar haul of gold coins.

That was on Saturday, 7 September, the weekend that all the British still based on the Athenée Palace looked askance at the front page of the city's leading daily, *Universul*. The war, it seemed, had caught up with their own capital. The headline read: LONDON A SEA OF FLAME.

They had not known it was *Der Tag*: the virtual climax of the Battle of Britain, which was to peter out after 15 September, the onset of the Battle of London, which history was to call the Blitz. What they sought, on that warm Saturday afternoon, 7 September, Ben Robertson later explained, was perspective: a chance to view the next stage of the battle from well outside the city limits. So Robertson and Vincent Sheean had piled aboard Ed Murrow's Sunbeam-Talbot convertible, driving out through the miles of slate-roofed slums east of Aldgate, following the line of the Thames through Limehouse and Stepney to Gravesend on the estuary.

All three were correspondents with impeccable sources, but no word had reached them that following a 24 August raid on Berlin, the Luftwaffe had switched priorities. From now on, for fifty-seven nights without respite, the target would be London.

Instead, like boys let loose from school, they bought enough apples to fill three steel helmets, paying a farmer two shillings (tenpence), then, chancing on a haystack at the edge of a turnip field, lay down to munch apples and doze in the sun.

When the sirens sounded and the ack-ack began its urgent pounding, that was no more than routine from Dover days. When the first British fighters soared overhead, intercepting the first wave of German bombers, that, too, was routine. But when more waves of German bombers, a second, a third, then a fourth passed overhead in glinting dragonfly formation, heading for the docks, and the vast columns of smoke began to rise over London, this was very far from routine.

Nor were any moments routine in the twelve hours of fearful

martial bombardment which followed. At 6.30 pm, when the all
clear sounded, the three had sought refuge in a pub for a pie and a
pint. At 8.10 pm, the siren wailed again; they returned to the
haystack. Yet out of that long and awful night they afterwards
retained only fleeting impressions. Robertson recalled it as 'a night
like the Revelation of St John'; he had no memory of repeating over
and over the childish jingle, 'London is burning, London is burning.'
Sheean remembered prophesying that 'the fire they set this night
would consume them, too, before it was quenched', but, though
fluent in five languages, he did not remember cursing in all of
them. Murrow remembered most, for on the Sunday night his CBS
broadcast from Studio B4 in the basement of Broadcasting House
would be followed by 30 million American listeners, tuned to his
sepulchral lead-in: 'This . . . is London.' In Murrow's recollection,
'The fire up the river had turned the moon blood-red . . . huge pear-
shaped bursts of flame would rise up into the smoke and disappear
. . . the world was upside-down.'

'He was concerned, very concerned . . . that if Hitler and Co
were not stopped here,' Godfrey Talbot, then a BBC colleague,
would recall, 'the next stop was Manhattan.'

Closer to the target area, other American warcos shared this
same concern. 'They are living through hell,' Raymond Daniell
cabled the *New York Times*, 'and behaving like angels'; even in the
lawyers' district of Lincoln's Inn, miles from the blazing heart of
dockland, Daniell was conscious of bombs 'like blows being rained
upon an inert body' and 'the big bombers that danced like moths
round that great fire'.

Farther west, on the roof of Lansdowne House, an apartment
block off Berkeley Square, Quentin Reynolds witnessed the raid in
company with his new flatmate, Robert Low of New York's *Liberty*
magazine. Appropriately, Reynolds, who for millions of Britons and
Americans was to become almost the apotheosis of the Blitz, found
this raid 'as exciting an ordeal as I imagine living in the Athens of
Pericles must have been'. For paradoxically, he found 'the constant
threat of death seemed to make people really alive'.

Appropriately, too, about this time a cable from a group of
wellwishers reached him from New York: 'WE ARE MISSING
YOU HERE. WE HOPE THEY ARE MISSING YOU
THERE.'

It was Ed Murrow and his companions who saw the true aftermath of 7 September. Long after 3 am they had returned to the

inn at Gravesend, slumping into bed without even removing their
clothes, in tiny bedrooms lit by the wavering glare of many fires.
Much later that morning they drove back to London through the
still-burning East End. As the car picked its way through rubble-
blocked streets, they saw for the first time the devastation wrought
by more than 600 Luftwaffe bombers: the truckloads of glass, the
cars 'with stretchers racked on the roof like skis', the ruptured gas
mains, searing and flaring, the red buses lined up to evacuate the
homeless – 'Men with white scarves around their necks ... Dull-eyed
empty-faced women ... most of them carried little cheap cardboard
suitcases and sometimes bulging paper shopping bags. That was all
they had left.' Or, as Sheean, with memories of Spain, cabled in a
NANA dispatch: '... moving, ever moving, like the poor in all wars,
taking to the roads'.

Overnight, a new London was revealed to these outsiders seeing
most of the game. Barely nine months ago, the earliest on the scene
had reported on a silent city where the loudest sounds had been 'the
solitary honk of a bus' feeling its way through the blackout, the
tapping of a blind man's cane. On moonless nights, a man might
find himself completely lost in a city of seven million souls. All that
was now in the past. Now the nights began with the chilling rise and
fall of the siren, the uneven throb of the bomber engines 15,000 feet
overhead, 'like a witch in a child's dream', the urgent scurrying of
feet in search of air raid shelters, the manic fury of the ack-ack's box
barrage over 200 square miles of greater London, as the white beams
of the searchlights stabbed and probed the sky.

In this new city, strange sights and experiences had become the
norm. It was a weird unnatural life, even for the birds, observers
reported, for they awoke and sang when the searchlights turned
night into day. On one night, Molly Panter-Downes of the *New
Yorker* spotted waiters and chefs racing a raw sirloin of beef from a
Pall Mall club that had been hit into a club whose kitchen still
functioned. It was with awe that Ben Robertson heard Sir Walter
Monckton, Deputy Director-General of the Ministry of Information, recount how he and a lone woman had fallen face down as
bombs fell in the Haymarket. A minute later, checking on her
welfare, he found that she had no head. It was with incredulity that
Robertson and the Australian Eric Baume, not far from blazing St
Clement Danes Church, saw a West Indian warden, crowned by a
white steel helmet, emerge from a nearby shelter. 'Well, gentlemen,'
he greeted them, beaming, 'history is being destroyed. Yes, sir. But

it will be reborn.' With that he disappeared.

'Where do you sleep?' had become the key question, noted Ralph Ingersoll, the recently arrived publisher of the New York daily *PM*, quite displacing the weather as the opening gambit of conversation. Many Londoners, he soon found, 200,000 of them all told, slept far below ground, in 'the lost land of Arp', for in every street 'dimly illuminated signs which read simply A.R.P. [Air Raid Precautions] point to the nearest shelter'. In one long night's per-egrination, Quentin Reynolds was witness to an entire city 'surviving in caves', eighty feet down in underground railway stations, their squatting figures throwing forlorn shadows on the tiled walls, bedded down on floors gritty and buff-coloured from leaking sandbags. For all the talk of equal sacrifice, London was still a city of haves and have-nots, although this was not a topic encouraged by the censors. At the Dorchester Hotel in Park Lane, Ingersoll noted, the rich slept deep in the bowels of the earth, in air raid shelters with reserved partitions, marked out by pink and blue silk curtains. In the lobby of the Ritz in Piccadilly, Virginia Cowles saw a greater informality: simple beds of pillows and mattresses improvised by guests in black pyjamas or siren suits, with the sister of the exiled King Zog of Albania shaking down on the floor outside the restaurant.

'We lived like milkmen and farmers in the biggest city in the world,' Ben Robertson reported, recalling wryly the mass bedding-down at nightfall, the mass exodus from the Tube at sunrise, and like all of them he paid unstinting tribute to the Londoners and the 'Elizabethan fire in their guts'. But he reflected, with something like wonder, 'the Blitzkrieg was to teach us that war was not so bad as the fear of war'.

Between 7 September and 13 November, an estimated 13,651 tons of high explosive and 12,586 incendiary canisters were showered upon the city. Now, as Quentin Reynolds was discovering, not only tiny red-brick homes were at risk, but buildings which had stood for two centuries before Berlin had even been founded. (Damage to places of public interest were released to the warcos within seven days.) Somerset House, where Shakespeare's will, among others, was held, lost its superb staircase. John Nash's curving Regent Street was ripped by a delayed action bomb. So, too, were the National and Tate Galleries, William Hogarth's panelled house in Chiswick, the gothic House of Lords and Wesminster Abbey. Churches, too, were under fire: Christopher Wren's St James's Piccadilly, close to Reynolds's own apartment block, Wren's much admired St

Stephen's, Walbrook, St Mary-at-Hill, St Dunstan-in-the-East and the Church of Our Lady of Victories.

Out of this concern was born the project which for millions of Britons as well as Americans established Reynolds as the authentic voice of the city under fire: a seven-minute documentary film, *London Can Take It*, a concept of his old friend Sidney (later Lord) Bernstein, then deputy head of the Ministry of Information film division. Directed by two emerging talents, Harry Watt and Humphrey Jennings, with what Sheean called Reynolds's 'rumbling bass drawl' as commentary, the film achieved triumphant October premieres in London's West End and on Broadway. For the first time, audiences far from the front line heard the whining shuddering roar, like an express train flashing from a tunnel, that signalled a high-explosive bomb, and the sizzling blue-white glare that marked a cluster of incendiaries. Equally they saw the familiar scene that marked every London dawn: the moraines of timber and lath and plaster, the torn window curtains, the fine glitter of powdered glass covering the pavements like hoar frost.

Missing only were the smells Reynolds had come to know too well: the harsh acrid stench of cordite from HEs, leaking gas and blue London clay, charred wood and pulverized plaster.

Unknown to many cinema-goers other features, on the Ministry of Information's 'stop' list, were missing from *London Can Take It*. Under a new Chief Censor, Rear-Admiral George Thomson, a retired submariner plagued by stomach ulcers, a more liberal policy was now becoming apparent; in Thomson's view, the more the truth was told, the higher stood morale. Yet some prohibitions remained constant to the end. The names and localities of damaged buildings – apart from historic monuments – were forbidden until twenty-eight days after a raid. Raids on factories went unreported. In newsreels of blitzed streets, at least one building must remain intact. Any item calculated to spread terror was suppressed: the presence of unexploded bombs (UXBs) and the Luftwaffe's new and lethal land mines, actually sea mines eight feet long, descending silently at 40 miles an hour on green silk parachutes, packed with 2200 tons of dynamite.

The stench of the Thames, after London's main sewer outfall was destroyed on 6 October, remained an untold story. So, strangely, did the location of 3000 pictures from the National Gallery despatched to a disused slate quarry in Wales, along with many of the British Museum's treasures. The RAF's home and enemy losses, although dutifully cabled to the United States, often proved inaccurate when matched against the Luftwaffe's.

To most warcos even these stringent vetoes made sense of a kind. But inevitably, as in the Battle of Britain, petty bureaucracy reared its head. When Reynolds submitted a Sunday night's broadcast script berating Germany, the BBC at once objected – 'Many of our Sunday night listeners are churchgoers. It is all right to hate the Germans on weekdays but not on Sundays.' It took an appeal to Alfred Duff Cooper to clear that script. Raymond Daniell was in equal trouble when explaining how 'the silver stream of the Thames pointed out the way to London'. Although this was a landmark known to every German bomber pilot, the censor blocked it: 'It would give the enemy important information.' Before hanging up the phone Daniell, exasperated, flung back, 'I suppose if I said the Amazon instead of the Thames it would be all right.'

One hour later the cable editor of the *New York Times*, in the main office on West 43rd Street, was bemused to read Daniell's intimation that 'the silver stream of the Amazon river pointed the way to London'.

Yet the Americans were given greater facilities than most, and they knew it. 'The British wanted the publicity in America,' Mary Welsh of *Time*'s London office remembered, 'and lowered their defences against US reporters.' There were cogent reasons for this. Even before Roosevelt's landslide re-election victory on 5 November, the United States had at last been coming through with help of a kind. On 28 September, the first of fifty over-age flush-decker US destroyers had reached British ports: a horse trade in return for America's right to defend and fortify eight British-held Atlantic bases like Newfoundland and the Bahamas. Roosevelt, like Ed Murrow, saw Britain's survival as paramount. Ahead, in March 1941, loomed the promise of Lend-Lease: the President's decision to supply Britain with munitions for free, to be paid for in kind when the war was over.

Thus any warco reaching London from New York via the Trans-Atlantic Clipper to Lisbon soon became a warco-about-town – 'No door was closed, no voice unkind,' Sheean chuckled wryly. Ben Robertson swiftly found himself welcome in the social whirls revolving round Diana and Alfred Duff Cooper and Nancy Astor and her husband Waldorf. Raymond Daniell's contacts ranged from the society hostess Sybil, Lady Colefax, to the former Chief of the Imperial General Staff, General Edmund Ironside. At one party in St James's he chatted affably with Queen Elizabeth (now Queen Elizabeth the Queen Mother), enchanting in powder blue and cheerfully sipping White Ladies, a heady brew of Cointreau, lemon juice and dry gin, with the best of them.

For the warcos, with space to report their findings, proved friends indeed. Until the war's end, the *New York Times*'s daily imprint of 500,000 copies carried an average 217 columns; to extend full coverage to the war news, advertisers were cut down to a scant quarter page and no help-wanted ads could exceed two lines. By contrast Fleet Street, following the fall of Norway and the rationing of newsprint, was in dire straits; the *Daily Express*, down to six pages from July 1940, was reduced to four before the Blitz ended. Thirty news items to a page became the inexorable rule.

It was an imperceptibly changing world that they had come to report. Chamberlainism was dead: the Old School Tie was going fast. 'You must understand that a world is dying,' Murrow strove to impress on his listeners on Sunday, 15 September. 'The old values, the old prejudices, all the old bases of power and prestige are going ... this war has no relation with the last one, so far as symbols and civilians are concerned.' And Clare Boothe noted that 'The era of "Have you heard ... ?"' had been supplanted by a newer, grimmer resolution.

Like the Britons whose lives they were reporting, the warcos were learning to adapt. All too soon a change of residence became a way of life. One newcomer, J. Norman Lodge, transferred from the AP office in Dublin, was bombed out of his digs three times within a week before reporting, 'My clothes have been so thoroughly smoked that everything I wear smells like Genuine Harris Tweed.' One of the first to move had been Daniell, bombed out of his Lincoln's Inn flat as early as September. After twice switching offices from 162A Queen Victoria Street to the fiendishly crowded Reuters building at 85 Fleet Street, he finally moved himself and his five-strong editorial staff into the Savoy Hotel, billing the paper for both office and bedroom space. 'I never quite got over the feeling that I was playing a part in a Noel Coward comedy,' was his later reaction to this rarefied atmosphere, although his girlfriend, the *Times* staffer Tania Long, adapted more swiftly. On one occasion, when dining in Daniell's suite, a bomb shook the hotel so vigorously that a chunk of plaster from the ceiling landed in Tania's soup. 'Please,' she begged the room waiter, deadpan, 'no more croûtons.'

Reynolds himself stayed put at Lansdowne House until the

spring of 1941, at the time the Blitz was virtually over, when the Ministry of Food requisitioned the entire block. Then, as Robert Low departed for the Middle East, Reynolds, along with Arthur Christiansen, the *Daily Express* editor, who had evacuated his family to the country, followed Daniell's example and took a suite at the Savoy. A longtime resident at Lansdowne House, 'Chris' had taken readily to 'Quent', tickled by his neo-Wodehousian habit of address-ing all Englishmen as 'old bean'. 'Quent', in turn, was intrigued by 'Chris's' inability to brief a warco articulately, for all that emerged to indicate powerful prose was a staccato 'Whammo! Whammo! Whammo!'

In 'Tich's Bar' where the warcos foregathered, on the Embank-ment side of the Savoy, presided over by bartender 'Tich' Massara, Reynolds was, on the surface, the life and soul of a very long-drawn-out party. At times, the tales grew as uproarious as the barrage across the river: how Reynolds, Low and Christiansen had all evacuated Lansdowne House in their pyjamas and dressing gowns at the height of an incendiary raid, but it was Christiansen who had presciently snatched up a bottle of brandy, prompting Low's snappy appraisal, 'This is why Chris is an editor, and you and I are only reporters.'

It always prompted a gale of laughter and a fresh round of drinks, but behind the jovial façade Reynolds was already sick at heart. In too short a time, he had seen more than most, and the knowledge that much worse was to come haunted him; he was perhaps the first of his generation to echo William Howard Russell's heart-cry: 'Cursed is he that delighteth in war.' 'I never really learned to enjoy the ... raids,' he wrote, many years later. 'I hated and dreaded them, but like everyone else I learned to live with them.' Nor was this hindsight. In a letter that he wrote at this time, his revulsion was made plain. 'I've seen too many women and kids pulled out of houses dead to get any exciting kick out of this,' he confessed. 'It's just horrible – not exciting ... the New York papers shouldn't send war correspondents over here; they should sent sports-writers. This is a new sport, but still it is a sport! It is called shooting fish in a barrel!'

To outsiders like himself, one factor was plain: the security bred by three centuries of freedom from war on their own soil had given the English an invincible sense of superiority. Few among them could now conceive of being beaten. Pierre Bourdan, chief of the newly created London-based Agence Française Indépendante, never forgot an interview he was granted around this time by Sir Archibald

Sinclair, Churchill's Under Secretary of State for Air.

Studying a huge wall map of the world, Sinclair told Bourdan seriously: 'We shall probably lose Egypt, Malta, Aden, the Middle East, perhaps the Indies, Singapore, and, I'm very much afraid, dear old Gibraltar, too.'

As he reeled off this formidable list, like a geography master, Bourdan gazed at him in disbelief. Then, shaking his head and frowning, Sinclair confided: 'Yes, I very much fear it will be five or six years before we win this war.'

At 9 am on Monday, 9 December, a morning of bright sunlight across the Nile Valley, the winning of World War Two no longer seemed beyond the bounds of possibility. At GHQ, Cairo, seven war correspondents – those few whose editors still felt that the theatre held some potential – had gathered in the office of the C-in-C, Middle East, General Sir Archibald Wavell. As he leaned against his desk, clad informally in shirt-sleeves, Alan Moorehead noted that for the first time since he had known him the taciturn, withdrawn Wavell was smiling slightly. Soon enough he heard that Wavell had reasons.

'Gentlemen,' he led off, 'I have asked you to come here this morning to let you know that we have attacked in the Western Desert. This is not an offensive ... you might call it an important raid. The attack was made early this morning and I had word an hour ago that the first of the Italian camps has fallen.'

To men like Moorehead and Alexander Clifford, who had endured long months of idleness following the fortunes of besieged London, this was heartening news. ('It was difficult to convert the news that St Paul's Cathedral and the Strand were being bombed into a clear visual image,' Moorehead confessed later.) In their own theatre of war the stalemate had seemed to stretch forever. On 13 September, just as anticipated, Graziani's Italians, 80,000 strong, had launched an offensive across the Egyptian border, hoping to make a clean sweep to the Suez Canal. Outnumbered, the British had fallen back according to plan. In a headlong four-day advance the Italians pushed sixty miles beyond the frontier, to reach the mud-hut village of Sidi Barrani. Here they paused to consolidate their gains, fanning out in a semicircle of seven defensive camps. The British, meanwhile, fell back eighty miles further into Egypt, to the sponge-fishers' village of Mersa Matruh – the terminus of a narrow-gauge supply railway from Alexandria.

Moorehead, like his colleagues, had more than once made the 300-mile journey from Cairo to Mersa, bowling along the good macadam road past the weary date palms and the coarse grass poking from the hot grey ground, within sight of a spotless white beach. It was there, well in advance of any pitched battle, that the analogy between the desert and sea warfare first struck him – inspired, perhaps, by a tour of duty with the Mediterranean Fleet.

'Each truck or tank,' he reasoned, 'was as individual as a destroyer, and each squadron of tanks or guns made great sweeps across the desert as a battle squadron at sea will vanish over the horizon ... there was no front line ... we hunted men not land, as a warship will hunt another warship, and care nothing for the sea on which the action is fought.'

It was at Mersa, too, that Moorehead experienced his first *khamsin* sand storm, which picked up 'the surface dust as finely as baking powder', to blow it 'thickly into the air across hundreds of square miles of desert'. In an unreal yellow light, sand and grit seeped through the closed windows of a car, matting one's hair, penetrating one's ears and nostrils. 'I hate them,' Moorehead was to write in 1941, 'and I hate the desert because of them,' yet it was from the desert that he was to send the dispatches which marked him out from other men.

At dawn on 10 December, their journey to the front began. At the best of times, as Moorehead and Clifford knew, it was a day and a half's journey from Cairo. But in the wake of an unexpected British victory – achieved, they discovered, through total surprise and the use of newly arrived 30-ton Matilda tanks, their three-inch armour impenetrable to Italian guns – this proved to be the worst of times. Cars broke their half shafts. Dispatch riders broke down. In the days that followed, the warcos hitchhiked and made do without sleep to catch up with that evanescent front line.

Only by degrees did the magnitude of the triumph dawn on them. What Wavell had planned, since only 30,000 troops under Lieutenant-General Richard O'Connor were available to him, was a five-day raid, with Buq Buq, twenty-five miles west of Sidi Barrani, as his halt line. His first objective, the fortified camp of Nibeiwa, had fallen at 7.15 am on 9 December – one hour and forty-five minutes before he summoned the warcos to GHQ.

Such was the confusion, Moorehead recalled later, that the correspondents could do little more than trail in O'Connor's wake. Yet, as he also admitted, this was a new kind of reporting that perfectly suited his eager terrier-like temperament – 'exasperating, exciting, fast-moving, vivid, immense and slightly dangerous'. There was little scope for notetaking, but Moorehead, unlike the *Express*'s star man, O'Dowd Gallagher, rarely took notes – 'It is a very fragile and fortuitous thing, this moment of the first impression but with me it is indelible, and no matter whether I am dealing with places or people I seldom altogether forget it, or perhaps see so clearly again.'

His first impressions of Nibeiwa, that mighty encampment with a four-mile circumference, more than confirmed this. From the moment he set foot within its stockade, every sight was proof that the Italians had 'wanted to be masters of the desert. They made their lives comfortable and static. They built roads and stone houses . . . they tried to subdue the desert. And in the end the desert beat them.'

Evidence of that ambition was everywhere about him, as the soft sand blew endlessly, obliterating 'piles of food, rifles, boxes of ammunition, the carcasses of animals'. Foraging in more than thirty dugouts, beneath huge signs bearing the Mussolinian exhortations he remembered from the streets of Rome – 'Chi Se Ferma è Perduto' ('He who hesitates is lost') and 'Sempre Avanti' ('Ever onward') – he found evidence of a luxury unknown either to Wavell or O'Connor. There were officers' beds with clean sheets and chests of drawers filled with linen, polished jackboots and 'great blue cavalry coats that swathed a man to the ankles'. With their own food supplies in doubt, Moorehead and the others fed splendidly on Italian leavings: 'Parmesan cheeses as big as small cartwheels', tins of frozen hams and anchovies, followed by bottled cherries and greengages, washed down with Recoaro mineral water and 'giant barrels of Chianti'.

Across five miles of landscape the ground was strewn with letters: the soul of a nation laid bare in the sand. There were many written 'in a thin spidery schoolboy scrawl . . . full of warm superlatives like *carissimo . . . benissimo*'. Some were infused with wishful thinking: 'We shall soon be at Alexandria. We shall soon now be exchanging this hellish desert for the gardens on the Nile.' Yet in many Moorehead found a core of hard common sense. 'We are trying to fight this war as though it is a colonial war in Africa,' one letter-writer insisted, 'but it is a European war in Africa fought with European weapons against a European enemy. We take too little account of this in building our stone forts and equipping ourselves with such luxury. We are not fighting the Abyssinians now.'

Yet in the bleak months following Dunkirk, Mussolini's forces under the Governor General of Italian East Africa, the Duke of Aosta, had seized parts of the Sudan and Kenya and all of British Somaliland. So was this, Moorehead wondered, the turn of the tide?

As they journeyed northward, towards the coast beyond Nibeiwa, it seemed that it was. 'Things had gone with a precision and speed that outstripped all communications.' The Matildas had fallen upon Sidi Barrani itself, and everywhere 'groups of Italians began bobbing up from their trenches, waving white handkerchiefs, towels, shirts and shouting "*Ci rendiamo*"' ('We surrender'). Everywhere Italian lorries, guns and deserted storage dumps told the same story. Towards Buq Buq, Moorehead and the others beheld an astounding sight: an entire division was being marched back into captivity, a 'stupendous crocodile of marching figures stretched away to either horizon', shepherded by British soldiers patently outnumbered by 500 to one. On 16 December – one week after the fighting began – Sollum, northwest of Buq Buq on the coast, fell, and with Sollum, Halfaya Pass, Fort Capuzzo, Sidi Omar, Musaid, and a new line of forts several kilometres long which the Italians had built on the lip of the escarpment. The bulk of the Italians would surrender at Beda Fomm, nearly 300 miles inside Libya.

For the first time the warcos who made the desert their beat had been well and truly blooded. Both food and petrol gave out at intervals: precious hours were wasted each day ranging the desert in search of abandoned Italian dumps. At night, all slept huddled in one car for warmth, cursing the useless impedimenta of camp beds and washing buckets with which Public Relations had burdened them. Clifford went down with sandfly fever and jaundice and could not eat for three days, finally breaking his fast with a lethal diet of tinned plum pudding and whisky. On 17 December, it was high time to return to Cairo for Christmas.

On the face of it, the score was phenomenal. At least 30,000 prisoners had been taken, including five generals. Hundreds of guns, lorries, tanks and aircraft had been captured, along with millions of pounds' worth of equipment. The Italian advance to the Nile had been smashed and the last Italian soldier driven from Egypt. After the deep humiliation of Norway, Dunkirk and British Somaliland, Moorehead felt, 'the prestige of the British army [was] restored.'

It was small wonder that he could report with zest: 'Our stale descriptions could be published fully when at last they did arrive in London and New York.' In essence, the tide had equally turned for him. 'It was a job that was forever a little beyond one's reach. But I personally emerged from it ... very glad to have been there and much wiser than when I went in.'

IV

Hitler Likes To Start Things On Sundays

(18 DECEMBER 1940–14 SEPTEMBER 1941)

Much later, armed with the precious gift of hindsight, Alan Moore-head was forced to a wry admission: the wisdom he had celebrated on leaving the desert in December 1940 paled before the experience he had acquired before 1941 was out. As an impulsive twenty-nine-year-old, one key element in a warco's life had escaped him; the fortunes of war.

For much of that year, Moorehead lived life on two levels: a tranquil domestic round in a first-floor flat overlooking the green lawns of the Gezira Club, together with Lucy, who had arrived by flying-boat in August in a blue-and-white maternity dress, their newly born son John, and Hassan, their *safragi*, who made all things possible. Their unlikely and permanent houseguest was Alexander Clifford, yet notably it was Clifford who adapted to this newfound domesticity, the regular hours and the set meals, more readily than Moorehead himself. It was Alex, as John's godfather, who looked after him on the nurse's day off, and Alex, more often than not, who steered his perambulator over the Gezira lawns or awoke to quieten his crying in the night.

For Moorehead his first real intimations of success were a heady time. All at once he was the centre of the now fashionable theatre of war, for Cairo, in the spring of 1941, was *the* place to be. After fifteen months in the doldrums, vindicated only by the Battle of Britain, the British had contrived to win a positive victory, and accreditations to GHQ were sought as eagerly as tickets to a May ball. From the paltry seven correspondents who had clustered round Wavell's desk

69

on 9 December, the total had swollen to ninety-two by June, and more were arriving daily.

There were manifold reasons for this. Alarmed by Italy's reversal in Libya, Hitler had come to his Axis partner's rescue, and on 12 February *Generalleutnant* Erwin Rommel had arrived in Tripoli to command a newly formed German Afrika Corps. On 24 March Rommel, a master of tank warfare, had struck back at the British so forcefully that by 9 April three British generals – Lieutenant-General Philip Neame, VC, O'Connor's successor, O'Connor himself, and Major-General Michael Gambier-Parry of the 2nd Armoured Division – were prisoners of war, and all Libya, aside from the gadfly garrison of Tobruk, on the coast of Cyrenaica, had been abandoned. It was a defeat that by late June 1941 had cost Wavell his command, but with an adversary like Rommel, the legendary 'Desert Fox', at centre stage, the Western Desert had become a war worth reporting for British and Americans alike.

There were other urgent reasons for warcos to converge on Cairo. Over intimate supper parties in Moorehead's Gezira flat and in Shepheard's bar the stories were told in excited detail; following months of tension, the fragile Balkan infrastructure had fallen apart. Scores of correspondents were now seeking fresh fields, not only a tranquil land where cables could be drafted but a safe haven from the swooping hawk-shapes of Luftwaffe bombers.

The débâcle had been foreshadowed as far back as 28 October, when Benito Mussolini, bent on scoring off Hitler for preempting the oil-rich regions of Romania, had sent four ill-equipped Italian divisions storming into Greece. The time had come for *Il Duce* to prove to *Der Führer* that he too could invade and conquer. To his surprise, the Greeks had fought back like tigers; within weeks the Italians were in headlong retreat, surrounded at the ports of Durazzo and Valona, their backs to the sea. But despite Churchill's quixotic – and impractical – offer of military aid, Premier Ioannis Metaxas had summarily declined. Above all, he feared German intervention.

How much he feared it was made abundantly plain to all those who hastened to the scene: Clare Hollingworth, the *News Chronicle*'s David Woodward, the petite Betty Wason of CBS (known to her colleagues as 'Demi-Tasse'), Christopher 'The Bishop' Buckley of the *Daily Telegraph*, prone to quote either Shakespeare or the Lord's Prayer in moments of stress, a cherished colleague of Moorehead's in the desert and later still of this writer's in the Far East. On the face of it, here was another war in the Finnish mould, with 'gallant little Greece' now hogging the headlines: the warcos were always men and women to espouse the cause of the oppressed. Thus David Woodward wrote movingly of the Greek columns trudging to the front through stinging rain, with flowers wedged in the barrels of the 1897 rifles their grandfathers had carried in the war against the Turks. At Koritza, on the Albanian front, Betty Wason marvelled at the forty-five-strong Hellenic Air Force, 'in machines that resemble packing crates strung with wings'. In these same Morava Mountains Clare Hollingworth, swaddled in sweaters and a long sheepskin coat, was so proud to share the soldiers' lot that she slogged at their side in mud eight inches deep, never once changing her clothes in seven weeks. Then, as now, it was in her nature to shrug off danger – 'I'm more terrified of being stuck in a lift than being shot.'

Yet all along, cowed by the fear of German intervention, the Greek High Command sought to play down the heroism of their troops. All mention of 'The Axis' or even of Germany was forbidden; the German Legation still functioned in Athens. Although November saw some thirty correspondents at the front, those still remaining in mid-March were summarily recalled to Athens; their presence in Salonika was seen as 'a provocation' to the Germans. Much Greek censorship was 'blind', whereby a correspondent never knew if his messages had been cut or even killed, but enough of it was open to cause painful scenes. Clare Hollingworth, for one, never forgot the passionate cry of one American agency man whose story had been cut to ribbons: 'Mr Zafiris, I'm not gonna be angry! I'm not gonna lose my temper! I'm not even gonna complain! I'm just kinda hurt.'

An early arrival on the Grecian Front was 'Bumblebee' Dimbleby, all set to cover the war in a style befitting the BBC's man in Athens. Along with the *Daily Telegraph*'s Arthur Merton and a Gaumont British News cameraman, Dimbleby was bound for the front in a yellow secondhand Packard, which the *Mirror*'s David Walker described unkindly as resembling 'the poor relation of something out of the late Lord Lonsdale's garage', though its contents were suitably sybaritic: collapsible bedsteads, *pâté de foie gras* and tinned asparagus. For Dimbleby, it was an assignment remarkable on two counts. For the first time, like Quentin Reynolds before him, he saw war for what it was: 'a surfeit of carnage'. For the first time, too, he realized that the Greeks, like most others caught up in World War Two, were eminently expendable.

Essentially a chivalrous middle-class Englishman, with the

faults and virtues of his kind, Dimbleby until now had seen war as a question of national glory. Right – particularly English right – would fight evil, and right would prevail, as Neville Chamberlain had prophesied. Now he saw it as a struggle in which men, women, children and even animals would suffer and in this context, long afterward, he would remember a dozen mules, massacred by bomb blast near a mountain village, 'heads blown from bodies, legs bent and snapped with bloody bones sticking through the skin, the entrails of one … blown round its neck in a slippery red garland'; a man hit by shrapnel sitting in a doorway crying for help; two old women gaping at a shattered house which 'looked like a cake from which the icing had fallen away'.

'Let me add my voice to the chorus of praise for Greece,' he urged in one early dispatch. 'we have a new ally,' but all evidence suggests that his emotional, highly partisan recordings were axed by Broadcasting House. This, in a sense, was cruelly logical. The only troops available to bolster Greece would be stripped from the one theatre of war where the British were then triumphant: Libya.

Yet events were now moving swiftly. On 29 January, Premier Metaxas died of blood poisoning. His successor, an immaculate banker, Alexander Koryzis, belatedly accepted the British offer of help – made primarily to convince the United States that Britain would fight for causes other than her own empire. The average Greek was cynical, and with reason; of the 100,000 British troops offered, only 58,000 were eventually forthcoming. 'No matter who wins, Greece will be destroyed,' was a typical comment. Then, on 1 March, the Bulgarian Premier, yielding to reality, signed a pact with the Axis, in Hitler's presence, in Vienna. On 25 March, Prince Paul of Yugoslavia followed suit, although two days later an uprising of proud Serbian patriots deposed him in favour of his ward, King Peter II. This was only a temporary stumbling block for Hitler, from whose Bulgarian springboard a mass attack on both Greece and Yugoslavia would be launched at 5.30 am on Palm Sunday, 6 April 1941.

Older hands now harked back to Dorothy Thompson's dictum following the fall of Finland. If clarification was needed, the position of small nations in the world would now be clarified afresh.

In Belgrade, on that unforgettable Sunday, most warcos still on the Balkan beat were enjoying room-service breakfasts in their chosen venue, the Hotel Srpski Kralj. At 7.06 am, his binoculars dazzled by sunlight, Ray Brock noted sixty bombers – Heinkels,

Dorniers, and Stuka 87s – sliding towards the naked city. Then a whistling earsplitting inferno, outmatching anything known in the London Blitz, engulfed the streets of Belgrade. Whole buildings disintegrated, Patrick Maitland recorded, 'with a crack like a 100-yard whip'. Brock was transfixed by sticks of incendiaries 'clattering like tin trays to burn with a blue-white glare along the tram tracks'. On the city's main street, the Terazia, Maitland saw teak paving blocks, torn loose by the bombs, 'loom like a surreal mountain'. In its centre, young Leigh White of CBS saw a yawning crater thirty feet across, strewn with 300 torn and mutilated bodies.

In a raid which lasted almost seventy-two hours, with waves of bombers moving back and forth across the city like tractors ploughing a field, the horrors were not transitory. In the fashionable shopping centre, Kralja Milana, Maitland witnessed an unbelievable spectacle: a hundred merchants had been raising their shop shutters as the raid began and outside every shop, as if arranged by a macabre stage director, a body lay inertly, face down in the rubble. Robert St John, whose wife Eda had left for Istanbul, captured the impact of the scene inside the Sprpski Kralj: 'There was the sound of thick walls falling, fire ran in little rivers down the staircase; whole wagonloads of tiles fell, and no one screamed and no one spoke.'

At 9 pm on this same day, the second instalment of Hitler's 'Operation Punishment' was visited on Athens. A low-level raid on the port of Piraeus blew eleven ammunition ships sky-high, shattering windows seven miles away, closing down the entire port for ten days. With this one raid, the British campaign in Greece was virtually lost before it had even started. Six days later, Betty Wason reported, even the High Command conceded that Germany had conquered one-third of the mainland. At 11 pm on 23 April, Greece surrendered. 'The next time we looked out of the window,' came Betty Wason's testimony on 27 April, 'it was to see the Nazi flag flying from the Acropolis.'

From focal points of Yugoslavia warcos attached to the *Panzer* columns reported only unremitting speed: a speed that, day and night, never dropped below 50 miles an hour. From the blitzkrieg jumpoff point, Vienna, W. B. (Bill) Courtney, a likeable fair-haired Irishman from *Collier's* magazine, noted that 'this lunge down more than 1200 miles through the Balkan heart of Europe' was akin to 'a hitchhike on a comet'; as the dust-choked columns churned on, priorities were ruthless. Ten minutes after a breakdown, a Panzer 'worth hundreds of thousands of dollars' would be nosed off the road for salvage – 'all, perhaps, on account of a dirty 50-cent spark plug.' Traffic control was streamlined; a full Panzer division stretched for more than sixty miles, yet from each tank turret a black-clad crewman, signalling with a red-and-white circular disc, controlled the speed of those who followed. Cecil Brown of CBS, aiming to meet that attack head-on along with the American military attaché, Lieutenant-Colonel Louis J. Fortier, heard the same refrain like a litany in town after town: 'The Germans are coming! The Germans are coming!'

On 27 April, following Yugoslavia's surrender, the warcos were shamefully conscious of living out a cliché – 'I've been making strategic withdrawals all the way across Europe,' grumbled the *Daily Mirror*'s David Walker. For, once again, the only logical outcome was flight.

In Greece – despite the censor's fierce denials – it was Dunkirk all over again, with the British pulling out by night from seven ports still unclaimed by the Germans. Among them, on a Greek steamship crammed with 1000 other souls, was AP's Edward Kennedy, who counted himself the war's sorest correspondent to date; in a headlong two-day retreat with the British to Piraeus, he had tumbled from his truck to take cover from strafing planes no less than fifty times. Richard McMillan of UP, a phlegmatic Glaswegian, recalled that he was one of 11,000 men embarking from the port of Nauplion with his American colleague Hank Gorrell. The last word belonged with the sardonic Alexander Clifford, who was briefly on assignment: 'All we need now is a rubber boat, a false set of whiskers, and a Bolivian passport.'

For many, these last Balkan weeks were a time of hair's-breadth escapes. Along with Russell Hill of the *New York Herald Tribune* and Leigh White of CBS, Robert St John fled from Belgrade to the Adriatic shore at Budva. In a 20-foot sardine boat, the *Makedonka*, lacking a compass and victualled only with prosciutto, bread and slivovitz, they started for Corfu. Dive-bombers killed their pilot; in ensuing raids, both St John and White were wounded, the latter critically, his right femur shattered in four places. When the craft finally reached Athens, White wound up in hospital, temporarily a German captive; in the course of four agonizing operations, he lost about fifty pounds in weight. But St John and Hill kept going; on 18 April, twelve days after the attack on Yugoslavia, both men reached Cairo.

From the vantage point of his Gezira flat, Alan Moorehead

watched them come, an increasing influx of correspondents with every fresh steamship and caique putting into Alexandria. But for all of them the era of lone wolves was past: the foreseeable future was one of Conducting Officers and censors who did things by the book, as St John and the *Daily Mail*'s Terence Atherton were amongst the first to discover.

On their disparate journeys south both men had supped amply with horrors. In Patras, an RAF truck which had conveyed St John and the wounded Leigh White towards Corinth had later exploded when a bullet struck its petrol tank; the driver had been cremated alive. In Athens, where hospital staff was painfully short, St John had tried to give a lethal dose of morphine to a man whose hands had been blown off and whose intestines were hanging out. All one night he had listened to the whimpering of a five-year-old girl 'whose right arm hung in black tattered shreds'.

But when St John and Atherton set off at 5 pm from Cairo's Continental Hotel to submit their dispatches, they realized they had entered a land 'where they were still trying to fight a war in the Kipling tradition'. The censors – five in all, for a civil censor and a telegraph office censor had been added since Moorehead's first arrival – had all gone home. Nothing loath, the two men tracked them down, from club to club, from cricket match to swimming pool, to cocktail parties at Mena House, a popular hotel near the Pyramids. But 'these sleek young men in their spotless white uniforms' were gently implacable. Men with their guts sticking out who screamed for aspirin tablets were just not on. Little girls with shredded arms were unacceptable. An RAF driver could die of bullet wounds; he could not be cremated.

But why? St John asked in appalled fascination.

Because, the young censor explained, patting the distraught correspondent gently on the shoulder, 'We must lean over backward in trying not to make war seem horrible. Death by bullet wounds is all right. Death by cremation is not very pleasant to think about.

'Very good for America, but we mustn't let the people back home in England, the people in the Empire, see how bad things are.'

All that spring, and even in the previous autumn, the capitals had been alive with rumours, as insistent as static in the ether. If Ray Brock, of the *New York Times*, en route to neutral Turkey, was among the first to hear the whisper, he was by no means the last. The truth of Pierre Laval's prophecy to Virginia Cowles as France fell was becoming ever more apparent: Adolf Hitler's true enemy was his old ally, Josef Stalin.

On a soft May night at Constanza on the Romanian shore of the Black Sea, Brock, following a precipitate flight from Belgrade, was a transient in the Carlton Hotel, awaiting the departure of the steamer *Dacia* to Istanbul. (Mary Brock and Slatko, the terrier, had already departed for Cairo.) Over coffee and liqueurs with the English-speaking manager, Brock commented idly on the busy presence of grey-clad German officers, both Wehrmacht and Luftwaffe, in the hotel lobby and corridors. 'What do you make of it?' he asked the manager. 'Are they just manoeuvring and practising?'

The manager was incredulous. 'Manoeuvring?' he echoed. 'Practising? Why, my friend, all the world knows that Germany is at last about to wipe out the Bolshevists. Why, in six weeks they'll be in Moscow.'

In Ankara, the Turkish capital, Brock's immediate boss, Cyrus L. Sulzberger, the nephew of the *New York Times*'s publisher, was inclined to be sceptical. 'This stuff has been in the wind for a long time,' he commented. 'Let's tone it down a bit.'

And that much indeed was true: the rumour had long persisted. In October, as far back as King Carol's flight from Bucharest, Eda, the perceptive wife of Robert St John, had grown intrigued by the German tanks, parked with the willing complicity of General Antonescu, along the street outside their apartment block, Strada Vasile Alexandri. Each tank she spotted was guarded by a private soldier, and at night the street came alive with the firefly flicker of torches as each man on duty sat intently, conning the same pocket manual. It took only an elementary ruse – a friendly *Guten Abend*, the offer of a glass of beer – to discover the manual's title: *Russian For Beginners*.

Towards Christmas, Pierre Huss, the plump suave head of INS in Berlin, heard an intriguing tip, although no censor on Goebbels' staff would have passed it for transmission. Around Rastenburg and Lötzen in East Prussia, the farmers and field workers were bewildered: an official circular from the local branch offices of the Nazi Party had forbidden them to prepare their fields for spring planting. Those living closest to the frontier were instructed to move their livestock and bodily possessions inland, though all available draft horses must be held for requisition. By degrees, it seemed, the area was being transformed into a vast military operations zone.

This would have come as no surprise to Drew Middleton, AP's

peripatetic man around the neutral capitals of Europe. It was in March 1941, in a bar near the Casino at Estoril, Portugal, that a British intelligence officer he had met with the BEF in 1939 made casual reference to the forthcoming invasion, 'as though it was well-known'. In New York, Middleton passed this nugget to his Foreign Editor, John Evans, but Evans, like Sulzberger in Ankara, hedged his bets. A drive to the east instead of the west seemed the tallest of tales. Supposing this was disinformation planted by the British to foment trouble between Russians and Germans?

In the first week of June the sources hardened. Following weekly custom, Britain's urbane Foreign Secretary, Anthony Eden, gave a group of American correspondents, Middleton among them, a non-attributable briefing over the teacups at the Foreign Office. Eden's statement was unequivocal: intelligence sources revealed 120 German divisions deployed along the Soviet border. Warnings had already been routed to Stalin from both Churchill and Roosevelt. 'Your Excellency will readily appreciate the significance of these facts,' Churchill had stressed.

At this point, AP's London Bureau Chief, Robert Bunnelle, reached a decision. 'The story should be written and written hard,' he decreed, and at his bidding Middleton did just that. Promptly, on Thursday, 13 June, Tass, the official Soviet news agency, knocked it and knocked it hard – 'A clumsy propaganda manoeuvre of the forces arrayed against the Soviet Union and Germany, which are interested in an intensification of the war.'

What neither Middleton nor Bunnelle knew at that moment was that the story had, in a sense, already broken.

Six thousand miles from London, in Tokyo, another newsman, the hard-drinking Richard Sorge, ostensibly the representative of the *Frankfurter Zeitung*, had amassed a formidable dossier of German intentions, though not for transmission to his editors. As early as 15 May, the Russian-born Sorge, for eight years a Moscow agent, had passed on full details of Operation Barbarossa to his spy master by W/T. Yet only silence followed, and Sorge was to lament increasingly, 'Why has Stalin not reacted?'

Another Tokyo newsman, Joseph Newman, newly appointed Bureau Chief of the *New York Herald Tribune*, was also wondering. The same tip had reached him from Branko de Vukelitch, a Yugoslav employee of the news agency Havas, who was, unknown to Newman, a trusted Sorge lieutenant. All Newman knew – like his counterparts at AP, UP and the *New York Times* – was that 'Vuki' was leaking the story to any correspondent who would seize on it.

But his colleagues were understandably chary. Over lunch at the American Club, Newman raised the rumour with Charles 'Chip' Bohlen, a longtime Soviet expert, newly posted to the US Embassy, but Bohlen was dubious: the Red Army was in such poor shape that Hitler could wring any concessions from Stalin without declaring war. Walter Duranty, in Tokyo on a visit for the *New York Times*, was equally dismissive. 'The chance of a war between Germany and Russia is about as good as frying snowballs in the summertime,' he chuckled.

Censorship rules in Japan were explicit; any correspondent could telephone a story direct to New York provided that the censor had first read over the text. Accordingly, in the last week of May, when 'the invasion story had reached the point when I could feel it in my bones,' Newman submitted his dispatch. The hours seemed to drag until his telephone rang again: 'Newman-*san*, it is all right. You are being connected with New York.'

Days passed, then weeks, but no reaction was forthcoming – from New York, Moscow, or any other world capital. They've killed it, Newman thought resignedly, but weeks later a batch of out-of-date *Tribunes* landed on his desk. He found it finally – on page 21 of the business section in the issue of 31 May:

TOKYO EXPECTS HITLER
TO MOVE AGAINST RUSSIA

Newman struggled with conflicting emotions then, familiar to every war correspondent: elation that the story had been printed at all, chagrin that a suspicious Foreign Editor had virtually consigned the scoop of a lifetime to oblivion.

Even by 1941 standards Richard Dimbleby thought it a bizarre campaign. Security was as totally lacking as shock tactics; at 2 am on Sunday, 8 June, the forces that breached the frontiers of Syria in a three-pronged drive from Palestine, Iraq and Trans-Jordan were advancing boldly in bright moonlight, cheered on by the martial strains of Free French bands blasting out *La Marseillaise*. Even their banners were at cross purposes; before any shot had been exchanged, a white flag of truce was hoisted beside the tricolour as they marched.

It was one of the many minor theatres of war in which the British strove to maintain their Middle Eastern foothold, and it was notable only as the first and last time that Frenchmen raised their hands against Frenchmen.

As an adversary Syria, held under mandate by Vichy France, was admittedly in the minor league. But as a staging post for German planes which landed at Aleppo airport to abet a shortlived rising against the British in Iraq, she stood condemned. It was a move to which Admiral Jean François Darlan, Pétain's Vice-President, anxious to curry favour with Germany, had readily agreed. But to Churchill, the thought of a German foothold in Syria, the back door to the Middle East, was intolerable. When General Charles de Gaulle, leader of the Free French forces, trumpeted a protest, Churchill was sympathetic. If the French were ever again to fight as allies, it would be on North African soil or not at all: de Gaulle could fly to Cairo to map out a Syrian campaign.

On the night of 7 June, Dimbleby had his briefing on that campaign in the Press Office of the King David Hotel, Jerusalem. Since the Free French under their Field Commander, General Paul Louis le Gentilhomme, could muster only 6000 troops out of the 50,000 now loyal to de Gaulle, the force would be augmented by two Australian brigades, an Indian infantry brigade, and British cavalry units whose officers had brought their own hunters from the English shires – 'Almost as many sprigs of the nobility as Henry V had led to Agincourt,' one correspondent rhapsodized.

Unlike Alan Moorehead, whose star was in the ascendant, with both the London *Times* and the *News Chronicle* eager to syndicate his *Express* dispatches, Dimbleby's was in steady decline. Already he sensed that a move was on within the BBC to oust him from the Middle East, and intuition did not fail him; the knives were indeed out for 'Master Richard', as the BBC's Controller (Home), A. P. Ryan, dubbed him scathingly. Peremptory telegrams from the accounts department constantly sniped at his expense sheets. To Ryan, who saw correspondents in the field as no more than junior local reporters, Dimbleby's assumption that he *was* the BBC was especially irksome. 'Tell us only what you are told or hear and see on the spot,' ran one curt rebuke. 'Don't include generalizations about the war at large.' Only the urgent intercession of Middle East Command, who saw his true value, saved Dimbleby from recall.

It was a far cry from the Rolls-Royce and the thoroughbred horses of his dreams, but at twenty-seven he was still ebullient enough to shrug this off. 'I could look back and forward from the driving seat of my truck,' he reported with the habitual Dimbleby zest, 'and see our column winding its way through valleys and over hills and the mountains of Lebanon for miles in front and behind.' But as that column wound inland from Tarshiha on the Palestine frontier, neither he nor the *Daily Telegraph*'s Arthur Merton realized they were en route to report a civil war. Within hours of the frontier crossing, the German ground staffs had been evacuated from all the Syrian airfields. The only enemy facing the Free French was thus the Vichy French.

It was still a war rich in incongruous contrasts. From the first, the Australians were under orders to wear slouch hats, not steel helmets, until actually fired upon. At Tibnine, ten miles beyond the frontier, the mayor approached Lieutenant-Colonel A. B. Macdonald, the Australian commanding Dimbleby's column, with a novel request. Could he telephone to Tyre, their next objective, to enquire if the invaders would be welcome? Only when the answer was affirmative did the column press on.

Yet, as Dimbleby reported grimly, the fighting on the banks of the malarial, thickly wooded Litani River, the first stand of the Vichy French, was 'some of the fiercest yet seen in the Middle East'. But as the war rumbled on for thirty-four days, over dry chalky highways, through squalid stone villages, the tragedy of fratricide was most often averted. One battalion of the Free French Foreign Legion found itself face to face with a sister battalion of the Legion fighting for Vichy. As the troops prepared to open fire, they realized they were facing old comrades. On both sides, then, guns were pointed to the sky, and the two commanders agreed to a mutual withdrawal. 'It was a poignant situation,' Dimbleby reported.

This was richly acceptable material to the BBC's News Editor, R. T. Clarke, but when Dimbleby followed up with a ringing affirmation of Middle East policy as he saw it – 'We can and must afford to ignore the feelings of the Vichy authorities and the French Army in Syria, dangling like a red and blue puppet on the end of a string jerked by Hitler' – tempers at Broadcasting House rose dangerously. Following this first dispatch, recorded in Tyre after sixteen hours on the road, Dimbleby's star was further on the wane.

In the end, as he was swift to underline, Syria was essentially a campaign of re-education. On the road leading north to Sidon, Dimbleby was intrigued by the sight of an elderly white-haired British Army captain, whose French was fluent, interrogating batches of captured Vichy officers. 'He treated the men with the skill of a kindly schoolmaster,' Dimbleby told his listeners, 'so much so that he reminded us of "Mr Chips" ... generally he called them *mes petits* ... he explained how the Germans were planning to turn Syria into a great base for an attack on the Suez Canal and Egypt ... "It's to fight *them* that we come into Syria. We aren't your enemies and you aren't ours. It's the Boches we're after"'.

Some were amazed, as Dimbleby saw; others, unwilling to go into action even against British troops, were so upset they burst into tears. 'They went down the line with a new idea in their heads and time to think about it.'

Plainly, the thinking was positive, for by 20 June, the Vichy French were as anxious to evacuate Damascus, the Syrian capital, as the invaders were to seize it. Thus, one day later, at 1.30 pm, Damascus 'fell' before an onslaught of two Free French colonels, two Australians, a British major and two armoured cars. The Allied Army, following up later with Dimbleby to the fore, had to bypass the main street altogether – not because of war or barricades but because the authorities were renewing the tram tracks. Their triumphal entry into the city wound, to spirited applause, through the heart of the red-light district – 'some of the meaner quarters of the town,' in Dimbleby's tactful phrasing.

That night, in his first dispatch from Damascus, he quoted General le Gentilhomme, who had granted him an early interview, his left arm in a sling as the result of a wound. It was an admirably muted message. 'Tell people in France and in Britain and in America that we haven't come here as conquerors to claim a victory,' was the General's summing up. 'There's been no victory in Damascus ... if there has been any victory, it's been against Hitler.'

In 1941, Adolf Hitler's presence brooded like a shadow over millions of lives. 'Armed as never before we stand at the door of the New Year,' he had rallied his Wehrmacht in January, and this was not an empty boast; for six months his troops had manned the ramparts, unchallenged, from the North Cape to Sicily. He stood as supreme master of 250 million Europeans – 'more civilized white human beings,' estimated the INS pundit, H. R. Knickerbocker, 'than ever before came under the tyranny of a single despot.'

The spectre of Hitler, and of such compliant satellites as Vichy France, was foremost in the mind of forty-five-year-old Ben Lucien Burman in March 1941, as he approached Brazzaville in the Congo, capital of French Equatorial Africa, stifling under a brassy sun.

A homespun Kentuckian, whose stock in trade was folksy bestsellers (*Steamboat Round the Bend*), Burman was currently a roving war correspondent for both the Scripps-Howard newspaper chain and the *Reader's Digest*. Now, as the climax of an intricate chain of contacts, he was on the eve of a world exclusive: the first press interview ever granted by Charles de Gaulle as leader of the Free French.

For Burman, these first days were inspirational. Along with his wife, Alice, an accredited war artist, he was installed in the stately riverside house which was de Gaulle's residence in Brazzaville but in his absence served as a guesthouse. Each day, he lunched with General Sicé, Senior Medical Officer in the French Congo, who had secured control of the colony for de Gaulle. Three months before the General's Syrian venture, Burman was already meeting up with the new refugees arriving daily in answer to de Gaulle's appeal – 'scholars and aristocrats, peasants and fishermen, sailors and carpenters, bakers and doctors and pale bank clerks'. Often on the radio he heard coded messages directed to camel troops escaping from Vichy-held Senegal, guiding them across the wastes of the Sahara to Free French Fort Lamy in the Chad, or to British territory in Nigeria. At times there were terse counter-orders from Vichy Radio: Stop them at any cost.

Each day, from the tiny telegraph office, Burman dictated fresh dispatches to the Scripps-Howard offices in New York, retailing the exploits of men risking everything to join de Gaulle. Here was proof, he cabled, that the spirit of France, 'entombed beneath the swastika in Paris', was being reborn along the Congo, Joseph Conrad's 'heart of darkness', thousands of miles distant.

It was news, he thought, to give the US State Department food for thought, for unlike Britain, Roosevelt still maintained an ambassador in Vichy, Admiral Eugene Leahy, in the hope that a continuing dialogue would help Marshal Pétain retain control of the French Fleet and keep the Germans from French North Africa.

It was an illusion which prevailed until Burman met de Gaulle – 'after which I viewed him with horror.'

On the surface, the meeting was as cordial as could have been hoped for. Over five o'clock tea, in what now served as the two men's mutual house, de Gaulle, lighting one Gauloise cigarette from another, amply confirmed rumours that had been current in Paris in Quentin Reynolds's time, when the General had served briefly as Under Secretary for War. Even when France still had the capacity to resist, Pétain had been bent on capitulation. 'I should have been very happy with the interview,' Burman conceded, instead of experiencing 'the most uncomfortable hour and a half of my life'.

Of course, de Gaulle was notoriously an egotist. A six-foot-four-inch ramrod, ascetic and humourless, he saw himself like the Sun King, Louis XIV, as the embodiment of French honour. Even so, Burman was unprepared for the reality. 'There was an intellectual arrogance in his speech and manner, a disdain for the rest of humanity such as I had never encountered in a human being. Here was a man so wrapped up in his own consciousness it was as if no one else in the world existed. I agreed completely with every word he spoke, but they were uttered with such a bitterness, a fanaticism that might lead anywhere.'

One thought troubled Burman above all: to date his dispatches had championed de Gaulle's cause on the basis of meeting his adherents. Now he had grave doubts. 'Was this towering figure who was the chief of the Free French a possible fascist, who when he achieved power would be little better than the dictators he sought to overthrow?'

In this moment, Burman became perhaps World War Two's first correspondent – but not the last – to exercise self-censorship. He quite consciously 'took sides'. Any attack on de Gaulle would be an impetus for the corrupt defeatist regime that was Vichy. And a boost for Vichy was, inescapably, a boost for Hitler. It was as simple as that.

So he would put down the facts, Burman decided, 'without any dubious personal interpretation', and he was as good as his word. As a rallying cry throughout his report, de Gaulle existed; as a personality, he did not emerge at all. 'Here astride the equator, France miraculously survives,' Burman wrote. 'Vichy considers all men here traitors ... but they are the men to whom France will someday erect its monuments ... This is no longer the heart of darkness. This is the Congo, the cradle of New France.'

Three months later, de Gaulle's fortunes were at last looking up. Not only Syria but almost all world sympathy was lost to Vichy at one stroke. 'Vichy has gone straight into the arms of the German government,' charged the angry old US Secretary of State, Cordell Hull; de Gaulle's status would be reluctantly acknowledged from this time on. It was, as Richard Dimbleby might have reported, another victory against Hitler.

In Jerusalem's King David Hotel, almost 160 miles south of Damascus, Dimbleby was overwhelmed by the news. It was the early afternoon of Monday, 23 June, and until now, after a sixteen-hour drive through the night, he had been preoccupied mainly with physical discomfort: his hands on the steering wheel had grown blue with cold and his thin khaki-drill bush jacket had afforded almost no protection against the icy wind. But all this was now forgotten; the incredible had happened. One day earlier, on 22 June, 1941, 186 German divisions had lanced into Russia.

Dimbleby's reaction was instantaneous. From Jerusalem to Broadcasting House went a message that a score of eager-beaver warcos had already dispatched: SUGGEST EYE MOSCOWARDS SOONEST.

But 'Master Richard' would not be going 'Moscowards'. Nor, for that matter would Alan Moorehead, Alexander Clifford or, in the immediate future, Quentin Reynolds. Not even Martha Gellhorn was in the running, although technically at liberty following a six-month working honeymoon on the Canton front of the Sino-Japanese war. (Somewhat to her own surprise, she had married her longtime lover, Ernest Hemingway, in Cheyenne, Wyoming, in November 1940.) The absence of warcos was not hard to fathom; too many of their colleagues had sold the Red Army short in the Winter War of 1940. No Foreign Editor would despatch a star reporter to a front that might crumble within weeks.

The initial pace of the German advance only confirmed that decision. On the first day, as the legions rolled on like a vast travelling workshop, trailing a pungent blue vapour of Panzer exhausts, through a glowing Van Gogh landscape of sunflowers, surprise was total: 10,000 prisoners were taken, 1200 aircraft destroyed on sixty-six airfields. Averaging twenty-two miles a day over rutted cart tracks, the Panzers were moving so fast the supply wagons could not keep up. Hitler's lifelong aim – to provide the *Lebensraum* for German's millions, wiping out the hated cradle of Bolshevism and harnessing the vast resources of slave labour – seemed suddenly within his grasp.

Despite the months of cocktail-bar rumours, no newsman 'in the censor-tight cylinder of Moscow' had foreseen the attack. On 22 June, almost all were resident agency men fluent in Russian, like Henry Shapiro of UP and Maurice Lovell of Reuters; the AP's shy, diminutive Henry Cassidy was so unprepared he was holidaying at Sochi on the Black Sea. Only Harrison Salisbury – not then the distinguished historian of the siege of Leningrad, but an unknown cable editor on UP's foreign desk, almost 5000 miles away in New York – had an inkling that something was afoot. Mindful of Greece and Yugoslavia, he had pieced together an undated lead story for the Sunday morning editions, explaining, 'Hitler likes to start things on Sundays.'

Those few on the spot could only marvel at the spirit of the people. Like the Londoners of 1940 the Muscovites, essentially a pliant people after twenty-four years of Communist rule, had been swift to adapt. 'Ivan Goes Calmly To War', was the keynote struck by Henry Cassidy in the first dispatch following his return, for the longest queues visible were those stretching two deep, waiting placidly to enter Lenin's Tomb. Two other eminent observers were just then checking into the National Hotel, the photographer Margaret Bourke-White and her brand-new husband, Erskine (*Tobacco Road*) Caldwell, both on assignment for *Life* magazine. (In this first idyllic year she was 'Honey-chile' and he was 'Skinny'; they split up eighteen months later.) Few telling details escaped Margaret Bourke-White; behind Moscow's closed doors and darkened windows, she found a fierce activity afoot. At factory benches, couples were working side by side; husbands were teaching their jobs to their wives before departing for the front. Teenagers patrolled at twilight, warning householders of faulty blackouts, checking sandbags and water pails. All younger children had been evacuated from the city – placed in the care of Moscow's manicurists who now had sterner tasks to perform.

Camouflage, Cassidy reported, loomed everywhere. The gold onion domes of the Kremlin vanished beneath a coating of battleship grey. The Bolshoi Theatre was hung with canvas, painted with false entrance doorways. Anti-aircraft batteries, screened by leaves, lay secreted in the clusters of pine and birch dotting the city. Each night 750,000 people bedded down beneath the blue and gold mosaic ceilings of the Moscow subway stations – 'exactly what Metro-Goldwyn-Mayer would think an air raid shelter should look like,' the noted film director Sergei Eisenstein sniffed to Margaret Bourke-White.

Another newcomer, a veteran of the fall of France, was forty-year-old Alexander Werth, born in St Petersburg of a Russian engineer father and a British mother. Although raised in an anti-Bolshevik tradition, Werth, now on assignment for both Reuters and the London *Sunday Times*, was soon to prove as devout a fellow-traveller as his colleague, Ralph Parker of *The Times*. Aptly, Werth's arrival coincided with Stalin's first address to the nation since the invasion, his 3 July speech embodying the ferocious 'scorched earth' policy of the Great Patriotic War. 'Whenever units of the Red Army are forced to retreat, all railway rolling stock must be driven away. The enemy must not be left a single engine, or a single railway truck, and not a pound of bread nor a pint of oil. The *Kolkhozniki* [collective farm workers] must drive away all their livestock, hand their grain reserves to the State organs for evacuation to the rear ...'

Fighting talk in this vein, even from an arch-Communist, was the stuff of life to Winston Churchill, who had already broadcast a stirring polemic, in part reprinted by *Pravda*: 'Any man or state which fights on against Nazidom will have our aid ... we shall give whatever help we can to Russia and the Russian people.' On 12 July, Britain and the Soviet Union became uneasy allies in the war against Hitler.

For despite all ideological differences, the priorities of *realpolitik* would prevail. Although many American newspapers were outraged to contemplate their country's involvement – 'The principal difference between Mr Hitler and Mr Stalin is the size of their respective moustaches,' stated the *Wall Street Journal* – Franklin Roosevelt saw Hitler's extirpation as the first item on any democratic agenda. After unfreezing Soviet dollar funds enabling them to buy weapons, and ensuring that the Neutrality Act would permit American shipping to enter ports like Vladivostok, he sat back to await the Russians' shopping list. On 8 July he got it: a staggering two billion dollars' worth of requirements, including 3000 pursuit planes and 3000 bombers.

On the morning of 30 July Henry Cassidy got an excited call from a tip-off man: Did he realize that 'Garrigopkins' was in Moscow? Since the Russians habitually converted 'H' to 'G', this was Cassidy's first clue that 51-year-old Harry Hopkins, Roosevelt's gaunt, sallow Personal Adviser, a man who had only narrowly survived an operation for stomach cancer, had reached the city for talks with Stalin.

At 8 pm that night, pale and tired, 'with one thin leg dangling over the other as he slumped in his chair', Hopkins received the press for his first conference at Spaso House, the Embassy residence. Yes, despite America's continuing neutrality, Roosevelt intended to aid Russia with both immediate and longterm supplies. To be sure, Hopkins and Stalin had discussed in detail the arms, munitions and material which America could provide. Off the record, Hopkins had also interceded to smooth the path of Margaret Bourke-White, who had learned to her fury that Stalin had imposed a wartime ban on all photography. But even a dictator recognized that a lady said to possess 'a lens for a heart', who had arrived with five cameras, twenty-two lenses, four portable developing tanks and 3000 flash bulbs, was not one to be gainsaid. The ban was lifted; Stalin, his impassive face pitted with pockmarks, posed for a close-up; Hopkins himself acted as her photographic courier back to the States.

Next day, following a second meeting with Stalin, Hopkins bade the press farewell. Despite the brevity of his mission, he seemed curiously sanguine. 'My short visit here has given me even more confidence that Hitler is going to lose,' he assured the newsmen.

Then a curious thing happened. Until this moment, Hitler's advancing armies had done even more than was expected of them. On 14 July, in just nine hours, they had breached the 1100-mile-long Stalin Line, a ribbon of redoubts stretching east of the Pripet Marshes. Three hundred miles to their northwest lay Moscow.

But suddenly, along 400 miles of line, the order had come: Prepare for defensive positions. Panzers, motorized units, pioneers, artillery, infantry – one million men in all – were frozen in their tracks.

The Anglo-Russian alliance was soon a reality in more than words: a combined military operation that culminated, for the best of strategic reasons, in a sizeable landgrab. Both sides were learning fast from the ruthless pace of Wehrmacht takeovers.

The land they coveted was Iran – most especially the British-subsidized Anglo-Iranian oilfields, now, in August, vulnerable to a German attack from Russian soil. Another bone of contention was the 2500-strong workforce of German civilians employed by Iran's railways and telegraph systems and in industrial plants – plainly a latent fifth column. While the British, as early as 8 August, demanded an 80 per cent reduction of Germans by September's end, the Russians were of sterner mettle. They called for positive action in three days – raising the bogey that they might beat the British to the start line. Trust between allies was, as always, at a premium.

It was a gamble the British could not afford to take, as Richard Dimbleby was soon to discover. Early in July, he had been temporarily exiled to Ankara, briefed to open up a direct broadcasting channel between Turkey and Great Britain. Regular dispatches from

Ankara, the BBC hazarded, might strengthen the bonds of Anglo-Turkish friendship, since both the capital and Istanbul had become fertile fields for German propaganda. Typically, it was not until Dimbleby was enjoying his first holiday in months, in Istanbul's Park Hotel, that an urgent cable reached him: UPFOLLOW QUICKEST REPORTS HERE RUSSOBRITISH ACTION IRAN IMMINENT.

Back in Ankara, on 27 August, the salutation was terser still: GET TEHRAN QUICKEST.

It was a belated start, for all that. Two days earlier, at dawn on 25 August, the first British columns were rolling across the Iranian border from Iraq. Indian troops, landing at the port of Bandar Shahpur, on the Gulf, seized the world's largest oil-cracking plant at Abadan. Simultaneously, down the shores of the Caspian Sea, came the mechanized Cossacks of General Max Sinenko, their western column closing on Tabriz, their eastern on the port of Bandar Shah.

Dimbleby, by contrast, travelled a rougher road – typical of the exertions demanded of, and gladly accepted by, a correspondent in this second year of war if a news 'beat' was at stake. The direct route ran through Erzurum, but this led to the Russian zone, and the Russians, as suspicious then as later, were offering no right of way. The swiftest approach was thus on the Taurus Express to Baghdad, a journey facilitated by the British Embassy's Counsellor, who converted him to a fully fledged courier with the aid of a diplomatic bag. Dimbleby's goals were now twofold: to see the expulsion of the Germans from their last foothold in the Middle East and to meet the Russians in the field for the first time.

Luck was with him. In the sweltering spice-scented streets of Baghdad, he met up with an old friend, James Holburn, an imperturbable Scot, also en route to Iran for the London *Times*. By mutual consent they chartered 'an elderly Chevrolet saloon and its fat Persian driver' to drive them 800 miles through the mountains to Tehran. Though the fare for the one-way trip was a then extortionate £50, few other drivers were willing to leave Baghdad. Their own man hinted so darkly at 'bandits and robbers' that Holburn, with impeccable logic, finally countered, 'If we're going to be killed anyway, why do we need to pay you at all?' Once more, Dimbleby had won himself courier status, with Embassy bags for Tehran and Moscow; as they jolted towards the northern fort of Karmanshah, he guarded those bags in the rear, while their combined luggage toppled onto him 'with awful regularity'.

It was a hazardous journey. At midnight on the first day a group of ragged men gathered in the road 100 yards ahead, 'shouting and waving rifles and sticks'; the driver, unnerved, made to slow down. 'Get on, damn you, get on!' Dimbleby yelled and as the driver slammed his foot on the throttle Dimbleby, lunging with a heavy Thermos flask, brought it violently down on the hand of a man clinging to the Chevrolet's side. The brigand toppled sideways; as the car bucked convulsively, another man, scrambling onto the boot, fell heavily backwards. In the small hours, both warcos reached Karmanshah unscathed.

At first light, Dimbleby sought out the major in charge of the local British brigade to demand a military escort. 'You don't expect me to spare my men for everyone who has trouble in this godforsaken place, do you?' the major exploded, but Dimbleby, in the shape of his courier's passport, had his answer pat. 'This says,' the major ventured, after a lengthy perusal, 'I've got to give you an escort if you ask for it.' Dimbleby was smug. 'That's the idea, but I'm sorry I had to compel you.'

In this way, escorted by two truckloads of Wiltshire Yeomanry, Dimbleby and Holburn reached Tehran. It was a piquant entry into a city fully as individual as Damascus: an unreal world of golden domes and shaded verandahs and carriages drawn by mangy horses, jolting over cobbled streets. The situation, in a phrase then beloved of communiqués, was 'fluid'. The Shah, sixty-five-year-old Reza Pahlavi, a trigger-tempered despot wont to kick errant ministers in the crotch, was on the point of abdication under Anglo-Russian pressure. His son, twenty-one-year-old Prince Muhammed Reza (himself dethroned in 1979) only awaited the approval of the Majlis, the National Assembly, before succeeding him.

There were other niceties of protocol. Before Dimbleby became the first foreigner to broadcast to London from Tehran, a Cabinet meeting was called to discuss it. The request was approved, but the radio station, on the city outskirts, was still manned by German engineers – 'surly Nazis,' in Dimbleby's ultra-British book. 'I'm here to relay to London,' he told them, 'as brusquely as I could', 'and you'd better see that it goes through.'

To nobody's surprise but his own, they did, and a jubilant Dimbleby noted in his diary: 'Broadcast direct ex-Tehran to London . . . at 1.30 pm. Complete world beat – justifying journey here!!! BBC lead 2.30 and all evening bulletins, quoting *in extenso* . . .'

It was a historic feat of its kind – a 2300-mile round trip to make one 1000-word broadcast – but these were historic times. After twenty-three months of war, the nations arrayed against Hitler were closer to a meeting of minds; on 9 August, in the quiet haven of Placentia Bay, Newfoundland, Churchill and Roosevelt, meeting for the very first time, had drafted the Atlantic Charter, a vague declaration of post-war aims after 'the final destruction of Nazi tyranny': in fact, little more than a pious expression of mutual goodwill.

In Tehran, too, at the first meeting of British and Russian troops, the goodwill was equally palpable. At Karaj, five miles from the capital, the Russians, in loose grey smocks over blue breeches, carrying old-style needle-type bayonets, flocked forward to pump hands with the British, while marvelling at the voluminous khaki shorts of the Gurkhas. As a good war correspondent, Dimbleby had inveigled his way into the military attaché's car, and it was as an accepted member of the Legation that he sat down for the first vodka toasts of the war, with the British colonel and the Russian General Novikov.

It was a moment to savour in later years, when the camaraderie of wartime seemed no more than an empty sham. The colonel, it seemed, was speaking for all of them, after so many loving cups and libations: 'Splendid fellows, these Russians, yes, splendid fellows.'

V

Oahu! We've Got A War On Our Hands

15 SEPTEMBER–7 DECEMBER 1941

It was one of the most coveted datelines of World War Two, yet fewer than a score of correspondents achieved it. Purely by chance, as September dawned, luck was on the side of an elite minority – nine men and two women – for in that first week, the Russians bloodily repulsed German offensives at both Smolensk and Bryansk. Now the need for American war material clinched the issue with Nicolai Palgunov, the bearded myopic Chief of the Soviet Press and Censorship Bureau. On 15 September, eleven warcos won the supreme distinction of the dateline: *With The Red Army*.

At 8 am on that Monday, a five-strong cavalcade of wiry little 10-horsepower M–1 automobiles set off down Moscow's Mojhaik chaussée heading for the cobbled, fir-lined Vyazma–Smolensk highway. At intervals, red and white striped barriers like horizontal barber's poles, manned by military traffic police, checked their progress. Their ultimate destination was Vyazma, 135 miles northwest, a 700-mile round trip on the Intourist model which lasted seven days, and the journey, as Cyrus L. Sulzberger of the *New York Times* summed up neatly, 'assumed that we saw no real action but could not manage to hide valuable impressions'.

The travellers were dressed, noted AP's Henry Cassidy, in 'a bewildering assortment of costumes'. Predictably, the star turn was Margaret Bourke-White, in a yellow sweater borrowed from an interpreter, topped by a leather coat of fire-engine red, although Alexander Werth in an evil-smelling yellow-white jacket of Siberian dogskin, which his colleagues christened 'Fido', ran her close. Not to be outdone, Sulzberger wore plus fours below a waterproof silk garment complete with hood and zip fastener, which he claimed was a Yugoslav skiing jacket – 'a white shiny tunic of the Isadora Duncan school,' scoffed Margaret Bourke-White. Charlotte Haldane, of the London *Daily Sketch*, wife of the scientist, had a brown London fire warden's uniform under a blue leather coat preserved from the Spanish Civil War. Only Philip Jordan of the London *News Chronicle*, asserted his status as a true Briton, in a natty war correspondent's uniform.

At times it was a journey to tax the patience of saints. Along the rutted sandy side roads, the average progress was two and a half miles an hour. On the third day, Charlotte Haldane recalled, slashing rain slowed the pace further still; ten hours on the road included a two-hour struggle to coax the cars up a steep hill. The entire week, Margaret Bourke-White recorded mournfully, was a photographer's nightmare: the cloud parted to reveal sunshine for exactly sixteen minutes.

Yet on the Central Russian front, as Wallace Carroll, a recent arrival for UP, paid tribute, they were meeting 'a young army all the way through' and 'this young army was eager to learn'. From Vyazma's grandiloquently named International Hotel, a two-storey stucco building sickly-sweet with the smell of insect repellent, they were ushered into the presence of the men who commanded, and the men who counted. Lunch on the first day – caviare, vodka, cabbage soup with sour cream, chicken with rice and sweet pink wine – preceded a trip to the local aerodrome to meet Major-General Georgi Sakharoff, with the 'ice-blue eyes, perfect teeth and the cheery grin of the world's ace pilots'. Supper – a replica of lunch – brought a guest of honour to the table: Major-General Vassily Sokolovsky, Chief of Staff to Marshal Semeon Timosenko, 'tall, handsome, impeccably turned out, polite, and very intelligent', as befitted the architect, seven years later, of the Berlin blockade.

The armament they glimpsed, such as it was in those first months of Russia's war, was impressive nonetheless. At the aerodrome Wallace Carroll was quick to spot the salient points of the MIG–3, Russia's new fighter, 'a cross between the American Curtiss P–40 and the British Hurricane'. Nearby, Cyrus Sulzberger was conscious of the 'fast low-silhouetted T–34 tanks that were to become so famous and endured as a standard weapon right through the Korean war and even Vietnam'. All such details, so carefully noted, were as carefully excised from their dispatches.

At one point their soldier-drivers, who carried hand grenades along with their cranks and tools, took extra precautions; axes flashed and their cars swiftly vanished beneath a leafy canopy of silver birch and fir saplings. It was here, only 800 yards from the German lines, that the old Russian hands scored over the others. Thus, in daily communiqués, Alexander Werth, with his St Petersburg upbringing, could distinguish between 'fierce', 'stubborn' and 'heavy' fighting, nuances which entirely foxed his fellows. In those front-line conditions, the bearded, leonine A. T. (Alfred Thornton) Cholerton, for sixteen years the *Daily Telegraph*'s man in Moscow, was in his element – nibbling wild white mushrooms which he gathered each time the cars ground to a halt, daily nauseating the fastidious Sulzberger by chomping raw fish, suspended by their tails, for his breakfast.

From this part-time tour, which took in everything from underground first-aid posts to Red Army clubs, also sited in dugouts yet equipped with grand pianos and electric lights, the warcos bore away one indelible impression: that of an army schooled after the dictum of Alexander Suvorov, a General who had flourished under Catherine the Great, 'Hard on the training ground, easy on the battlefield.' In the world of Generals Sakharoff and Sokolovsky, an officer could be broken to private or given an eight-year suspended gaol sentence for overstaying leave. A man could be shot for an offence that in the United States would merit only the guardhouse. 'The maggot gnaws the cabbage but it dies before it's done,' was a survivor's proverb that they heard quoted more than once. Or, as Solovsky told them, 'The Blitzkrieg had developed into a continuous grinding of the German war machine. The process resembles Verdum, but in terms of ten or one hundred times the destruction.'

On the final day, as if in irrefutable proof of that impression, Nicolai Palgunov, like a skilful impresario, brought them to the battlefield of Ushakovo.

It was Cyrus L. Sulzberger, the mercurial twenty-nine-year-old *New York Times* man, who, by common consensus, filed the most vivid account of Ushakovo. This was a village, he reported, that had 'lost one of its three dimensions. Now it had only length and breadth: there are no vertical elements save a couple of gateposts and a small wooden obelisk on a mass grave ...'. The grave, fenced in by evergreens, was topped by a silver star which bore a mass inscription: 'For those who died in this place in the struggle against German Fascism, 29 July–5 September 1941.'

'The slightly sour smell of death hovers over [Ushakovo],'
Sulzberger reported. '... Ruined rye crops are brown with rot ...
Crows and magpies peck at the blood-soaked earth ... puddles of
water are still dyed with unmistakable stains of blood ...'

Under the vast and empty sky, nothing that any of them had
ever seen had prepared them for this. 'There, like monster footprints,
are the holes dug by the Russian shells that followed the retreating
Germans ... Here, beside piles of stretchers, is a great pile of turned-
up earth, 400 yards square, where the Germans had swiftly buried
their dead as they withdrew.'

What followed was, inevitably, anti-climax. On 23 September, Palgunov's party had been once again deposited at the two Moscow
hotels that to the very end spelled home to the warcos: the old-
fashioned National, facing the Kremlin across Red Square, with its
huge rooms and monstrous plastron chandeliers, and the cavernous
Metropole, once the revolutionary headquarters of the White Guard,
whose suites habitually ran to grand pianos. And once here, the
deadening daily routine began all over again.

By late autumn, some twenty-five correspondents were covering
the Moscow scene, lured there by the Red Army's indomitable stand,
and all their days blended into one. Each morning, from 9 am to 12
noon, they remained captive in their hotel rooms, dependent on their
secretary-interpreters for monotonous droning literal translations
from the four-page Soviet dailies: *Red Star* (the top military paper),
Pravda (the Communist Party mouthpiece), *Isvestia* and *Komsomol
Pravda*. The gist of these stories was rarely headline material. If
German atrocities sometimes featured in the bulletins, the likeliest
items concerned collective farms, field hospitals and infant crèches.

To boost their own morale, the warcos employed puerile ruses
to hasten their cables, once approved, to the telegraph company and
thus scoop their rivals. AP and UP used two fourteen-year-old girl
runners, Zena and Venus, both 'as fast as fawns'. A slight edge
was enjoyed by Harold King of Reuters, who bribed the Turkish
Embassy's motorcyclist – known, naturally as 'The King's mes-
senger' – whenever the ambassador was away.

Sometimes The Desk, whether in London or New York, would
relieve the tedium with a mind-boggling query. Thus UP's London
Bureau once cabled Moscow urgently: was it true that Marshal
Semeon Timoshenko, the People's Commissar of Defence, was actually 'Timothy Jenkins', son of a Welsh miner, who had emigrated

to Russia? The unglamorous reality: Timoshenko, born forty-six years earlier in Bessarabia, was a former farmhand until he enlisted with a Tsarist cavalry division.

Correspondents fresh to Moscow soon embarked on a crash course: the facts of life, Russian-style. Wallace Carroll had left London in July armed with three 'crunch' questions to which UP wanted hard answers: How strong was the Red Army? How strong was Stalin's government? How long could the Russians hold the Germans in check? His quest convulsed Henry Cassidy, who had covered Moscow for AP since 1940. Russian secrecy, Cassidy explained, was so obsessive that one military attaché had probed for months to discover the basic pay of a Red Army private – 10.50 roubles a month, or eight shillings – without success.

Obsessive secrecy in turn bred suspicion or incomprehension, stumbling blocks that every warco faced when confronting the censors. Following her Vyzama visit, Charlotte Haldane was in temporary trouble for stressing the Red Army's 'bulldog tenacity'. What really did this signify? Only the explanation that the phrase commonly symbolized Winston Churchill's jaw – and was thus acceptable to British workers – saw her story through. Yet a bland article by Henry Shapiro concerning Soviet trade was killed altogether: it had mentioned the import of dyestuffs. To the censor, whose English was rocky, this had been interpreted as weapons (stuff to make people die) and hence a military secret.

What frustrated the newsmen above all was the interminable time-lags. At the Foreign Office press department, where all stories were vetted, a four-hour wait was commonplace but eight-, ten-, even twenty-four-hour delays were not unknown. This left, as PM's publisher Ralph Ingersoll complained wrathfully, barely two hours a day to gather news. Even a correspondent as innocuous as Charlotte Haldane perforce took her turn on the treadmill. As correspondent of the *Daily Sketch* – known to Fleet Street as the 'Clean and Clever' – her remit was to furnish one story daily to intrigue the British housewife: the price of mushrooms, department store opening hours. But these, too, took their place in Palgunov's shuffling queue.

The focal point of this imbroglio centred on the biweekly conference of sixty-three-year-old Solomon Abramovich Lozovsky, Vice-Commissar for Foreign Affairs and official spokesman for the Soviet Information Bureau, an old Bolshevik who had escaped from prison more times than any living Communist. Punctually at 5 pm on Tuesdays and Fridays, Lozovsky held court in the former Greek Legation, around a green baize table flanked with bottles of lemonade and Narzan mineral water. Overtly the conferences were friendly, as the goatee-bearded Lozovsky, eyes twinkling behind his rimless spectacles, parried the correspondents' questions with flippant one-liners, reminding Alexander Werth of 'an old boulevardier sipping his Pernod or *café-crème*'. In reality, the meetings were a mirror-image of Dr Goebbels' in Berlin: a calculated attempt to quash the whole story of Russia's battle with her former ally.

If the questions were predictable, so too were the answers. What was the unnamed city which that day's communiqué reported retaken by the Red Army? 'My dear sir. If the army wanted you to know the name of the city, then the communiqué would have said it.' If the Germans had lost 700,000 soldiers in the last fortnight, how great were the Russian casualties? 'It's hard to make an exact count.'

Just as he had tangled with Goebbels in Berlin and Pierre Comert in Paris, it was destined that Quentin Reynolds would in due time clash with Comrade Lozovsky.

That Reynolds should have reached Moscow at all was luck rather than persistence. An initial application through Ivan Maisky, the Soviet Ambassador to London, had been turned down: *Collier's* already had one Moscow representative, Alice Leone Moats, a comely blonde with a smattering of Russian, and official policy was one newspaper, one correspondent. It was William Averell Harriman, millionaire's son and merchant banker, Roosevelt's newly created 'Defense Expediter', who came up with the solution. Briefed by the president to 'keep the British Isles afloat' – and hence their Russian ally – Harriman was bound for Moscow on a lend lease mission, along with Lord Beaverbrook, Churchill's new Minister of Supply. Would Reynolds be willing to serve as the mission's press attaché?

Using the same diplomatic leverage that had served Dimbleby so well in Baghdad and Tehran, Reynolds had arrived in Moscow in the last week of September – to be installed in the mighty two-room suite at the National Hotel once occupied by Leon Trotsky.

As an old pro, Reynolds readily passed on every usable snippet to the impatient correspondents, but it was he alone who had direct access to Harriman, Beaverbrook and the forty-strong Anglo-American mission. It was because of this, after the mission's maiden session on 28 September, that he first crossed swords with Lozovsky.

Beaverbrook, conferring with Stalin, had been impressed by his knowledge of technical matters. The British Hurricane, Beaverbrook had stated with all the confidence of a former Minister of Aircraft Production, had 1350 horsepower. Stalin had smiled faintly. 'No,' he corrected. 'It has 1250' – a story that Reynolds was swift to release and Lozovsky was as swift to veto. The item was discourteous to a British minister.

Reynolds protested. As a press baron, Beaverbrook had recognized a good story and authorized its release. 'It was a good joke on Beaverbrook,' Reynolds urged, 'and he himself laughed at it.'

Lozovsky's gaze was steady and unwavering. 'The story would serve no useful purpose. We will not pass it.'

Even so, it was Reynolds, on the night of 1 October, who glimpsed the great and infamous at close quarters, when Stalin invited the entire mission to a state dinner at the Kremlin. This was not an occasion to which correspondents were privy, but Reynolds, as a temporary diplomat, saw it all. As the guests, more than a hundred in all, nibbled pastry sticks from passing trays, he had time to register unflattering impressions. Foreign Minister Vyacheslav Molotov, standing alone, 'wore a Groucho Marx moustache, and most of the time looked as if he were watching someone sucking a lemon'. Lavrenti Beria, head of the dreaded NKVD, 'looks like a family physician until you get close to him'. Deputy Foreign Minister Andrei Vishinsky, chatting with Harriman in French, looked rosy-cheeked and benign: 'Everything about him was warm – except his eyes which looked like two bits of coal in the snow.'

Lastly there was Stalin, clad in a pepper-and-salt gabardine tunic buttoned to the neck, 'a rather bow-legged little man ... a shattering contradiction of the public image ... who carried his atrophied left arm close to his body to minimize the defect'. 'I hope you like Moscow,' was his murmured greeting to Reynolds, as translated by the Soviet Ambassador to Washington, Constantin Oumansky. At a later date, Reynolds thought, it was a British correspondent who best caught Stalin: 'He looks like the kindly Italian gardener you have in twice a week.'

It was an aptly Lucullan setting for the three-and-a-half-hour banquet which followed: a pillared French-style dining room, lined with banked arum lilies, its sixteen-foot-high double doors inlaid with gold-leaf carving and the arms of Catherine the Great surmounted by golden cherubs. It was equally a Tsarist feast which followed, in which caviare gave place to sucking pig, soup, fish and two varieties of game, a banquet at which Stalin, drinking twenty toasts, downed an entire bottle of champagne.

Only one factor, as Reynolds understood it from Harriman, marred the success of the four-day mission; without counting the cost to Britain, Beaverbrook had time and again yielded to the Russian front Great Britain's share of Russian supplies. Yet later events would prove Beaverbrook farsighted. For the foreseeable future, Britain's war role would be mainly peripheral, feinting at Rommel in the Western Desert. In the months to come, the entire war would hinge on the success or failure of Russian resistance.

Already the Black Sea ports of Odessa and Sevastopol were under siege. From 8 September Leningrad, the white city of Peter the Great, once St Petersburg, was to endure a blockade of 900 days, lasting until January 1944. Now Moscow, too, was threatened. The German advance, halted by Hitler on 30 July, at the time of Harry Hopkins's visit, was once more a reality. Intent on securing the fertile lands of the Ukraine and subduing Leningrad, the cradle of Bolshevism, the Führer had decided that Moscow could wait. But on 2 October, with the Ukraine collapsed and Leningrad besieged, he ordered a new offensive, Operation Typhoon, whose target was Moscow.

On 15 October Moscow was abruptly a city on the move. Although Stalin and the Politburo were staying resolutely put, almost two million people – including 500 factory complexes and their 200,000 workers – were moving east, among them the staffs of all foreign embassies and all foreign correspondents. The end of the road for Reynolds and his colleagues was now Kuibyshev, formerly Samara, the terminus of the ancient caravan routes from India and China, 525 miles distant. To those sceptical Muscovites remaining, it was an exodus derisively known as the *bolshoi drap* 'the big skedaddle'.

Five days later, after travelling 'hard' on wooden benches in the unlighted, unheated compartment of a thirty-three-coach train, Reynolds, Sulzberger, Cassidy and Miss Moats reached Kuibyshev – 'a sprawling city on the Volga River ... so far east of the war zone that it was not blacked out'. In the Grand Hotel, which Sulzberger pictured as 'like the provincial inn in a Dostoyevsky novel, crowded ... and redolent with cabbage, both cooked and digested', all of them faced a working life now innocent of bathtubs and central heating, with only one lavatory for each floor.

At first, the idea of quitting was far from Reynolds's mind. In a warco's life, hardship and discomfort had always gone hand in hand with luxury: on the eve of leaving Bordeaux, unshaven and in filthy uniforms, Reynolds and Kenneth Downs had unashamedly invaded the Chapon Fin, a gourmets' paradise, to lunch off *sole Marguery, entrecôte à la Bordelaise* and appropriate wines, finishing off with an 1856 brandy. It was a paradox he debated one afternoon with the *News Chronicle*'s Philip Jordan, on a bleak Kuibyshev street packed out with stumbling sheepskin-clad peasants and raw recruits.

'Here we are in a snowstorm, wading in slush, and there isn't a taxi to be had,' Jordan pondered. 'We'll get to the hotel wet and freezing, but with 200 dollars between us we'll still have a problem finding a hot drink. And yet there are people who think war correspondents lead glamorous lives.'

Reynolds had reservations. There were places, he thought, despite the drabness and misery, where warcos could lead fulfilled lives, but given the monolithic wall of distrust and evasion Kuibyshev was not one of them. That much was plain when, desperate for copy, he blocked out a feature concerning Kuibyshev itself – 'a colourful city which had suddenly sprung from obscurity into world-wide prominence'.' Here's one you won't be able to cut out,' he told Nicolai Palgunov triumphantly.

He had spoken much too soon. A standard 2500-word *Collier's*-length feature was blue-pencilled down to 400 words.

In the run-down Foreign Office building, Reynolds had his final showdown with Solomon Lozovsky – a confrontation which the Vice Commissar, with all the might of the Soviet Union behind him, won hands down. (Eight years later, as a reward for his loyal vigilance, Stalin put him before a firing squad.) As if to a slow-witted child, Lozovsky explained, 'People are not interested in what you eat and drink. They are not interested in the Kuibyshev ballet or the marionette show you write about ... Save such stories for after the war. Important things are happening. Write of them.'

Then, as if in refutation of this, he added smugly, 'Tass is telling the people of America all they need to know.'

Reynolds was not party to a later meeting between Lozovsky and the *New York Herald Tribune*'s Eve Curie, the dark, aloof daughter of Pierre and Marie Curie, discoverers of radium. It was then that the Vice-Commissar had told her bitterly: 'We are not going to forget quickly the way the Soviet Union has been calumniated, insulted and attacked, day after day, month after month, for

twenty-five solid years in the countries that are now our allies ...
Trust cannot come so quickly.'

In any case, there had been no need. Reynolds had felt the
antipathy all along in his blood and bones. 'I'm leaving as soon as I
can get out,' he told Lozovsky now. 'I can't earn a living here. None
of us can. We're taking money from our papers and magazines under
false pretences. Will you fix my exit visa as soon as you can?'

On 12 November, when Reynolds and Alice Leone Moats hitched
a ride on a plane to Tehran, the one remaining military enigma was
Japan.

To be sure, Japan's status had been made plain in September
1940, when her man in Germany, the slim, suave Saburo Kurusu,
had joined the Axis in Berlin – to recognize 'the leadership of
Germany and Italy in the creation of a new order in Europe', as
William L. Shirer cabled CBS. But when her Foreign Minister, the
tranquil, pipe-puffing Yosuke Matsuoka – described by the Havas
news agency as 'an English country gentleman painted yellow' –
visited Berlin in March 1941, Japan's commitment had seemed less
certain. Urged by Hitler to attack British possessions in the Far East,
Matsuoka had only smiled politely. Two weeks later in Moscow, on
Easter Sunday, Matsuoka had signed a five-year neutrality pact with
the Soviet Union.

In mid-July, entering the war game for 'defensive purposes',
Japan had pressurized Vichy France into accepting land, sea and air
forces 500,000-strong in southern Indo-China; Darlan, always eager,
as in Syria, to truckle to the Axis, had temporized, then accepted.
As a warning shot, Roosevelt had frozen Japanese assets in the
United States, banning the export of all oil supplies.

In the event of war, his Cabinet cautioned the· Emperor
Hirohito, Japan had one year's oil supplies at best – but for those
units of the Japanese Navy now in Camranh Bay, French Indo-
China, little enough oil would be needed to cover the 750 miles to
the British naval base at Singapore.

The British were unmoved. Their attitude, born of centuries
of imperial complacency, was summed up to Martha Gellhorn by
Colonel G. E. Grimsdale, Deputy Director of Military Intelligence,
Malaya: 'Japan has definitely missed the bus.'

In Martha's unflagging itinerary, Singapore was just one more
waystation in her exploration of the Far East scene – a journey on
which her bridegroom, Ernest Hemingway, had been for a time a

reluctant companion. In Chungking, the capital of wartime China, she had interviewed both Generalissimo Chiang Kai-Shek, the president, and his wife, May-Ling Soong, overtly dainty, inwardly as abrasive as carborundum, a chainsmoker of mentholated cigarettes, 'said to be worth thirty divisions' to the General in his four-year war against the Japanese invader. She had visited the Canton front, which had resolved itself 'into a war of mountain strongpoints', she had surveyed 'the ticking time-bomb of Hong Kong', another outpost of the British Empire, where Hemingway had privately expressed the opinion that in event of war 'the garrison would die like rats'. In Surinam, the last outpost of the doomed Dutch Empire, she heard the coolies labouring in the bauxite mines lament their Queen, now exiled in England – 'We sorry for Missy Wilhelmina.'

Lastly, there was Singapore, then, in the summer of 1941, the stuff of which myths were made.

This was the myth that Martha Gellhorn – and all the war correspondents – knew had been sixteen years a-building. It was, in the eyes of the propagandists, a £60-million floating dockyard, yet another 'impregnable fortress', although its only defence was six 15-inch naval guns pointing mutely out to sea. The concept was infinitely reassuring: a frontal assault on the naval base could be held off for ninety days, after which the British Fleet, in the true tradition of the Seventh Cavalry, would arrive to the rescue.

From the pillared splendour of Raffles Hotel, Martha viewed a spectacle at once so colourful and so improbable that she was forced to think, against her will, of 'a Hollywood set out of Cecil B. deMille'. For Singapore was, all unconsciously, a movie in itself: a polyglot medley of 'rickshaws and Rolls-Royces ... Indian officers with beards and bright turbans, Australian troops in rough-rider hats, English officers like actors impersonating English officers ... taxi-dancers ... Malayan royalty, orchids for five cents a bunch, gin slings, gossip, intrigues, parties and a possible war'.

'All that is really needed,' was Martha's sardonic comment, and few warcos came more sardonic, 'is Miss Marlene Dietrich in the role of a waterfront siren, vamping the army, navy and air force.'

This movie scenario – as she envisaged it – had a theme song, reiterated day and night by all the officers of the Services' Public Relations Office ('Aspro'), a song entitled 'I am not at liberty to reveal'. 'The suspicion grows,' Martha noted at this time, 'that there is very little to reveal ... all the stupidity which attends any actual war, the pompousness and paperwork and nuisances are in Singapore in force: but there is no war.' Better, she thought, to opt for a bit role in this movie: to eat fresh caviare, to go the round of the nightly dinner-parties, to succumb to the blissful euphoria of Sunday mornings at the Seaview Hotel, when the guests wound up their pre-lunch cocktail session with a rousing chorus of 'There'll Always Be An England'.

A part of the movie, understandably, had been cut: specifically, the Chinese coolies, 82 per cent of a population of 600,000, who worked in the rubber plantations and tin mines for 50 cents a day. 'This would be a grimy note and spoil the scenario.' The movie, of course, had a plot – 'There's a war on' – but the war in England, the England of Dunkirk, the Battle of Britain and the London Blitz was, in fact, 'farther away from Singapore than from New York'.

All movies needed comic relief, and in this category, Martha decided, you could include 'a really first-rate English snob' like the RAF officer who assured her that he would sit down for a drink with a sergeant pilot 'just like anyone else'. More comic relief still was furnished by the slouch-hatted Australians, who brought what Martha called 'the great blessing of laughter'. Reluctant to salute anyone but their own company officers, the Australians had finally agreed for the sake of example to salute the officers of a Scottish regiment in an adjoining camp. But after one busy Scot had drawn four salutes in a morning, the sentry called him to order: 'For God's sake don't come back this way again.'

No 'Aspro' officer would have accepted Martha's contention: 'The mood [of the movie] is "Business as usual", or rather "better than usual", since the nine large tin-mining companies made an average profit of 321% during 1940, and more is expected this year.' And her concept of the movie's happy ending – set down on paper in New York weeks later, far from 'Aspro's' prying eyes – would have shocked them profoundly: 'The music is "The Star-Spangled Banner" and there should be a beautiful shot of the Pacific Fleet steaming in over the opalescent China Sea.

'In case the plot works out, and there is actually a war, a real war, not a movie war ... the only happy ending there can be for Singapore is the US Navy, and Singapore knows it.'

Until late in 1941, the British saw the Japanese threat as still little more than hypothetical. To the disgust of Roosevelt's Chiefs of Staff, who had accompanied him to the Atlantic Charter meeting at Placentia Bay, their preoccupation was still the Western Desert – to which the Americans assigned number four priority, well below the United Kingdom, Singapore and the ocean trade routes. Still the British stuck stubbornly to their guns: their Middle Eastern presence might yet knock Mussolini's troops out of the war for good and all, and redeem the shame of the campaign in which Rommel had recaptured all of Cyrenaica save Tobruk.

Of all the Western Desert troublespots, none was such a thorn in Rommel's side as the beleaguered fortress of Tobruk. Captured by Lieutenant-General O'Connor's Australian contingents in January, besieged by Rommel after 8 April, Tobruk remained the one bridgehead that could repel Rommel's mass advance on Egypt. To hold Tobruk denied him the use of the only suitable port in Cyrenaica save Benghazi, 240 miles to the east.

When Alaric Jacob, a Reuters correspondent in the Middle East, arrived in Tobruk on 24 August 1941, he was well aware that he had arrived to report on a legend – a legend of shrugged-off endurance which Alan Moorehead, among others, had helped to foster when Tobruk fell in January. Fires were blazing in the town, furniture and household goods were strewn across the streets, yet on the mahogany counter of the National Bank Moorehead had seen a lone soldier, cheerfully frying the British Army's preferred diet, a pan of egg and chips.

At thirty-two, Jacob – who would ultimately succeed Moorehead as the *Daily Express*'s man in the desert – was an unlikely choice to give substance to an imperial legend. A confirmed Marxist since his time as a Washington correspondent six years earlier, he held firmly to the belief that 'there must be something radically wrong with a man who is not a socialist before he is thirty'. Despite his own imperialist background – his father had served under General Edmund Allenby, the conqueror of Jerusalem, in World War One, and there had been East India Company forebears – the ascetic Jacob would gladly have traded places with any correspondent soon to visit the Vyazma front. And in due time 'the privilege of living in the Soviet Union' was to be his, along with his wife, the novelist Iris Morley, accredited by *The Observer*.

Even so, Jacob, a seasoned reporter, did not sell Tobruk short. Its legend, in August 1941, was that of an impudent snook-cocking garrison, 220 miles square, a hive of grim activity peopled by 23,000 determined men – Anzacs, Britons, Indians, even a Jewish transport unit with a Star of David on their trucks – commanded by an Australian as tenacious as Rommel himself, Major-General Leslie

Morshead, known to his troops after the villain in the Flash Gordon comic strip as 'Ming the Merciless'. A port as awkwardly shaped as a clog, Tobruk's outer perimeter was a network of high artillery lookout posts and concrete dugouts, called the Red Line; two miles inland, the garrison was further protected by the Blue Line, a continuous minefield so thickly sown that the sappers themselves had lost track of them.

The accent, Jacob soon learned, was on the defensive–offensive: twenty-man patrols armed with bayonets and hand grenades, shod with sandals fashioned from old motor tyres, who launched nightly surprise attacks on Rommel's lines. Nothing, it seemed, had enraged Morshead more than the cock-a-hoop headline in one Australian daily: TOBRUK CAN TAKE IT. 'We're not here to take it,' he stormed. 'We're here to give it,' and Jacob's earliest unwitting *faux-pas* was to refer to the 'siege of Tobruk'. Although Tobruk was ringed completely by land and air, 'siege' was a dirty word.

For 242 days and nights, the eyes of the free world were focused on the men whom the Axis propagandists dubbed 'The Rats of Tobruk'. As a newcomer from the brightly lit fleshpots of Cairo, Jacob at first found the spartan routine bewildering: all headlights had been removed from cars, and a driver groping his way with a torch was likely to attract a fusillade of shots. The hardships were manifest. Beer was an almost unknown quantity, unlike the omnipresent desert fleas, which swarmed in the rocky dugouts. In the Red and Blue Lines, one scene was common to every strongpoint: men lying doggo for thirteen daylight hours on end under corrugated iron lean-tos, fighting boredom, weak from the sun, plagued by lice and dysentery. To stir above ground by day was to court a sniper's bullet and mealtimes were thus turned upside-down. Men breakfasted at 9.30 pm, took a hot lunch at midnight and dined before dawn.

Camouflage, Jacob noted, became the daily key to life or death. Helmets, even windshields, were daubed with anti-glaze paint: the tracks of walking men, as visible from the air as chalk lines on a blackboard, were smoothed clear with camel-thorn switches. Yet normal life of a sort went on among the dugouts. Six mimeographed newspapers flourished, from 'Tobruk Truth' to 'Mud and Blood'; the Catholic Church held services daily, and every few weeks Morshead rotated men to the coastal areas, to enjoy cricket matches and sea bathing. Even so, the UP's Jan Yindrich, a South African released after a two-month assignment, developed an uncontrollable facial tic.

Motionless in their dugouts, men dreamed impossible dreams, which they revealed to Jacob only reluctantly. Imaginary pails of iced beer replaced the brackish water, and corned beef and tinned herring vanished before T-bone steaks. Pets, if they chanced upon them, were cherished like pedigree prizewinners. One Anzac dugout acquired Myrtle, a tame magpie. As a sign that the troops accepted him, a British ack-ack battery introduced Jacob to their mascot, 'Larry the Lamb', an ancient sheep who relished corned beef. Each night a sentry was posted to guard him from would-be butchers.

In truth, Tobruk was never completely blockaded, since the harbour offered a seaward access to Alexandria, 394 miles to the east; it was from here that Jacob had arrived on the mine-layer HMS *Latonia*. But air cover was almost nonexistent, for Tobruk lay beyond the reach of Egypt-based fighters, and the harbour was littered with rusting wrecks bulging from the water like dying sea monsters, the harvest of 437 high-level raids by Stuka dive-bombers. It was with good reason, Jacob thought, as he departed from Alexandria on 8 September on the destroyer HMS *Decoy*, that the WDLF (Western Desert Light Flotilla), which ferried supplies to Tobruk, had been rechristened 'We Die Like Flies'.

Partially to relieve Tobruk and launch a second front to help their Russian allies, the British, on 18 November, launched their ill-starred Operation Crusader – with the grandiose objective of destroying all Rommel's armour and reoccupying Cyrenaica at one stroke.

At 9 pm on Sunday, 16 November, deep in an underground dugout at Bagush on the restless Mediterranean, General Sir Alan Cunningham, commander of the newly formed Eighth Army, had seemed confident that this could be achieved. 'A hoarse-voiced cherub of a man,' as Captain Sean Fielding of Army Public Relations recalled him, he told the pressmen sipping whiskies-and-soda, round a plain table: 'I am going to seek old Rommel out and destroy him and his armour.'

Among the warcos assembled that night, Alan Moorehead had conflicting feelings. It was now seven months since Rommel had sent the British packing from Cyrenaica, Libya's eastern province, and despite sporadic visits to Tobruk and Mersa Matruh, Moorehead's distaste for the desert war was deepening. 'I don't think ... I ever approached the front with any other feeling than that of dread,' he was to write in retrospect. 'We may have been caught up with the general excitement and wariness there at times ... but nearly always it was dread and nothing else.'

It was true that he himself had lauded the desert warfare as 'a knights' tournament in empty space' – innocent of houses and factories and civilians and animals. It was equally true that neither he nor Alexander Clifford nor Alaric Jacob ever 'saw' the battle as such. 'We were simply conscious of a great deal of dust, noise and confusion. The only way we could gather a coherent picture was by driving hard from one headquarters to another ... picking up the reports from the most forward units ... ' True, too, that he and Clifford had established over the months 'a network of tacit understanding and little habits' quite outside the ken of Lucy in Cairo, busy with her new job as secretary to Wavell's successor, General Sir Claude Auchinleck. In this Odd Couple relationship, it was automatically Clifford, versed in gourmet food, who cooked the rations, Moorehead who lit the stove, unpacked the truck and poured the nightly whisky ration into iron mugs. When turning in, Moorehead knew that Clifford's priority was a special pneumatic pillow; Clifford knew that, as a dedicated chainsmoker, Moorehead's was an ample supply of cigarettes.

And yet, as Moorehead would confess later, he was coming to share the revulsion from war that, unknown to him, had already gripped Reynolds and Dimbleby – although 'of course, none of this was apparent at the time. We all appeared to be splendid fellows together, and the façade of cheerfulness and willingness never for long broke down ...'

Even so, hopes for Crusader were high. At first light on 18 November, under a sullen downpour split by forked white lightning, the men of the Eighth Army heard the burst of machine-gun fire that signalled the 'off' as the force moved out from Bagush across the desert towards the Wire, the rust-corroded barrier six feet high that Mussolini had erected in 1932 to stop the Bedouins leaving Libya – 'like some great trek to the American west envisaged by a film director with delusions of grandeur,' thought Alaric Jacob, 'the lorries with their canvas tops looked just like covered wagons'.

For the first time since the mass Italian surrender at Beda Fomm, most men felt a warm glow of confidence. At last there was an abundance of everything – at least 118,000 fighting men, 700-plus guns, armoured tanks, among them 200 Chrysler M–3s, known as Honeys, the first US tanks ever to taste war. Unit after unit thrilled to the thunder of almost 650 RAF planes, crisscrossing the lowering skies – snub-nosed Hurricanes, big twin-engined Beau-fighters, even high-flying Fortresses.

Yet from Moorehead's viewpoint, it was 'a cold miserable and disheartening start for the battle. Bedraggled and wet, we trailed on in the wake of the soldiers. Every track we took was the wrong one ... no one seemed to have a clear idea of what was happening and where we were going.' His first consolation, at dusk on 19 November, was to see the Honeys go into action for the first time, with 'their ugly box-shaped turrets, their little waving pennants ... straight from the steel mills of America to the desert ... ' charging 'straight into the curtain of dust and fire that hid the German tanks and guns ... at speeds of nearly 40 miles an hour ... '. His second consolation was that Major Randolph Churchill, then heading the Middle East Army Bureau of Propaganda, would, through a combination of in-field censors and on-the-spot Lysanders, speed their stories back to Cairo for transmission.

All warcos had yardsticks of their own. To most men who crossed his path the Prime Minister's son was a truculent drunken bully, but to the Western Desert warcos, from the Marxist Jacob through the vaguely socialist Moorehead to the high-Tory Clifford, he could do no wrong. Randolph would get the story through on time.

The question was: What story? For the first few days, the only information that Moorehead could glean came in garbled fragments. Apparently puzzled by Rommel's failure to react to his first thrust, Cunningham had spread his armour on a seek-and-find mission across the face of the desert. From this elementary British mistake, Rommel was to profit richly.

On Saturday, 22 November, alone, Cunningham's 4th and 7th Armoured Brigades lost more than 100 tanks and the airfield at Sidi Rezegh, due south of Tobruk. What followed next day – which by chance was *Totensonntag*, the German 'Sunday of the Dead' – was stark slaughter. Time and again Rommel hurled his mass tanks at the British units round Sidi Rezegh, taking them on one after another and one after another knocking them out. These, unknown to Moore-head and his colleagues, were the heaviest casualties the British had yet endured in the desert.

Then, at 10.30 am on 24 November, Rommel brazenly led the entire Afrika Korps and two Italian divisions in a wild dash for the Wire, a forty-mile-long column bent on spreading chaos among the

British rear echelons like wolves stampeding a flock of sheep. It was a move that Eve Curie, a complete newcomer to the desert, found singularly disquieting. 'We were moving against the stream,' she realized suddenly as her truck groaned forward from the Wire. 'Scattered groups of lorries were already evacuating equipment and men in a hurry ... ' On hastily returning to the base camp, 'a surprise awaited us: everything had been packed up in our absence'. Over 1000 square miles of desert, confusion spread like fire under a leaning wind. Retreat became total. Columns of inky smoke stained the desert as clerks fired secret records. Signallers fumbled frantically to coil up the miles of wire which made up the telephone networks. Entire units – British, German and Italian – became hopelessly entwined. 'Libya was a madhouse,' Alexander Clifford reported. 'The operational maps now looked like surrealistic masterpieces.' 'All day, for nine hours we ran,' supplemented Moorehead, who had been caught at the moment of retreat literally with his pants down, pelting for the getaway truck armed with a spade and a roll of toilet paper.

Back in Cairo, Moorehead viewed with resignation the uproarious headlines on the newsstands: ROMMEL IN ROUT – ROMMEL SURROUNDED. Despite Randolph Churchill's liberal in-field censorship, GHQ Cairo had opted for nothing less than unqualified victory. 'Little or nothing,' Moorehead carped, 'had been allowed out about our losses or the German gains ... The breakthrough had been ignored.'

Ignored, too, was the fact that on 26 November Auchinleck had relieved Cunningham of his Eighth Army command; a Cairo hospital was to diagnose him as suffering from both mental and physical fatigue. The shortcomings of the Honeys – whose 37-mm 2-pounders were only effective at 800 yards' range – had been glossed over. Tobruk *had* been relieved, but narrowly, after four bloodstained days.

As yet, Moorehead thought, the High Command had still to grasp that the public was by now resigned to delays, even defeats. 'What the public disliked intensely was having its hopes raised high, only to be plunged into the disappointment of reality later on ...

'The old bad dictum that you must always give the public good news had been the thing they had fallen back on in their distress.'

Clark Lee was by no means certain but it looked as if the American public, like it or not, would soon be forced to digest the worst news of all. After just over two years, World War Two was reaching out to shatter a dream they had nourished since the Armistice of 1918: a dream of splendid isolation.

It was Friday, 14 November – two days after Reynolds's departure from Kuibyshev, two days earlier than General Cunningham's Crusader briefing – and in a noisy bar on the Shanghai waterfront, the thirty-four-year-old AP correspondent was listening hard and saying little. He had the sick, deflated feeling that he was sitting on the scoop of a lifetime – one that he could in no way use.

Any attempt to capitalize on it, Lee knew, would imperil his informant, Sergeant Hajime Matsui of the Imperial Japanese Army, who had only set up this rendezvous to pass on a friendly warning from his colonel. After five and a half years in the Far East, Lee had put down deep roots there: although he had been critical of Japan's invasion of China, he was known to respect the Japanese people. And everyone knew that his wife was a native Hawaiian, Princess Liliuokalani Kawanankoa.

'It has been ... called to the colonel's attention that you plan to go to the United States on home leave in about two months,' Sergeant Matsui hazarded gently. 'The colonel wishes to point out that except for two Dutch vessels and one French, no departures are scheduled from Shanghai. There is a possibility that after the next ten days there may not be any way to get out.'

Translated, Lee thought, 'the shooting might start any time after the next days,' and he was swift to heed the advice. Contact with a friendly Dutch shipping agent secured him a cancelled berth aboard the 8000-ton *Tjibadak*, outward bound for Manila the next morning. But at journey's end, all thoughts of a reunion with the Princess in San Francisco were in vain. The cable awaiting him suggested further trouble: REMAIN MANILA UNTIL FURTHER ORDERS STOP REGARDS KENPER. 'Kenper' was Kent Cooper, AP's general manager in New York.

Not for the first time, Lee harked back to an interview he had been granted in 1939 by Lieutenant-General Masaharu Homma, then commanding the Japanese forces blockading Tientsin. 'I think that every American believes he can handle any two Japanese soldiers,' Homma challenged Lee genially, as if an American–Japanese war was already a foregone conclusion. 'At any rate, we are proceeding with this in mind, and we are prepared to lose 10 million men in our war with America. How many are you prepared to lose?'

This was intelligence that Lee had not hesitated to pass on to

Lieutenant-General Douglas MacArthur, in his penthouse on the fifth floor of the Manila Hotel. As recently appointed chief of the US Army forces in the Far East, MacArthur had already won the correspondents' approval, both as a flamboyant personality and an incisive commander: he was, summarized Clare Boothe, using the words of one of his rankers, 'a hell-to-breakfast baby, long and lean', using 'ten-dollar words delivered in a million-dollar manner'.

In that same Manila Hotel, twenty-five-year-old Melville Jacoby, *Time*'s man in the Phillipines capital, was keeping a watchful eye on Japan's Saburo Kurusu, who had formally aligned Japan with the Axis fourteen months earlier. En route to Washington for talks with Secretary of State Cordell Hull, he was distinguished by his black morning coat, despite the tropical heat, his 'cat-about-to-swallow-the-canary smile' and his deft evasion of correspondents' questions.

Jacoby, though, like a canny checkroom attendant, had singled out one telling fact: Kurusu's meagre baggage had suggested his stay in Washington would be the shortest possible.

Nor could it feasibly have been otherwise. As Theodore H. ('Teddy') White, *Time*'s man in Chungking, was already informing The Desk in New York, Japan was reaching crisis point. Kurusu's instructions were quite finite: Japan's troops would be withdrawn from southern Indo-China to northern Indo-China if America reversed her embargo on oil and steel and gave Japan a free hand in China. Since the US had long supported Chiang Kai-Shek morally and financially this was a course she could not in honour pursue. In this case, White stressed, using an old Chinese metaphor, the 'Japanese would have been caught ... like a turtle in a bottle'.

The eyes of Japan – but not of America – were thus focused on the US first line of defence, of which the core was the Hawaiian island of Oahu, the base of the US Pacific Fleet at Pearl Harbor. From 1931 on, every member of each graduating class in Japan's naval academy had been asked one $64,000 question: How would you launch a surprise assault on Pearl Harbor?

On 7 December, a bright Sunday morning with a light northeast trade wind caressing the green cane fields and the ninety-six vessels of the Fleet making ready for morning colours on Battleship Row, 353 carrier-borne aircraft of the Imperial Japanese Navy gave the answer to that question.

At 8 am Frank Tremaine, the UP manager in Honolulu, awoke abruptly with a roaring in his ears but although he and his wife

Frances had stayed late at a dinner-party he didn't think it could be a hangover. All at once he recognized it as anti-aircraft fire – yet Sunday morning was an unlikely time for practice. Trampling his wife's party dress from its hanger as he rushed for the phone, he put in a long-distance call for San Francisco. 'It's an attack by Jap planes,' he shouted to Frances. 'I put in a call for SX. If it comes through, you tell them everything you can see.'

At 8.30 am, as Tremaine headed for the Army Public Relations Office at Fort Shafter, Mrs Tremaine, phone in hand, was giving the San Francisco Office a blow-by-blow account of Roosevelt's 'date that will live in infamy': the mighty grey ships obscured by shimmering geysers of water, the columns of blood-red smoke spewing skywards, the hurtling hornet-dives of the Japanese bombers. At least she was fully alerted. Joseph C. Harsch of the *Christian Science Monitor*, newly arrived in Hawaii, was departing for a swim, but first awoke his wife to tell her, 'Darling, this is a good imitation of the raids you get in Europe.' En route by steamer to a new assignment in Egypt, AP's Tom Yarbrough felt priorities had been confused. A ship's officer assembled all passengers to announce: 'It seems there is a state of undeclared war between Honolulu and the US'.

A few knew that it was the real thing. In Washington DC, UP's Arthur DeGreve, who had received confirmation from the White House, found the teletype inoperative: he reached the New York news desk by phone, yelling as soon as contact was made:

'This is DeGreve in Washington – FLASH – White House announces Japanese bombing Wahoo.'

'Bombing what?'

'Wahoo, dammit, Wahoo.'

'Spell it, for Pete's sake.'

'O - A - H - U - Wahoo! We've got a war on our hands.'

VI

Our Forces Are Holding Firmly On All Fronts

8 DECEMBER 1941–8 NOVEMBER 1942

Now the war was as wide as the world, but even though Pearl Harbor had changed the face of history, the news was slow to travel. In the wardroom of the cruiser HMS *Repulse*, heading northeast from Singapore through the South China Sea, it was 7.30 am on 9 December before Cecil Brown of CBS and the *Daily Express*'s O'Dowd Gallagher heard President Roosevelt in Washington DC, asking Congress for a declaration of war on Japan. Ten hours later, they learned why: another radio bulletin brought the first skimpy news of Pearl Harbor. At once, *Repulse*'s captain, William Tennant, summoned Brown to his sea-cabin. Gripping his hand, Tennant said feelingly, 'I am very glad to have an American reporter aboard.'

That gesture said everything. After twenty-two years and twenty-five days, the two-ocean war had reached the United States. In a world where thirty-seven nations were now at war, Britain and America were at last united by a common enemy, a common hurt.

But Brown, like Gallagher, had distinct reservations about this trip. Promised a four-day sortie with the Eastern Fleet, both men had jumped at the chance – convinced they would be quartered aboard HMS *Prince of Wales*, Britain's newest 35,000-ton battleship, known since she had borne the Prime Minister to his Placentia Bay meeting with Roosevelt as 'Churchill's Yacht'. Since *Prince*'s arrival in Singapore as a deterrent had been widely publicized, her presence could be mentioned: in the eclectic world of the warcos, *Aboard Prince of Wales in the Gulf of Siam* had seemed an irresistible dateline.

Now, thanks to an inevitable muddle by 'Aspro', they had been bundled aboard *Repulse*, and their only dateline would thus read *With the Eastern Fleet*. The whereabouts of *Repulse* – like her sister ships that made up this patrol, the destroyers *Electra*, *Express*, *Vampire* and *Tenedos* – remained a closely guarded secret.

Although Admiral Sir Thomas 'Tom Thumb' Phillips, the diminutive C-in-C, had signalled from *Prince*, his flagship, 'We are out looking for trouble and no doubt we shall find it,' both warcos had written off the next four days as wasted. The realization that this was still, despite all, a time for loners had not struck them. Nor had they divined that they alone were destined to write the epitaph of battleship power, British or otherwise.

At 6.30 am on 10 December, expectations quickened slightly. Reaching his observer post on the flag-deck, Gallagher, who had struggled into oil-stained overalls, heard *Repulse*'s loudspeaker cough into life: 'A signal has just been received to say the enemy is making a landing at Kuantan [140 miles north of Singapore]. We are going in.'

As the gun crews took up action stations, Gallagher and Brown piled for the wardroom. If shooting was imminent, a quick breakfast of cold ham, coffee, bread and marmalade seemed thoroughly in order.

By 7.50 am, eight miles off Kuantan, only palm trees shimmered behind a shoreline which rose by degrees to haze-shrouded mountains. 'I think we are too late now,' *Repulse*'s flag officer announced. 'Think they have all gone.'

If such was the case, it was not for long. At 11.07 am the loudspeaker blared again: 'Enemy aircraft approaching – action stations!' From the flag-deck, Brown and Gallagher saw them clearly: nine Japanese aircraft, flying in line astern at 12,000 feet, 'stretched out across the bright blue cloudless sky like star sapphires of a necklace'. As if by reflex, flames belched from the *Prince*'s ten new-type 14-inch guns.

Word came that, rather belatedly, Admiral Phillips had now signalled Singapore asking for air cover.

Bombs came hurtling, 'like ever-enlarging tear drops'; they struck the sea ten yards away, and *Repulse* shuddered; a titanic geyser of water swamped her decks. At 11.18 am, the Japanese intention was plain; they were singling out the two capital ships. *Prince* and *Repulse*. Both hit back with their Vickers multiple pom-poms, the 'Chicago pianos', firing 2000 half-inch shells a minute. Throughout all this, Brown, the laconic Ohioan, and Gallagher, the cynical South African, were scribbling in fascination – one noting the black paint on the funnel-shaped gun muzzles 'rise in blisters as big as your fist', the other the empty cordite cases tumbling from the guns' scuttles, as if from a berserk fruit machine.

Repulse rocked again, more violently. Pieces of paint showered from the deck above the flag-deck. A bomb had scored a direct hit on the catapult deck, ploughing through the port hangar to ignite the cruiser's one Walrus float-plane. From the tortured notes of a bugle, Gallagher discerned 'that most sinister of all alarms at sea – "Fire!"'

At 11.21 am, *Repulse*'s answering fire paid off: half a mile astern, a Japanese bomber, one of seven downed by *Prince* and her escorts, hit the South China Sea trailing black smoke. But at 11.40 am Brown scented trouble – '*The Prince of Wales* seems to be hit. She's reduced her speed' – and more trouble was in the offing. Distant specks had appeared, and were soon identifiable: nine torpedo bombers, 'circling four or five thousand yards away ... circling in a huge sweep'. Some were diving head-on, some from astern. The torpedoes, nose-heavy, made only faint splashes before streaking towards *Repulse*. It was 11.45 am.

At 11.51 am, Captain Tennant signalled *Prince*, four cable lengths ahead: 'Have you sustained any damage?'

The answer was bleak: 'We are out of control. Steering gear is gone.'

By 12.01, twelve torpedo bombers were attacking *Prince* and *Repulse* from all angles. But only *Repulse* could twist and snake violently, bent on evasion. The stink of cordite, the warcos noted, was now overpowering; the cruiser's decks were littered wastefully with empty shell cases and dying men. At 12.14, replying to a query, Tennant signalled Admiral Phillips: 'We have dodged nineteen torpedoes thus far, thanks to Providence.' But neither Providence nor air cover was on hand at 12.20 pm.

'Stand by for barrage,' the communications pipe sounded, as the torpedo bombers approached, then, 'Stand by for torpedo.' The torpedo struck twenty yards astern of the flag-deck; to Brown, thrown four clear feet, it was as if the cruiser had 'crashed into dock'. Mesmerized, Gallagher was watching another torpedo as it 'churned up a thin wake', driving straight for the immobile *Prince of Wales*. A second hit her, then a third, and Gallagher watched her 'turning slowly over on her port side, her stern going under and dots of men jumping into the sea'. Then another torpedo took *Repulse* on her port side, and Gallagher, hurled against a bulkhead, heard Tennant's last command echo over the dying ship: 'All hands on deck! Prepare to abandon ship. God be with you.'

Automatically Gallagher checked his watch; 12.25 pm. By now *Repulse*'s list 'had developed so fast you could see it'. As a good warco he thought automatically of Kipling:

> Hit, and hard hit! The blow went home,
> The muffled knocking stroke –
> The steam that overruns the foam –
> The foam that thins to smoke –

Then he jumped from the torpedo-blister into the black velvety carpet of oil two feet deep that coated the South China Sea.

After temporarily losing touch with Gallagher, Brown had done the same; both men now made two of the 2800 survivors on a sea dotted with bobbing heads, 'packed like a football field', as the destroyers among the escort moved in to pick them up. But more than 800 lives had been lost, among them Admiral Phillips and *Prince*'s captain, John Leach.

It was past midnight on 11 December when HMS *Electra* deposited Brown, still shaking with exhaustion and slathered in oil, back at Singapore's much vaunted naval base. In the interim he had had much time to reflect. In barely two hours, Japanese bombers had accomplished more than Hitler's submarines and Stukas in two years of war. (At Pearl Harbor, he would learn later, the US had suffered greater naval losses than in the whole of World War One.) But returning to the naval base, his first thoughts were all for Gallagher, a colleague he was convinced was lost.

'Gallagher? Oh, he's just fine,' an officer from *Repulse* speedily reassured him. So much recovered, in fact, that he had already left the naval base for Singapore, eighteen miles away.

All compassion spent, Brown lost no time in calling for a Navy car. Gallagher dead was a man enshrined in memory – 'a swell guy, a great reporter and a courageous fighter'. Gallagher alive was a deadly rival who might ensure that the London *Daily Express* announced the death of battleship power hours before the Columbia Broadcasting System in New York had heard a word about it.

Neither Gallagher nor Brown had any monopoly on grim tidings. As their colleagues were reporting ruefully, port by port, fort by fort, the Far East was now invested.

At 2 am on 8 December, following three soaring red flares from their headquarters ship, 100 motorboats breasting nine-foot waves brought 24,000 men of the 25th Japanese Army ashore at Kota Bharu, Malaya – forty-eight hours earlier than the Kuantan landings reported to *Repulse*. At 7 am, thirty-six Japanese fighters wiped out the entire island air force – seven planes – at Hong Kong's Kai Tak airport. On the same day, with the same ruthless precision, the Japanese hit Clark Field, sixty-five miles north of Manila, destroying all but three out of thirty-five Flying Fortresses. Three days later, at noon on 10 December, eighty bombers winged their way unopposed to Cavite, eighty miles southwest of Manila, the only American naval base in the Far East beyond Pearl Harbor, and pounded it to rubble.

Everywhere it was the same melancholy story of too little and too late. Overnight, the Japanese were seen for what they were: hardy, fearless warriors, whose sharpshooting was accurate up to 1000 yards, equipped with slit-toed rubber shoes that helped them climb swiftly and silently, men able to survive for five days on minimal rations of rice and fish. Thirty miles south of the Malayan frontier, it took barely 800 of them fifteen hours to broach the deservedly forgotten Jitra Line, designed as a divisional strongpoint for three months. Then they forged down the peninsula towards the Johore Causeway dividing Singapore from the mainland. Neither anti-tank defences, fire-traps nor underwater mines existed to stall their back-door advance; barely enough artillery ammunition was in place to fire twelve rounds a day.

By 11 December, an ambitious plan to defend Hong Kong from the mainland along an eleven-mile redoubt called the Gin Drinkers' Line – once a rendezvous for alcoholic picnics – had been abandoned. For the British, a retreat across the harbour to the thirty-two square miles of Hong Kong island was the one way out. In Manila, where MacArthur's troops were as poorly equipped as the British had been in Norway, the outcome was again inevitable. By 24 December MacArthur, declaring Manila an open city to spare civilian lives, had transferred his headquarters to Corregidor, the 'Gibraltar of the Pacific', a three-mile-long rocky fortress thirty miles away across the bay. His troops, armed with ancient water-cooled machine guns and mortars more fitted for junk piles, effected a gallant fighting retreat twenty miles west to Bataan, infamous in American history as the rugged twenty-five-mile-long peninsula where 75,000 of them became POWs in April 1942. Their besiegers were the 14th Army of General Masaharu Homma – who had signalled Japan's willingness to sacrifice 10 million men to AP's Clark Lee.

Only Rangoon, the Burmese capital, was spared until 23 December – when the first Japanese air raid on the docks area left more than a thousand dead. Two days later, on Christmas Day, the bombers returned. By then almost 250,000 people had quit the city, and the end was predictable. Only one British armoured brigade and one infantry battalion was earmarked to defend Rangoon: no further reserves could be sent.

It was against this background that Winston Churchill became the first British Prime Minister ever to visit the United States in wartime, along with his Chiefs of Staff, for in the light of America's eleventh-hour involvement, three crucial questions had now to be resolved. Would Roosevelt stick to his avowed Atlantic First policy, with Germany as the number one enemy? If so, how could Japan be slowed down in the Pacific in the interim? And how could an Allied command be coordinated through the vast theatres of the Atlantic and the Pacific?

The fate of nations would be decided by the answers to these questions, and so, too, would the destiny of the warcos. As the planners pored over their charts, so the Foreign Editors would pencil in itineraries over the next three years.

In most of the United States, the mood was staunch. 'What they said – tens of thousands of them' reported *Time* magazine, 'was, "Why, the yellow bastards ... we'll stamp their front teeth in."' Long lines piled up outside the recruiting offices: the year's end would see 28,349 men newly enlisted. But in downtown Honolulu, only ten miles from Pearl Harbor, Robert Casey, a roly-poly correspondent of the *Chicago Daily News*, still found nerves at snapping point when he arrived on Friday, 19 December.

Here, just as in London and Paris, Berlin and Moscow, the streetlamps had gone out. The few military cars in evidence crawled with blue-painted headlights. Silent, frightened groups of people huddled in the lobbies of hotels and boarding houses, listening for the first cry of the siren that would herald the Japanese return. Their faces wore 'the blank expressions of men coming out of the ether'. 'This town is sitting right on the edge of its chair,' Casey reported, 'all ready to get up and run somewhere.'

At the submarine base's Saturday morning press conference, held around a long table in the Officers' Club, Casey found the same unease. True, a handful of the Fleet's surviving officers had been mustered to tell their stories – but none of them, stressed the public relations officer, Sam Riddick, could be mentioned by name, any more than the ships. One battleship, the *Arizona*, ran the Navy's official story, had been lost, and another, the *Oklahoma*, had capsized, but would soon be righted – a fiction hard to grasp for all those at Pearl who could see both battleships, along with the *California*, the *Nevada* and the *West Virginia*, fifty feet down in the diamond-clear water.

Even the UP's Wallace Carroll, the survivor of sundry brushes with Comrade Lozovsky in Moscow, confessed that the Soviet methods were 'liberal indeed compared with the cable censorship which the United States established for a time after the attack on Pearl Harbor'. One military censor in Washington seemed to mirror the mood of the moment: 'I wouldn't tell the people anything until the war is over, and then I'd tell them who won.'

It was no lone example as Clark Lee, now chafing in Manila, was among the earliest to testify. From first to last, Lee charged, the keynotes of Philippine censorship were 'inefficiency, inconsistency and lack of understanding', operated for the most part 'by naval reservists who had no experience in their jobs'. The bombing of Clark Field was a closed book, and thus no mention could be made of the desperate need for planes to replace the devastated Flying Fortresses. An account by Lee's colleague, Russell Brines, of how and why MacArthur had yielded up Manila never reached the AP office in New York: the censor had quietly buried it. Even stories from Corregidor, where Lee and his fellows had retreated along with MacArthur, were vetoed by the General. Given the near impenetrable blackout, it was not surprising that the Foreign Editors in the United States were groping in a fog. 'Another first-person eyewitness story,' requested one *Time* cable, 'but this week we prefer Americans on the offensive.'

Incensed, Shelley Mydans, who with her husband Carl failed to escape internment, flashed back: 'Bitterly regret your request unavailable here.'

All over the Far East, almost without exception, the face of officialdom was the face of deceit. Even so, the warcos were registering their small vivid vignettes for later publication, as if relays of candid cameramen had focused their viewfinders over the 2400 miles separating Manila from Rangoon. In Hong Kong, which Churchill had stressed would be resisted 'with the utmost stubbornness', Gwen

Moorehead, (*Daily Express*), left, with
ander Clifford (*Daily Mail*) in the Western
rt, 1941

ha Gellhorn and Ernest Hemingway at Sun
y, Idaho, 1940

Noel Monks (*Daily Mail*), left, sur
the Siegfried Line with Winston
Churchill and Montgomery, 1945.
They are surrounded by war
correspondents.

Ernie Pyle

owd Gallagher (*Daily
ress*), third from left, with
r survivors aboard the
royer *Vampire* after the
edoing of H.M.S. *Repulse* in
South China Sea, 1941

ntin Reynolds, war
espondent for *Colliers*
azine

e Hollingworth, the war
espondent for the *Daily
graph*

Leland Stowe, (*Chicago Daily News*), the 'warco' who helped topple the Chamberlain governmen

Edward R. Murrow, CB? correspondent in Londor throughout the war

August, 1944, Robert
a's camera focuses on
man prisoners of war
civilian reporters
nded up in the channel
of St Malo

rmandy, June 1944.
ert Capa follows US
atroopers moving
ugh the deserted town
aint Sauveur

The eve of D-Day. *Life* photographer
Robert Capa records troops embarking
on small craft in Weymouth Harbour

D-Day, 6 June, 1944. The chaos of
Omaha Beach as pictured by Robert
Capa

group of US war correspondents visit London to mark the fifth anniversary of D-Day.

chard Dimbleby (BBC) poses beside Berlin's Brandenburg Gate, 1945

An exclusive shot by the author's cameraman, Joe Waddell: the dejected retre of the Japanese from Singapore, September, 194

The raising of the Stars and Stripes on Iwo Jima, February 23, 1945: a Pulitze Prize winning picture by Jo Rosenthal for Associated Press

Dew, who freelanced for both *Newsweek* and NANA, was twice hailed by a three-man Japanese peace mission en route to the Governor, Sir Mark Young: 'Cameraman? Don't you want to take our pictures? Wouldn't you like our names?'

'There must be vigorous fighting in the inner defences,' was the official word, but Gwen Dew saw the reality in the ferry trip she took across the harbour with a company of wounded men, watched over by a nurse who was herself bleeding profusely. 'You are wounded, you must stop,' one man expostulated. 'I must go on,' the nurse replied, 'and I am dying.' She was dead before the ferry reached the island's capital Victoria. Hong Kong fell, as Hemingway had foreseen, on Christmas Day 1941.

'Today we stand beleaguered in our island fortress,' proclaimed the GOC Malaya, Lieutenant-General Arthur Percival, on 31 January, as the last allied soldiers fell back across the Johore Causeway, adding, 'with firm resolve and fixed determination we shall win through.' But Ian Morrison, seconded to the London *Times* from the Ministry of Information's Far Eastern bureau, saw a different picture. 'The world wanted to be sold Singapore,' he concluded.'It wanted to believe that Singapore . . . was a bulwark against Japanese aggression in the Pacific . . . The legend grew.' But by 8 February, as the black smoke from burning oil dumps blotted out the Singapore sun, Morrison knew it was as Martha Gellhorn had predicted; there would be no 'firm resolve', no 'fixed determination'. Prudently he hitched a ride on a Dutch freighter bound for Batavia, capital of the Dutch East Indies. Singapore fell on 15 February.

One day earlier, Eve Curie had reached Rangoon – which was to fall on 8 March – to recognize instantly the 'ghastly odour of defeat, of retreat, of fear . . . the emptiness, the unforgettable silence of the large cities in danger'. Yet Rangoon, pronounced that day's communiqué, was perfectly 'calm', and next morning an interview with Burma's Governor, Sir Reginald Dorman-Smith, only 'produced a handsome artificial smile in support of his statement that Rangoon would hold'. With every fibre of her being, Eve Curie yearned to bring him down to earth: 'Why do you take all this trouble? I am French. I *know* what a defeat looks like.'

Up country from Rangoon, it seemed that some officers knew it too. In Mandalay, Burma's ancient pagoda-dotted second city 250 miles north, *Time*'s Jack Belden witnessed a spectacle that surely pointed the way towards the end of the white man in Asia. At 11.03 am on Saturday 4 April, Japanese bombers pinpointed the major

Chinese Army supply base 'as a scientist fixes a bug beneath a microscope . . . and stabbed it with hundreds of explosive plummets. Out of each plummet rose a splash of flame; fires sprang out of wooden houses, and soon half of Mandalay was ablaze.'

Far from the fires, on the city outskirts, Belden found a police official with a glass of whisky in his hand and asked him, 'How many people have been killed?' But the officer didn't know. 'Maybe four hundred. Maybe four thousand . . . Everything will be all right tomorrow. We'll fix everything then.'

Along with UP's Darrell Berrigan, Belden moved on to meet a colonel. He was stumbling down the steps of his house, supported at the elbow by a junior officer who said, 'I don't think you should talk to these gentlemen, sir.'

'We just wanted to ask you something about the fire,' Belden explained.

'Well, I haven't got time now,' said the colonel simply. 'Besides, I'm drunk.'

It was not until much later that Belden was able to file a dispatch quoting one of Chiang Kai-Shek's divisional chiefs of staff: 'As the Japanese are fighting both the British and us, they are looked on as friends.' The ultimate Japanese aim – to sever the last link between India and their old enemy, China – was only a question of time.

Some Far Eastern officials did, indeed, feel qualms of conscience. Late in February – three weeks before MacArthur, following presidential orders, pulled out of Corregidor on a hazardous 2000-mile journey to continue the fight from Australia – Lieutenant-Colonel Herbert Harries, a cool, correct West Pointer, took Clark Lee aside in a corner of the fortress's grim 100-foot-long Malinta Tunnel. As MacArthur's press spokesman, Harries had time and again dished out the communiqués that served as pabulum for the Philippines and the entire Far East: OUR FORCES ARE HOLDING FIRMLY ON ALL FRONTS.

'You know, I felt like hell reading you those lies in a pontifical way every day,' Harries confessed. 'But it had to be done. We were trying to deceive the enemy and to conceal the fact that we were withdrawing into Bataan.'

One man, in due time, was to tell much of the truth: Lieutenant-General Joseph W. 'Vinegar Joe' Stilwell, a crabbed fifty-nine-year-old China veteran whom Roosevelt, late in December, had furnished to Chiang Kai-Shek as Chief of Staff, partly as an incentive to Chiang to stay in the war. But on the China–Burma front, Stilwell found only dire confusion. Major-General Harold Alexander, charged by Churchill to save Burma, saw only one possibility: to save the British troops by a 900-mile withdrawal to India. By 5 May Stilwell, whose Chinese Fifth and Sixth Armies were fast disintegrating under Japanese pressure, saw that he, too, must withdraw. Dogging his footsteps to the very end was *Time*'s Jack Belden.

A footloose thirty-two-year-old native of Brooklyn, Belden had been nine years in China, switching from English teacher at Peiping University to roving reporter when the Sino-Japanese war had begun. Thus he knew Stilwell, warts and all: a leathery, aggressive warrior but still an abysmal diplomat, wont to blow his top on the slightest provocation. When that time came, Belden wanted to be there.

On 7 May, Stilwell's epic retreat began. His objective now was India. His Chinese Army units were one day's march behind him, but with him was a party 114 strong, including an American Baptist doctor, nineteen Burmese nurses, plus, in Belden's words, 'a polyglot party of weary, hungry, sick American, British and Chinese Army officers, enlisted men, Naga, Chin and Shan tribesmen, and a devil's brew of Indian and Malayan mechanics, railwaymen, cooks, refugees, cipher clerks and mixed breeds of Southern Asia'. At their head, leading at a dogged fixed pace of 105 steps per minute, which became known as the 'Stilwell Stride', marched 'Vinegar Joe'.

Stumbling ahead along elephant trails, eking out half rations with berries and plants, Stilwell, Belden noted, 'alternatively performed the services of company commander, mess sergeant, gun-bearer and guide', loading the truly sick onto the twenty mules that accompanied the party. Alternatively wheedling and tongue-lashing the stragglers, many of them stricken with dysentery and heat exhaustion, he had brought them by 13 May to the wide, fast-flowing Chindwin River. Ahead of them now lay a fifty-mile march over a 7000-foot mountain pass, and through more cloud-enveloped jungle, until they reached the moist green tea plantations of Assam, north-eastern India. Not one member of the party was lost.

And Belden's instinct was proven right. At the end of a nine-day trek in which the refugees had averaged fourteen miles a day, 'Vinegar Joe' did have something to say: a statement which encapsulated the whole sorry Far Eastern story in two sentences. He delivered it to the assembled press in New Delhi on 25 May, and since a three-star general had said it, the censor had no option but to pass it.

'I claim we got a hell of a beating. We got run out of Burma and it is humiliating as hell.'

For almost fifty American warcos time, in the spring of 1942, hung heavily. On 11 December 1941, Hitler, duly honouring the Tripartite Pact, had declared war on the United States; on the same day, Mussolini followed suit. Like their brethren in Tokyo and Japanese-held territories, the newsmen in Rome and Berlin, along with the embassy and consular staffs, became detainees, pending exchange formalities.

To men who knew a good cliché when they saw one, this was a God-given opportunity to study their captors at close range. Happily, almost without exception, they conformed to national stereotype. At the Grand Hotel Jeschke, Bad Nauheim, the eighteen correspondents headed by AP's veteran Louis Lochner found the Germans were universally *förmlich* – punctiliously correct. The hotel might be spartan and cold, but there was a freedom of thought unknown in Hitler's Germany. A University in Exile sprang up, sponsoring everything from Shakespearean recitals to musicales and spelling bees.

One early phenomenon puzzled Lochner: an overnight conversion to Catholicism. Twenty diplomatic families, all practising Catholics, were soon joined at Mass by a line-up of forty or fifty, many correspondents among them. Attendance at Protestant services fell off dramatically. It was some time before Lochner – and the Gestapo – got wind of a thriving racket: North American 'Catholics', kneeling devoutly in their pews, were conducting a sacrilegious barter with their Latin American counterparts, cigarettes (which the Latins craved) in return for liquor (which the Americans painfully lacked).

The Italians, despite Mussolini, were *allegro* – cheerful, lively, good-humoured. A three-day spell in Rome's grim old Regina Coeli (Queen of Heaven) prison – to which the internees, following Italian custom, paid the taxi fare – gave place to ten days' lodging in the Pensione Suquet, a former brothel off the Corso Umberto. For the first time in three years' residence the AP's Richard Massock, escorted by a detective, had leisure to visit the city's zoo.

Even better things were in store. For five months, the correspondents were next housed in Siena's four-star Excelsior Hotel, equipped with their own clubroom which ran to a bar, a library, and bridge and backgammon tables. Although visits to tearooms, cinemas and department stores were permitted, technically no man could venture beyond the city's ancient walls, but free souls like the *New York Times*'s Herbert Matthews, armed with bicycles, freewheeled all over the Tuscan hills, snapping up black-market eggs to supplement the hotel's rations.

When Reynolds Packard, the UP Bureau Chief, pleaded urgent business in Rome this, too, proved no problem. Along with the inevitable detective, Packard was given first-class railway passage to the city, a room in the five-star Grand Hotel, plus a couch outside his door for the inevitable detective's greater comfort.

On 22 May 1942, once exchanges were completed and the newsmen from Siena and Bad Nauheim boarded the Swedish liner *Drottningholm* in Lisbon harbour, all were agreed that things could have been worse.

It was a different story in Japan. From the first, the Japanese had adhered to the law of Bushido – the unrelenting code of the samurai warrior caste – and all twenty-six correspondents in detention were treated as Roosevelt's spies. Otto Tolischus of *The New York Times* was mercilessly questioned for days on end, and forced to sit for hours on his heels. The *Chicago Tribune*'s John B. Powell suffered injuries in freezing prisons that were ultimately to prove fatal. None of them were to see the United States again until August 1942.

The *Time–Life* staffers Carl Mydans and his wife Shelley travelled an even rockier road. Interned in separate dormitories at the Santo Tomás prison camp, Manila, they were transferred seven months later to the Palace Hotel, Shanghai, subsisting on a $60-a-month allowance drawn from the Swiss Consulate. Red armbands singled them out as enemy aliens. Finally, exchanged in a 'one for one' deal, they boarded a Japanese motor ship for Goa, Portuguese India, for passage home on the Swedish liner *Gripsholm*.

At New York's Pier 90, Dmitri Kessel of *Life*, who was waiting to meet them, 'resplendent in war correspondent's uniform', wasted no time in pleasantries: there was still much work to do. 'Better hurry,' he advised them. 'They're waiting for you back at the office.'

That was on 1 December 1943; the wheel of war had spun many times since The Desk had cautioned Shelley Mydans: 'We prefer Americans on the offensive.'

On the face of it there had been news in plenty; the problem had been to report it freely. To the impatient warcos, the United States –

who had suffered not only Pearl Harbor but the loss of two strong-points in the west and north Pacific, Guam and Wake Island – seemed to have drawn into itself, a nation secretly tending its wounds. The old warhorse Ernest Hemingway had sniffed the scent of battle, but his former Spanish Civil War boss, John Wheeler of NANA, could offer no immediate assignment. At this nadir of the war, he reported, the armed forces did not yet want reporters on the fighting front.

Given the US Navy's post-Pearl identity crisis, newsmen like Robert Casey, now assigned to the Pacific Fleet, faced no easy task. Then, and much later, the official communiqué was regarded as 'the Bible'. No news could be divulged before the communiqué, nor could 'the Bible' be contradicted. Any correspondent on a major assignment automatically became part of the 'pool system'. Thus, on 8 May, when Stanley Johnston, a garrulous moustachioed Australian, was the sole newsman to participate in the Battle of the Coral Sea, every newspaper in the United States, as well as Johnston's *Chicago Tribune*, shared the story.

The irony was that Johnston never 'saw' the battle, any more than Moorehead or Alaric Jacob ever witnessed a clash of tanks in the Western Desert. The Japanese Navy's attempt to seize Port Moresby, New Guinea, as a prelude to the bombing and invasion of northeast Australia, was the stuff of which communiqués were made. It was the first battle in naval history in which surface ships, relying on their air arms, never fired a shot, but Johnston did not see the mass of American fighters and bombers which set the light carrier *Shoho*, one of Japan's major warships, fatally ablaze. 'How completely the carrier has displaced the battleship in importance in modern war,' he told his readers, pointing up the lesson of the *Prince of Wales*, but this conclusion, too, was based on hearsay.

What counted was the human element. Aboard the aircraft carrier USS *Lexington*, mortally wounded by five torpedoes on her port side, Johnston heard the engineer officer, Lieutenant-Commander H. R. Healy, advise her captain with the aplomb of a well-bred manservant: 'I would suggest, sir, that if you have to take any more torpedoes you take them on the starboard side.' It was Johnston, too, when the 'Lady Lex' was sinking, who was there to record an executive officer's last tribute: 'She never wavered. She kept her head up and went down like the lady she always was.'

Four weeks later, on 6 June, the US Navy was proving the passing of battleship power all over again, this time off the tiny coral atoll of Midway, when four of Japan's finest carriers were lost – the

Akagi, *Kaga*, *Soryu* and *Hiryu* – and more than 300 Japanese aircraft. Now another Chicagoan, Robert Casey, was an 'eyewitness' who could register no more than brief shipboard impressions. 'My God!' he recorded a Japanese patrol pilot's reaction, in flawless high-school English. 'The whole US fleet is out here!' By 10 June, as the ships returned to Pearl, the realization was sinking in that 'we have fought a major engagement – one of the biggest naval battles of all time . . . we . . . have taken control of the Pacific.'

Still the Navy's distrust of the press ran deep, and on the night of 6 June, when the first communiqué was issued, Stanley Johnston unwittingly found himself in dire trouble. At that moment, Johnston was 4000 miles from Pearl Harbor, in the Chicago office of his managing editor, James Loy Maloney, who greeted the news of Midway with undisguised contempt. The Navy, he harrumphed, was 'trying to balloon a skirmish into a big battle', and with that he relegated the story to an inside page. But Johnston protested violently. This, he was rightly convinced, was one of the biggest naval battles in history. From expertise gleaned from voyages with the Fleet, he blocked out an analysis of Japanese battle strategy, backed up with a study of the Japanese Navy from *Jane's Fighting Ships*. Accordingly, under the headline 'NAVY HAD WORD OF JAPAN PLAN TO STRIKE AT SEA', the story made page 1.

The repercussions were devastating. Johnston, it was charged, had imperilled US naval security. His estimate of Japan's naval strength could have tipped off the enemy that America had cracked her diplomatic cipher system back in August 1940. This was news to Johnston, for one, and a full-scale grand jury investigation proved nothing more positive than that Tokyo intelligence officers did not read the *Chicago Tribune*, but the case was still rumbling on in 1957, five years before Johnston's death at the age of sixty-two.

This was the shape of the war in the Pacific on 7 August 1942, when 16,000 United States marines, their green combat jackets bearing the one word 'FIGHT', scrambled ashore on Guadalcanal, the largest of the Solomon Islands, in the Southwest Pacific: an island ninety miles long by thirty miles deep, sickly-sweet with the stench of rotting vegetation. To the marines who stormed it, recorded Richard Tregaskis, a lanky (six feet seven inches) INS correspondent on his first war assignment, it would for ever be 'that effing island' or 'that unmentionable island', but to capture and hold it was the first stepping-stone on the long road to Tokyo.

For by the end of July, after three months in possession,

Japanese construction crews had carved a primitive runway across Guadalcanal, through meadows of razor-edged *kunai* grass growing four feet high, raising a primitive control tower and camp among the coconut palms. Now the Americans were taking the lessons of the Coral Sea and Midway clearly to heart. 'This sector of the war,' explained Ira Wolfert, a NANA correspondent whose descriptive writing was to net him a Pulitzer Prize, 'is being fought primarily for islands to be used as unsinkable aircraft carriers,' and for two and a half years American sights would remain fixed on that objective.

'It was a laboratory sample,' wrote *Time*'s John Hersey, presciently, 'of the thousands of skirmishes our men are going to have to fight before the war is won.' It afforded an example, Hersey thought, 'of how battle feels to men everywhere'. Richard Tregaskis had an inkling that how they felt was not hard to plumb. After dark, most camp singsongs inevitably wound up with a heartfelt chorus of 'Blues In The Night'.

One war correspondent, the AP's Vern Haughland, thirty-four, would have echoed that refrain with all his being. On 7 August, simultaneously with the marine landing, Haughland was aboard an army bomber over Guadalcanal when it ran out of fuel. Strapping on a parachute for the first time in his life, he jumped from 13,000 feet and landed safely. This was the beginning of a nightmare which was to endure, all told, for forty-two days and nights. For the first eight days, Haughland was in company with Lieutenant James A. Michael, one of the bomber's crew, as they inched painfully up mountains and slept beneath piles of wet reeds, but once they had separated, in the hope of finding help more speedily, Haughland was on his own. With a warco's singlemindedness, he kept a diary: of the day when he ate 'lots more reeds', of the riverbank, where he found 'some delicious berries on shore'. On some days he was drenched and exhausted by torrential rains, on others barely conscious and lightheaded. 'Where from here?' was his despairing entry on 9 September, his last before missionaries found him ten days later, exhausted and raving with delirium in a native village.

For all the marines on Guadalcanal, 'Where from here?' was equally a pertinent query. Understandably the Americans were still groping. Unversed in jungle lore, their instinct, John Hersey saw, was to hug the steep ridges from which their artillery could dominate the valleys. But the Japanese, with feral cunning, clung to the jungle. There the steamy stinking nights, alive with the chinking of insects, could erupt without warning in screaming Banzai charges, when the darkness split apart with firecrackers. 'Here was booming, sounding, shrieking, wailing, hissing, crashing, shaking, gibbering noise,' was one man's impression. 'Here was hell!'

Another aspect of the campaign troubled Richard Tregaskis. On 12 August he had travelled by motorboat to the green island of Tulagi, five miles off Guadalcanal, an early Japanese strongpoint. What he heard from General William H. Rupertus of the 1st Marine Division was not reassuring. Of Tulagi's 2000 defenders, only twenty-three had been taken prisoner alive. In the day's fighting, no one had surrendered voluntarily. Tulagi, in fact, had been a vast honeycomb of dugout caves filled with Japanese – 'each cave . . . had been a fortress in itself, filled with Japs who were determined to resist until they were all killed. The only effective way to finish off these caves . . . had been to take a charge of dynamite and thrust it down the narrow cave entrance.'

This could be a war without end.

At first the demands were muted, no more than chalked scribbles on a factory wall: SECOND FRONT NOW. But as the summer of 1942 drew near, they became more insistent, daubed in paint on bridges and railway arches: SECOND FRONT NOW! It became an issue boldly bannered in newspaper headlines and stridently declaimed at Speakers' Corner in Hyde Park on Sunday afternoons: SECOND FRONT NOW!!

The angry sincerity of the British was understandable. The brunt of World War Two was being borne by the Russians, and they knew it. Although no Allied warcos were allowed to visit Leningrad, its siege had been a reality since September 1941. In December, the pitiless Russian winter and a giant counter-offensive by Marshal Georgi Zhukov had seen fifty-three German divisions in retreat from Moscow – already the warcos were drifting back from Kuibyshev. But on 16 May Korch, the heart of Crimean industry, was to fall, followed by Sevastopol on 2 July. Soon Stalingrad would be a front-line city. The belief widely held by the British public, shared by the US Chiefs of Staff, was that the Allies must measure up to these sacrifices and open a second front.

One man who doubted the wisdom of this was Quentin Reynolds. Since returning from Russia he had carefully renewed his high-level contacts, and with profit. He had lunched with Winston Churchill at the Prime Minister's country retreat, Chequers; others who had talked off the record were Averell Harriman, Harry Hopkins and the new commander of American troops in Europe, General Dwight D. Eisenhower. Each man had told the same story: the American personnel needed for any large-scale liberation of Europe were only now being trained in Northern Ireland, fewer than 100,000 of them. None had arrived in Britain, nor had General Carl 'Tooey' Spaatz's Eighth Air Force, which still awaited the mighty airfields that would house their planes. All these lay in the near future – but not in time to stage a second front in 1942.

It was never more than briefly mooted, as Reynolds discovered. To placate the Americans, Stalin and all the clamant second fronters, there would instead be a 'reconnaissance in force'. On the night of Tuesday, 18 August, two miles offshore from Portsmouth on the bridge of the destroyer HMS *Calpe*, Reynolds was soon to witness this: the first ever Combined Operation, though with strictly limited objectives. No permanent beachhead was envisaged. The 10,000 raiders involved – half of them Canadians unblooded in battle – carried food, medical supplies and ammunition for one day only. In assaulting six separate beaches on a ten-mile front, they had two primary missions: to shatter two powerful coastal defence batteries and to examine and perhaps destroy a radio-location station.

It was to be the first time since the Allies had set foot on French soil in the débâcle of Dunkirk, and their destination, 100 miles southeast, was the old cross-Channel ferry port of Dieppe.

'We could see ships all around us,' Reynolds was to relate, ' . . . fat transports, heavy-bellied, with small invasion barges on their decks . . . long tank landing craft, low in the water', although no capital ships were in evidence and no RAF bombers overhead. One of nine warcos present, the *Daily Herald*'s A. B. Austin, thought it 'for all the world like a grimmer Cowes regatta'. But at 3.47 am on 19 August, as Dieppe drew nearer, something had plainly gone awry; the sleeping night 'awakened brilliantly in a riot of dazzling green and bright-red streaks'.

Word now reached *Calpe* as to the source of the explosions: a German tanker, escorted by E-boats a few miles to starboard, had seen landing barges going in and opened fire. 'This,' grumbled a young officer on the staff of Captain John Hughes-Hallett, RN, the naval commander, 'will upset our schedule'.

It was a masterpiece of understatement. As the ill-starred flotilla drew closer to the beaches, dawn was a golden flush above the cobbled streets of the old port, and it was plain that the Germans were now everywhere alerted. Aboard the *Queen Emma*, a converted

Channel steamer, twenty-eight-year-old Ross Munro of the Canadian Press sensed from the start that 'the raid had gone all wrong'. Even as the first infantrymen of the Royal Regiment of Canada poured down *Queen Emma*'s ramp and onto the beach, 'machine-gun bullets laced into them. Bodies piled up on the ramp ... there must have been sixty or seventy of them ... cut down before they had a chance to fire a shot.'

All along Blue Beach, the Royal Regiment's landing site, chaos reigned. Beside Munro, one officer was hit in the head; he sprawled across the warco's legs, bleeding badly. Six feet away, a crouching youngster lunging vainly for the ramp 'collapsed on the blood-soaked deck', as 'a streak of red-white tracer slashed through his stomach.' 'Christ, we gotta beat them; we gotta beat them!' he was crying as he died.

Floundering through loose shale to the sea-wall, Munro himself was stopped short as 'a string of mortar bombs whanged on the Esplanade.' Through a blue curtain of choking smoke, he groped his way back to the *Queen Emma*.

Aboard *Calpe*, the flagship, anchored within sight of the shore, the bulky Reynolds was essentially a passive observer. But on that tragic morning, there was much to see, and much to hear: 'the dull boom of six-inch guns ... the rattle of machine guns ... the high singing sound of the Spitfires,' the motor torpedo boats 'roaring throatily by, and large barges filled with men and guns ... moving towards the shore'. Although Reynolds did not know it, one warco, Wallace Reyburn of the *Montreal Standard*, had managed to struggle ashore with the South Saskatchewan Regiment, tailing them for six hours. His first intimation of this was when the young Canadian, ashen-faced, lurched into the wardroom 'then collapsed slowly to the floor'.

Reyburn was painfully wounded in the shoulder and the buttock, but his first conscious reaction, as he gagged down brandy, was, 'This is a hell of a story, isn't it?' Then he passed out cold. As proud as if Reyburn had been a prize pupil, Reynolds recorded: 'No school of journalism in the world could train a man to that.'

Reports were reaching *Calpe* every ten minutes, and few of them were good. Of the two coastal batteries, only one, assigned to Lord Lovat's No. 4 Commando, had been annihilated. Landing barges were pulling alongside to deliver the first wounded, and after nine hours offshore the destroyer was packed out with them, 500 silent men supine on the decks and in the wardroom. Nerves,

Reynolds sensed, were frayed to snapping point.

Then two things happened. 'Let's go home, for God's sake,' a wounded lieutenant shouted, struggling to his feet. 'I've had enough! Let's go home,' and his voice was shaking with sobs. Suddenly *Calpe* 'heaved upward, then lurched to port . . . and it was as though you'd hit a giant glass with a tuning fork, and the sound of it kept ringing in your ears long after the blow had been struck'. It was then that Joe Crowther, *Calpe*'s bluff Yorkshire mess steward, broke silence. 'Hear that new eight-inch gun of ours?' he boomed. 'Sounds just like a bomb hittin' us, don't it?' . . . 'Broke all the glasses in my pantry.'

There was, Reynolds knew, no eight-inch gun aboard *Calpe*, and a German bomb had fallen too close for comfort, 'but some of the tenseness that had gripped the wounded men left them'.

As the battered armada at last headed homeward, Reynolds went on deck, to seek out Major-General J. H. 'Ham' Roberts, the Canadian commander. 'It was tougher than you figured, wasn't it?' he asked and Roberts, drawing in a deep breath, had to admit it. 'Yes, it was tougher than we figured.'

It was true, as Reynolds found later, that many lessons had been learned for the future: the need for capital ships, for rocket ships and for saturation bombing, for a personal naval assault force, even, in the last resort, for a portable harbour. Yet the lessons had been learned at an appalling cost of Canadian lives: 2000 prisoners, nearly 1000 dead.

One lesson still to be learned was that of public relations. Ross Munro, for one, with a mass Canadian readership in mind, reached his Fleet Street office, still in his bloodstained uniform, to hammer at his typewriter for twelve hours flat out, dosing himself with Benzedrine tablets to keep himself awake. But the final Dieppe story, vetted first by Combined Operations headquarters, then by the Ministry of Information, was not released until 6.05 pm on 20 August – twenty-nine hours after the operation ended, sixteen hours after the warcos had returned to London. As a result Dr Goebbels' Ministry scored heavily: an attempted invasion, it announced, had been decisively repulsed.

Perturbed, Reynolds sought the counsel of the canny open-minded Kansan commanding the Americans in Europe, Dwight Eisenhower. Unknown to him, the General was just then studying the Dieppe results for purposes of his own, but he did try to give Reynolds comfort. He must in no way credit the German version,

Eisenhower said, but 'think of Dieppe merely as a dress rehearsal – a dress rehearsal for invasion'. With that Reynolds had to be content, remembering the old Broadway adage: a disastrous dress rehearsal always means a triumphant first night.

Or so he hoped.

At about this time, in Cairo and Moscow, two distinguished war correspondents were taking stock.

Unusually, Alan Moorehead was bound not for the desert but for the United States and Canada, a well-deserved holiday with Lucy and John after almost two years without a break. At this bleak time, it was typical of the eternally optimistic Moorehead, dedicated, as he confessed, to 'a pursuit of the impossible', to see only silver linings. 'The British could at last claim they had emerged from their blackest hour,' he wrote in July 1942. 'Egypt was safe at last.'

Few of his colleagues shared that faith, and with reason. On 21 June, Tobruk had finally fallen to Rommel, with the loss of 26,000 Allied troops, 2000 vehicles and 5000 tons of provisions. (Among the prisoners was Ronnie Noble, of Universal News, forced to destroy whole reels of exclusive film – 'It was like having teeth drawn!' – and AP's Larry Allen, who at once requested an interview with Rommel, though he thought it might be refused. It was.) But Tobruk was only the climax of seven months of seesaw battles, in which the British had fallen back fully 800 miles, and in this long-running desert drama the cast of characters was changing with dizzying speed. Auchinleck, Wavell's successor, was now replaced by Alexander, the saviour of British troops in Burma. Cunningham's successor, General Neil Ritchie, was in turn ousted by Lieutenant-General Bernard Law Montgomery, a newcomer to the desert.

Civilians in Cairo and Alexandria saw these as baleful omens. Customers fearing a financial crash drew one million pounds from Barclay's Alexandria branch in one day. A pall of ash and smoke hung over Cairo's British Embassy as records were hastily burned. In a replay of France, Belgium, Greece and Yugoslavia, the roads and trains leading from the cities were clogged with fleeing refugees. No word of this got past the censor, but of the six *Daily Express* staffers now assigned to the Middle East, only Moorehead could see, in that great cliché of 1942, 'the turn of the tide'.

As he viewed it, all Auchinleck's actions were logical. From Mersa Matruh, the sponge-fishers' village, from which the British had launched their first offensive in December 1940, 'The Auk' had fallen back to a line 240 miles inside Egypt, only sixty miles from Alexandria, a line forty miles long which the British had fortified in advance. To Moorehead, it was 'a reporter's paradise ... so short and compact you could visit the whole front in the course of a day'. It was unique in the desert 'in that no other line had a top and a bottom'. To the north, it was bounded by the Mediterranean: to the south it ended in the hills forming the impassable Quattara Depression. Throughout July, when Moorehead paid his first visit there, Rommel was pounding at it, but by the defensive–offensive tactics that had held good for eighteen months in Tobruk, Auchinleck kept him at bay.

Come August, and Moorehead and his family departed on the one-time luxury liner SS *Zola*, along with 1000 German POWs' for the United States – to find the same urge for a second front nagging at their collective consciences. It was his successor, Alaric Jacob, who now moved up the line, to dismount finally at a whistle-stop railway station, 'with a second-class waiting room, where an old poster fluttered in the desert wind – SPEND YOUR HOLIDAYS IN SUNNY PALESTINE' – and a worn board announced the destination: El Alamein.

In Moscow, the AP's Henry Cassidy had also taken stock and reached a decision. A thirty-two-year-old Bostonian, Cassidy had once been adjudged so shy that a Harvard vocational counsellor advised him to take up schoolteaching – 'You are too bashful to be a correspondent.' But when the need came, Cassidy, like any warco, could rise to it. And in October, the need had come to sound out 'Uncle Joe' Stalin on that vexed second front.

After two years in Moscow, Cassidy knew the ropes. Only transitory journalists – and pushy ones at that, like Margaret Bourke-White and PM's Ralph Ingersoll – gained direct access to Stalin. But Cassidy, unlike the transients, knew that private petitions to Stalin, handed through a gate in the southwestern corner of the Kremlin wall, which was the mail receiving room, sometimes got results.

On 2 October, working from his office suite in Room 273 of the Metropole Hotel, Cassidy tapped out a succinct letter to Stalin, outlining two key questions. What place did the possibility of a second front occupy in current Soviet estimates? Most importantly, to what extent was Allied aid to the Soviets proving effective?

The response was near-reflexive. Towards midnight on

3 October, the telephone rang in Cassidy's room. He must report at once to the Press and Censorship Bureau. Stumbling through the blacked-out city, Cassidy found Nicolai Palgunov awaiting him, 'peering through his thick glasses with a certain amount of respect'. 'The document that you are waiting for is here,' he said, pushing across his desk a typewritten sheet signed in violet ink 'J. Stalin'.

The dictator had come straight to the point. The importance of a Second Front? 'A very important, one might say, a prime place.' The effectiveness of Allied aid? There was a palpable barb in Stalin's answer, which AP subscribers were to carry worldwide: '... The aid of the Allies to the Soviet Union has so far been little effective. In order to amplify and improve this aid, only one thing is required; the full and prompt fulfilment by the Allies of their obligations.'

Stalin had no real cause for alarm. On two separate fronts, the Allies were now poised to more than 'fulfil their obligations'.

Everyone sensed that the Big Push was coming. The question was: when? Day after day, from August to October, the correspondents watched the British reinforcements streaming up to El Alamein: 41,000 men, 800 guns, more than 1000 tanks, including 300 of the new 36-ton Shermans that Roosevelt had made available. They noted, too, Lieutenant-General Bernard Montgomery's impact on his troops: thousands of them were fast becoming 'Monty men'. He was prickly, voluble, reputedly ruthless, a wiry grey-eyed disciplinarian with no time for 'bellyaching', yet for all that eminently approachable. His black Tank Corps beret festooned with the badges of every unit serving under him, he found time to take tea 'out of a battered mug with private soldiers he met along the way'.

As Montgomery's first biographer, Alan Moorehead extolled the way that he had welded the Eighth into his own private army – so uncritically that some suggested that this was a father-figure effacing the Micawberish Moorehead senior. But Alaric Jacob, for one, had distinct reservations about the teetotal non-smoking 'Monty'. 'He is not my cup of tea,' he wrote at the time. 'I am allergic to Puritans, and Montgomery is puritanical to the extent of being bad-mannered about it ... He is self-opinionated and in my opinion self-righteous.' In his diary, a week after arriving at Alamein, he noted sourly: 'Monty is very cocky.'

The 'Monty' stories in the Western Desert were already legion. 'In defeat, indomitable; in victory, insufferable,' was said to be Churchill's verdict; and another story had St Peter welcoming a psychiatrist into the pearly gates: 'You are just the man we want. God's not feeling well: he thinks he's Monty.'

Only one question was in doubt: if the battle about to be joined eclipsed any the desert had seen before, how would Montgomery measure up?

'Please put out your pipes and cigarettes,' came an officer's quiet injunction on the morning of 23 October, seconds before Montgomery entered the giant marquee erected for the press. Then, perched on a wobbly folding chair, a fly-swatter balanced on his right index finger, Montgomery began to talk. 'At ten o'clock tonight,' Jacob recorded his words, 'a battle will begin at Alamein and will be fought out by moonlight. It will be terrific – quite terrific. By dawn tomorrow, we shall know how we stand. There's no question of the ultimate issue ... this battle will be won.'

'We will proceed to hit Rommel for six out of North Africa,' he concluded, and UP's Richard McMillan explained in a muttered aside to the *New York Herald Tribune*'s Russell Hill that this cricketing metaphor equated with baseball's 'knock him out of the box'. As they filed from the tent, heading for cars bound for the front line, there was a spontaneous buzz of questions. 'What do you make of him? Either he's a great general, or ...'

That Friday night was one of eerie silence, broken only by the fitful call of night birds. The wide golden moon, hanging low over the desert, was so bright that noncombatants to the rear, courting sleep, tugged blankets over their heads to blot out the light. Conscious of history as men rarely are, each correspondent was trying to register one salient impression that would say it all. Russell Hill thought that the 2000 military policemen symbolized the precision of Montgomery's planning. Immaculate in their white gloves and red caps, they stood by to shepherd the tanks to their objectives along six separate sand tracks, each marked by tape, and to speed forward the water carts that would firm down the sand. Richard McMillan reflected sombrely that if this was the gateway for the British to Libya and Tunisia, it was equally the gateway to Cairo for the Germans. The BBC's Godfrey Talbot was intrigued by the gun commanders checking the snail-paced hands of their watches – 'pimples of sweat were on hands and foreheads, although the evening was now cool.'

Then, at 9.40 pm, with an earsplitting earth-shaking roar, the guns of Alamein spoke: 900 of them, one to every twenty-three yards of front, pouring a storm of fire onto the Axis positions that was plainly audible in Alexandria, sixty miles away.

Soon the British gunners were deaf from the thunder, and their thick gloves were burned through by the red-hot gun barrels. To the rear, the warcos were conscious of the ground vibrating under their feet 'like the skin of a kettledrum'.

As the shells burst among the Axis strongpoints, acres of mines went skyward, spewing geysers of rocky sand and jagged lengths of barbed wire. Under the murderous roar of 900 rounds a minute, blockhouses crumbled and dugouts caved in. Days later, Chester Morrison of the *Chicago Sun* found German and Italian soldiers who had dropped dead from the concussion of the exploding shells, with not a mark on their bodies.

Alaric Jacob was stupefied. Besides a battery close to the Hill of Jesus he had to brace himself, legs apart, to withstand the storm of the blast. 'This is the last war over again,' he realized. 'It's *Journey's End*. It's *Undertones of War*.' Dimly, above the clanking of tank tracks, he heard the heart-stirring skirl of bagpipes, as the 51st Highland Division, to the strains of 'Loch Lomond', moved up behind the sappers as they probed through the five-mile deep minefield which Rommel called 'The Devil's Gardens', clearing lanes that would allow the tanks to advance two abreast.

Unknown to the warcos, and even to Montgomery, Rommel was not then in command; at the moment of bombardment, he was 1500 miles away from the front, undergoing medical treatment in Austria. His deputy, General Georg Stumme, had been stricken with a coronary as the battle began. For almost two days, when Rommel hastily returned, the Axis forces were leaderless.

Still in a daze, Alaric Jacob was moving on, following 'a long curving caterpillar of great tanks', bathed in 'a sinister green-blue light'. Even at 5 am on 24 October the bombardment went on without pause, and everywhere flares dropped by British and German aircraft glittered overhead like chandeliers – 'The blue, green, yellow and white lights made the desert quite beautiful,' Jacob thought. At 8 am, after a brief drugged sleep, he and his colleagues were already interviewing the first of the German POWs. How far would the push go? a young officer asked Jacob. 'All the way,' Jacob answered confidently. 'That think I also,' the officer replied.

But by 26 October, confidence was abating. From the first, Montgomery's sappers had faced a nightmare task. Thousands of mines had been exploded by the barrage, but the sappers, although armed with long-handled mine detectors like flat disc-shaped vacuum cleaners, sought in vain to reap a lethal harvest of 500,000 mines: deadly S-mines, no larger than a can of beans, flat black Teller mines. On that Monday night, despite his months in the desert, Jacob could take no more than a few minutes at Dressing Station 86 of the 11th Australian Field Ambulance. 'In one cubbyhole a doctor was amputating an arm, in another ... ten men lay gasping on trestle tables having fresh blood pumped into them ... men with faces like soiled cardboard were slopped on a bench up against a wall ... The doctors worked like ... overworked butchers on a Saturday night.'

'This,' Jacob thought, 'is stuff no paper will ever print nor will any photographer record it.'

It was not surprising that in this fiery shambles, few warcos had any coherent picture of how the battle was going. 'Tight censorship had been clamped down, Russell Hill remembered, so that although dispatch riders stood by to hasten bulletins from the field, most newsmen were reduced to Cockney clichés: a sergeant boiling a billycan of tea on top of a burning jeep, grimy grinning privates giving the thumbs-up sign. Nevertheless they worried. 'Although the Germans were losing ground every night, we were not winning the battle,' Jacob had to concede, and the *Daily Telegraph*'s Christopher Buckley, versed in every campaign from Stonewall Jackson to the Dardanelles, would agonize at each day's press conference: 'Can *anyone* give me the tactical answer?' Most warcos then estimated 20,000 killed, wounded or missing – as against a final count of 12,500.

The crucial breakthrough came at 1.05 am on 2 November – and Jacob was there to witness it, from the shelter of a trench it had taken him three hours to dig. There was need to take cover: as 360 guns opened fire on a 4000-yard front, the cold blue desert night seemed to split apart. Like a steel shield advancing 100 yards every three minutes, the barrage poured a creeping cataract of fire upon mines and trip-wires. 'I felt more frightened that night than any other in the desert,' Jacob admitted, for the barrage was concentrated on the Rahman Track, four miles beyond, where Rommel's most powerful remaining artillery was then sited. Following the barrage, the New Zealanders of Lieutenant-General Bernard Freyberg, backed up by British armour and infantry, would decide the fate of Alamein.

It was with the smug air of a man in the know that Jacob, later that day, was able to reassure a major of the 7th Armoured Division, which had raced from the south of the line, spoiling for battle. 'Is everything going all right?' the major asked, plainly hoping that it wasn't.

'Couldn't be better,' Jacob disillusioned him. 'The whole line has been broken.'

It was small wonder that Montgomery was elated. Before dawn on 5 November, wearing a grey home-knitted sweater and khaki slacks, he was descending from his caravan to greet the correspondents. 'It was a fine battle,' he told them. 'Complete, absolute victory.' Then, using the old World War One term for the Germans, he added, 'Boches finished. Finished!'

It was almost – but not quite – true. After an estimated loss of 32,000 men, Rommel was retreating through the driving rain which now engulfed the desert, a tattered column forty miles long, fleeing 1400 miles across Libya, abandoning Tripoli, the capital, on 23 January, to seek sanctuary in Tunisia.

Already it was too late. Four days after Rommel pulled out, 107,000 men – two-thirds of them American – were making ready to go ashore from 500 ships riding quietly at anchor off the coast of French North Africa. It was the first joint Anglo-American venture of World War Two.

In their wake came the only war correspondent to become a legend in his own lifetime: Ernest Taylor Pyle.

VII

The Guys That Wars Can't Be Won Without

9 NOVEMBER 1942–5 JUNE 1944

Few young newsmen had the cards more stacked against them than Ernie Pyle. Recalling his debut as a novice reporter on the *La Porte* (Indiana) *Herald*, the city editor's verdict was unflattering: 'Mr Beal [the editor] and I thought we had picked a lemon. This young man, bashful and unimpressive, didn't look like a newspaperman to us.' Months later Pyle obligingly confirmed this impression: as a copy-editor devoid of news sense on the *Washington Daily News*, he relegated the arrest of Bruno Hauptmann, prime suspect in the Lindbergh kidnapping case, to the bottom of Page One. Even in later years, he would talk ruefully of 'the writing business, which I never should have entered in the first place'.

Yet on 22 November 1942 when Pyle, an inconspicuous forty-two-year-old sharecropper's son, 'with thinning reddish hair and a shy pixie face,' stepped ashore at Mers-el-Kebir, Algeria, his welcome from the grimy helmeted GIs was at once tumultuous. The veteran Al Jolson, who had arrived to entertain the troops, was baffled. 'Heck, he doesn't sing or dance and I couldn't figure out what he did to entertain them, but they acted like he was Mr God!'

To thousands of US troops on their first combat mission abroad, Ernie Pyle was almost as important: he was a voice from Main Street, a link with home. For almost six years, six times a week, his column had featured in twenty-four papers of the powerful Scripps-Howard chain, and in twenty-six others besides. Travelling some 150,000 miles across the western hemisphere, along with 'that Girl who rides with me', an oblique reference to Geraldine Siebolds Pyle, his wife, he had filed off-the-cuff reports on anything and everything that took his fancy: Alaskan gold miners, a squatter who painted pictures behind the Memphis city dump, even his problems with the zipper on his trousers. For 13 million stateside readers, Pyle was already Mr America.

On one London visit at the height of the Blitz, he had sent home gossipy tourist impressions of the wasteland surrounding St Paul's Cathedral, but he had lingered too briefly for the nightly threat of bombers overhead to impinge on him. ('Who are *they*?' he asked naively, when the Savoy Hotel's doorman told him, 'They'll be here in five minutes.') Pyle had thus arrived in Algeria with a refreshing lack of credentials: he had never reported a war in his life.

At first glance, it was a cut-and-dried campaign he had come to cover: fourteen eventful days had passed since the Anglo-American task force had stormed ashore at three points along the North African coastline. At Casablanca, the Vichy French had at first resisted stubbornly; at Algiers and Oran, resistance had been more sporadic: finally, on 10 November, Admiral Jean-François Darlan had ordered a Vichyite ceasefire. Promptly, before midnight on that day, Axis troops – ten German and six Italian divisions – had swarmed into unoccupied France, taking over full control.

Now the way ahead seemed clear for the three-column advance that the Allies had agreed in Washington DC back in June: a 450-mile dash from Algiers to secure the Tunisian ports of Bizerte and Tunis, sited on the Mediterranean at its narrowest point east of Gibraltar. These were seen as the staging grounds from which to breach Hitler's Fortress Europe along its southern ramparts. But Ernie Pyle had scarcely set out for the front before the advance, now only twenty-five miles from Tunis, ground to a halt. Longstop Hill, which commanded the entire valley overlooking the port, had already claimed 500 Allied casualties when merciless sheets of rain forced a withdrawal. The mud had become like a brute force, wrenching the rubber boots off men's feet, so thick that no vehicle could venture within a mile of Longstop. Reluctantly, General Eisenhower called off the advance.

The forces now stabilized along a 200-mile front stretching from Medjez-el-Bab, held by the British First Army, in the north, to Gafsa, the American stronghold in the south.

This was the situation, towards mid-January 1943, when Alan Moorehead, his family holiday cut short by the invasion, arrived in the British sector to marvel at the organization. Here were luxuries that the Western Desert had never seen – jeeps, cases of whisky, orderlies serving bacon-and-egg breakfasts – and from the correspondents' forward billet, in the Grand Hotel de Thibar, it was possible to venture out each morning, *see* tanks clash with tanks and drive back to write it up before dinner.

It was not a Tunisian perspective Ernie Pyle would have recognized; as a newcomer, Pyle was abiding by his own rules. Contrary to the age-old traditions – the warcos visited the forward outposts, quizzed the troops, then returned to knock out the story on their battered Remingtons and Coronas – Pyle returned to the US II Corps base camp at Tebessa only once in three weeks. For all that time he lived as the infantrymen lived, and this routine he was equally to follow in Sicily and Italy.

In those front-line weeks Pyle never once shaved – 'anyone clean-shaven is an obvious outsider.' Almost unintentionally, he became, in one man's phrasing, 'the GI's Boswell', and because the infantry were 'the underdogs ... the mud-rain-frost-and-wind-boys', he embraced them wholeheartedly. As warfare grew ever more mechanical, a soulless clanking parade of LCIs (Landing Craft Infantry) and LSTs (Landing Ship, Tanks), so Pyle, to counter the anonymity, focused on the men. When Pyle embarked on a night jeep ride, his companions were 'Capt. Pat Riddleberger, of Woodstock, Virginia, and Pvt. John Coughlin, of Manchester, New Hampshire'. On a small-hours patrol, the radio man ahead of him was 'Pvt. Lee Hawkins of Everett, Pennsylvania'. Late one afternoon, he shared a foxhole with 'Pvt. Malcolm Harblin of Peru, New York, a twenty-four-year-old farmer who has been in the Army only since June ... a small, pale fellow, quiet as a mouse'.

'This is always a fruitful procedure,' joked the *New Yorker*'s A. J. Liebling, 'because he [the journalist] can load up his dispatches with the names and the member papers in the home towns are glad to use them'. But Pyle, snuffling his way through a perennial head cold, scribbling his battlefield notes in pencil, careful to take a dozen carbons, saw his own technique as less of a circulation-builder than a just tribute. 'In the end they are the guys that wars can't be won without.'

And as Liebling himself had to admit, 'Pyle Set The Style'. Basically an afternoon-paper man, never attracted to 'spot news' or 'the big picture', his summaries punched the situation home as weightier pundits failed to do. Thus on 14 February 1943 when Field Marshal Rommel, as he now was, drove the green American

II Corps eighty miles back through Kasserine Pass, capturing 2300 GIs, Pyle's simplistic analysis put most average readers in the picture: 'Our predicament is damned humiliating, as Gen. Joe Stilwell said about our getting kicked out of Burma a year ago. We've lost a great deal of equipment, many American lives, and valuable time and territory.' But he comforted them, 'When the time comes the British 1st Army will squeeze on the north, the British 8th Army will squeeze on the south, and we will hold in the middle. And it will really be the British who will run Rommel out of Tunisia.'

This was the small-town boy approach, which some commentators despised, but the outstanding warcos were exactly that: men-in-the-street who knew what the man-in-the-street wanted to read. At times they defended themselves with spirit. 'We had to be much more accurate,' O'Dowd Gallagher maintained, 'because, in a small town, people *knew* what we were writing about.' 'You learned to get names right,' Richard Dimbleby concurred. Of Pyle himself, John Steinbeck, assigned to the war by the *New York Herald Tribune*, said at the time: 'He is the only one of us who has captured the thoughts and the voice of the GI.'

Ironically, Pyle was one correspondent who nourished no illusions concerning war; to him, Liebling wrote, it was 'an unalleviated misfortune'. Nor, as some claimed, did he idealize the GI; soldier obscenity sickened him and he was 'both intrigued and repelled' by the bestial acts committed by supposedly normal men. He could echo the hushed eulogy of a British general seeing Americans lying dead in their foxholes, rifles still grasped in the firing position – 'Brave men. Brave men' – yet confess to one lifelong ambition. If William Howard Russell had been the first war correspondent, Pyle wanted to be the last.

At this stage of the war he was one of the few newcomers to register with the public at large. Many of the older hands, whose bylines had become bywords, had moved on to other spheres. Hugh Carleton Greene, who had dropped the bombshell of war into the Polish government's lap, was now involved with the BBC's Overseas Service. Virginia Cowles was serving as Special Assistant to the US Ambassador in London, John Gilbert Winant. Clare Boothe had become the Republican Member of Congress for Connecticut. Others were out of circulation through no fault of their own. The BBC's Edward Ward and Harold Denny of the *New York Times*, both veterans of Finland, had become POW's after Rommel's great Crusader counter-attack of November 1941, although Denny was released the following August. Ben Robertson had died tragically in a Clipper accident in Lisbon Harbour.

Some were fulfilling an observer's role. Clare Hollingworth, in Cairo, commuted tirelessly to Tehran, Baghdad and Damascus; Ray Brock travelled the same shuttle from Ankara. Leland Stowe was plumbing the mysteries of Mahatma Gandhi's civil disobedience campaign against the British in India. William L. Shirer was currently a columnist with the *New York Herald Tribune*. Robert St John, still disgruntled by the British attempt 'to fight a war in the Kipling tradition', had returned to America to publish a bestseller, *From the Land of Silent People*, revealing the ugliest face of war.

Only Ernie Pyle – along with the diehards like Moorehead, Reynolds, Dimbleby and Martha Gellhorn – would see the war through, month by month, campaign by campaign, to the end.

Tunisia was a seven-month campaign – a battle for hills (called *djebels*) and ravines (known as *wadis*) a terrain of red rock ranges ribbed by meandering rivers, scattered with cork forests and with vineyards at first dappled with the scarlet and gold of autumn. It was a battle where the Allies faced the might of fifteen Axis divisions under Rommel and General Jürgen von Arnim, a Russian front veteran, which Germany was initially reinforcing at the rate of 1000 men a day. In this battle, the securing of airfields like Tebessa was of prime importance; when paratroopers of the US 509th Infantry Battalion spilled from their troop carriers, Jack Thompson of the *Chicago Tribune*, turning the scales at 190 lbs., dropped with them, although he had never strapped on a parachute before. Other airfields, like El Aouina, outside Tunis, were secured through bombardment by the 97th Bomb Group, an assignment covered by Margaret Bourke-White, the first woman ever to fly a combat mission, on 22 January.

When The Desk cabled her colleague, *Time–Life*'s Eliot Elisofon, as to how soon he would follow her example, Elisofon was understandably nettled: Miss Bourke-White was at that time sharing the commanding officer's bed. He retorted tersely that she had one piece of equipment that he didn't have.

Elisofon himself was one more proof that Ernie Pyle was 'setting the style'. On 30 March, when the Americans launched an all-out attack on El Guettar in central Tunisia, Elisofon's camera was focused on 'people who were not usually photographed in battle', the men who carried ammunition in $2\frac{1}{2}$-ton trucks to within three miles of the front, then returned by night to 'sneak it up to the guns'; the engineers searching for and disarming the thousands of mines; the Signal Corps men who repaired the wires to keep communications open.

'The history books of all previous wars were written as if the commanding officers themselves were doing the fighting,' acknowledged the AP's New York general manager, Kent Cooper, and the warcos in the field were now out to redress that balance. Thus on 7 April the link-up of Montgomery's Eighth Army, which had broken through the formidable Mareth Line dividing Libya from Tunisia, with advance patrols of General George S. Patton's II Corps was strictly an other-ranks affair. On the coastal plain southwest of the port of Sfax, it was Sergeant William Brown, a Devonian, who greeted the Americans: 'This is certainly a pleasant surprise.' Cyrus L. Sulzberger of the *New York Times* was on hand to record the reactions of Pvt. Perry Searcy, from Kentucky, and Pvt. Joseph Randall of State Centre, Iowa: 'Well, it's good to see somebody besides a Nazi.'

The Axis were now in full retreat up the central plain, towards the high mountains ringing Tunis and Bizerte. The key hills now were Hill 609, so named from its elevation in metres on old French maps, and the already contested Longstop. Since it controlled two roads to Tunis, Longstop could not be bypassed. At a cost of more than 3000 casualties, neither hill was bypassed.

In the reports of the time, the top commanders – Lieutenant General Kenneth Anderson, commanding the British First Army, Major-General Omar Bradley, replacing Patton, even the publicity-conscious Montgomery – took a back seat. The focus was on the fighting man, and for all those families who would never experience it, Moorehead reported on what it was like waiting to go over the top.

'They sat in their lorries, twenty men to a lorry. They had on their full marching kit and they smoked cigarettes. They sat in rows, not talking much, but their eyes were always going from one place to another and they gave the impression that they were listening, listening intently. Each man gripped something with his hands, a rifle, the tailboard of the truck, a cigarette – their hands never lay relaxed and open at their sides. They did not glance at their watches. They knew the time – each passing second of it. At each new explosion on the ridge before us – the ridge that presently they were going to charge – they did not move or show in any way that they had heard. Only their eyes kept travelling in the direction of the noise.'

Pyle's Tunisian panorama evoked something of the same tension, a war in which all contestants were most often 'little boys again, lost in the dark'. Theirs was a world, he reported, 'of tired and dirty soldiers who are alive and don't want to die; of long darkened convoys in the middle of the night; of shocked silent men wandering back down the hill from battle: of chow lines and atabrine tablets and foxholes and burning tanks and Arabs holding up eggs and the rustle of high-flown shells; of jeeps and petrol dumps and smelly bedding rolls ... All these it is composed of; and of graves and graves and graves.'

Sometimes, as on 7 May, it was briefly and wonderfully composed of tears and cheers and laughter – as the two forces, in an earlier prophecy of Patton's, 'pushed to the coast for a fight or a bath', the British armies streaming for Tunis, the Americans for Bizerte. In Tunis, at precisely 2.45 pm, Alan Moorehead was in the thick of it, to witness the total stunned surprise with which the Germans reacted: 'Hundreds were walking in the streets, some with their girlfriends. Hundreds more were sitting drinking aperitifs in a big pavement café ... In the hairdressing saloon next door more Germans struggled out of the chairs and, with white sheets round their necks and lather on their faces, stood gaping.'

In Bizerte, the AP's Wes Gallagher was leaving nothing to chance: two of his staffers, Hal Boyle and Graham Hovey, stood by like census-takers, noting the names and home towns of every American tank driver entering the port. Among the jubilant population, now making ready to unfurl the tricolour, some looked forward to the simplest of pleasures. A beaming youngster told NBC's John MacVane: 'We can now again see American films – Robert Taylor and Greta Garbo.' At Ferryville, a dozen miles from Bizerte, one man stopped Alexander Clifford's party to enquire: 'Have you any chewing gum? My wife is pregnant, and she has a craving for chewing gum.'

Among the 275,000 Axis soldiers taken prisoner at least one man, sensed the *News Chronicle*'s Philip Jordan, felt only profound disillusion. 'That's my Führer,' he said, taking a portrait of Hitler from his pocket on a Tunis street, then, unleashing a torrent of obscenity, he tore the picture into pieces. '— my Führer.'

Nine weeks later, on Thursday, 9 July, the Allies landed triumphantly in Sicily.

That was the good news, recalled Hugh Baillie, President of UP, who had begun his war surveying the barrage balloons from London's Park Lane Hotel, given out by the first communiqué in Sicily. Missing from this, and from all subsequent bulletins, was any mention of twenty-four American planes, mistakenly shot down by American guns, the paratroopers blown out to sea and drowned, the gliders carried off by the wind and smashed. Nor did the munitions ship that blew up in Algiers harbour, killing 1000 men, or the bitter fight of the Herman Goering Panzer Division on the beachhead near Syracuse feature in dispatches. Sicily, Baillie concluded, had to be an unvarnished success story – perhaps to chime with the pile-driving offensive the Russians had opened on the Orel–Byelgorod front.

It was in Sicily – and even more in the campaigns that followed – that the Machine was seen in action for the first time. Although no warco referred to it as such, its existence was known to all: its aim, on parallel lines to Germany's PK (*Propaganda Kompanien*) organization and the Japanese Domei agency, was to channel the presentation of the war, ensuring in the words of Byron Price, the US Government censor, that 'newspapers ... and broadcasting stations must be as actively behind the war effort as merchants or manufacturers'. As essential cogs in the Machine, some thirty Official War Artists (OWAs) now entered the Allied camp, men like Albert Richards, Richard Eurich, William Coldstream and Edward Bawden; all told they were to produce some 5000 studies, but almost always of ships and bridges and aircraft rather than men. 'Art was produced to order,' wrote their historian, Alan Ross, of what was essentially a sanitized public relations exercise from the start.

John Steinbeck, world-famous as the author of *The Grapes of Wrath* and *Of Mice and Men* long before his warco days, marvelled at his first glimpse of the Machine in action. 'Facts available in any library in the world came to be carefully guarded secrets,' he discovered, 'and the most carefully guarded secrets were known by everyone.' There was no written rulebook, but most often the warcos carried the rulebook in their heads. The self-censorship that Ben Lucien Burman consciously exercised two years earlier in his interview with de Gaulle was now a way of life: a way of life that might have been laid down by Charles Dickens's Mr Podsnap – 'Would it bring a blush into the cheek of the young person?' Thus there were no cruel, ignorant or ambitious commanders – perish the thought! There were no cowards in the armed services. It went without saying that all infantrymen were wonderful. Sicily, and later Italy, teemed with nubile girls, but it also went without saying that all infantrymen were chaste. There was no such thing as fornication. The war effort took pride of place.

One incident which yet made world headlines centred round General George S. Patton Jr, transferred from the command of II Corps in Tunisia to head up the Seventh Army in Sicily. Patton, known as 'Blood and Guts', was already famous among the GIs for his pearl-handled pistols, his lacquered helmet, his iron-fisted discipline and his gruesome oratory – 'We won't just shoot the sonsabitches – we're going to cut out their living guts and use them to grease the treads of our tanks.' Early in August 1943, visiting a military-hospital evacuation tent, Patton overreached himself. Chancing on a soldier he thought was faking illness, he slapped him across the face. Five days later, in another tent, faced with what he took to be another malingerer, Patton again slapped the man's face, called him 'a yellowbelly' and kicked him in the rump. As Patton stumbled from the tent, sobbing, the *Daily Mail*'s Noel Monks heard him erupt: 'There's no such thing as shellshock. It's an invention of the Jews.'

Since Eisenhower's censorship covered only military security, the story was thus wide open – the more so since the soldier singled out had been forcibly hospitalized after gallant service in Sicily and Tunisia. But Monks did not file it, nor did any of his fellow Britons. To them, it was an American 'family affair'. Instead the warcos petitioned Eisenhower, demanding that Patton should apologize to the soldier and to the officers of the Seventh Army. This left the Americans in a quandary – among them Quentin Reynolds, who had just arrived in Algiers.

Along with Demaree Bess of the *Saturday Evening Post* and Merrill 'Red' Mueller of NBC, Reynolds sought an audience with Eisenhower. The General listened miserably while Bess and Mueller documented their findings – including signed statements from doctors and patients – but finally managed a smile. 'You men have got yourselves good stories,' he said, 'and, as you know, there's no question of censorship involved.' But Bess, respectfully, disagreed. 'Quent and Mueller and I have been discussing what would happen if we report this,' he replied, 'and our conclusion is that we're Americans first and correspondents second.'

It was then that Eisenhower came clean. If the story did appear, he admitted, 'Georgie, the best armour man we've got, would be destroyed.'

In fact the story *was* printed – but not until four months later, by the Washington columnist Drew Pearson, who had already cleared it with the US internal censors. And by then the heat was no longer on; Patton had been reprimanded and apologized emotionally to all concerned; it rated as no more than what Philip Ure, of the London *Times*, called 'an unfortunate incident'. The Machine had triumphed again.

On one score, at least, the warcos were grateful: the Machine rarely tried to tone down their message that war was an enormity. Herbert Matthews, once more reporting for the *New York Times* after his long internment in Siena, was permitted to describe Sicily as a devilish war of mines – and on 6 August, when the vital north-eastern hill town of Troina fell, to depict 'a town of horror, alive with weeping, hysterical men, women and children who had stayed there through two terrible days of bombing and shelling'. It was to be a familiar pattern, Matthews noted later, 'all the way to Bologna – torn streets, heaps of rubble that had been houses, grief, horror and pain'. Ernie Pyle, too, saw that pattern: 'It all works itself into an emotional tapestry of one dull, dead pattern – yesterday is tomorrow and Troina is Randazzo and when will we ever stop . . .'

At first the tenacity of Axis resistance was uncertain. 'The Italians fought with great dash and spirit,' one American officer told John Gunther, another newcomer to the war. 'They really did. The bloody fools.' But the *Daily Telegraph*'s Christopher Buckley saw more encouraging signs. One was the abnormally large number of 'peasants' of military age – soldiers who had thankfully discarded their blue-green uniforms and returned to till their fields. Another was the formal surrender of the town of Noto on Sunday 12 July, once the Germans had abandoned it. Over a glass of wine in Noto's one hotel, the Mayor offered Buckley and the military governor a solemn toast: 'To Winston Churchill!'

Buckley was reading the signs aright. On 25 July, heartily sick of the Axis connection, the Fascist Grand Council deposed *Il Duce* of Fascism, Benito Mussolini. Although rescued from captivity by a daring German commando-style raid, Mussolini's writ would henceforth run no further than the puppet Salò Republic on Lake Garda, 500 miles from Rome. A new Italian government under the ambivalent old Marshal Pietro Badoglio now declared war on Germany.

Just as in Tunisia – and later in Italy – communications in Sicily were still the main bugbear. The old truth that had held good in the Crimea and at Bull Run was still as valid in Thibar and Syracuse: 'A war correspondent is only as good as his line of communication.' Did he 'isolate himself with the troops at the head of the hue and cry'? Alan Moorehead had agonized during one march on Kairouan, Tunisia, or should he 'stop and get a story off and then resume the chase on the following day'? Often the solution was sheer hard slogging. Mindful that their readers expected their news on the breakfast table, Moorehead, Clifford and Buckley, after graciously accepting the surrender of Taormina, Sicily, trudged eight miles back to where they had parked the car, then scorched the forty intervening miles to the press camp at Lentini.

Any failure to do so, they knew, would at once have prompted a flood of queries from their respective Desks: WHAT FOL-LOWUP EXYOU? WHY UNNEWS? or, the ultimate in sarcasm, WE STILL PUBLISHING YOU KNOW.

By 10 September, when Montgomery's Eighth Army and the US Fifth Army under General Mark Wayne Clark had gained precarious toehold on the Italian mainland, all of them were in line to become true connoisseurs of war. In the months ahead, the prime qualities that made up a correspondent – endurance, courage, self-reliance, above all, ingenuity – would be tested to the full.

Even old desert hands like Moorehead and Buckley had to master new skills: hugging whatever cover was afforded by hedges and walls, conscious that the middle of the track was most likely to be mined. A newcomer like John Gunther, well-known for encyclopedic surveys like *Inside Europe* and *Inside Asia*, now reporting for the NBC subsidiary the Blue Network, absorbed techniques he had never known existed; how to type sitting cross-legged on the floor of an abandoned villa, even how to type on one's knees in a fast-moving jeep. If roast chicken and Chianti sometimes featured on the menu, the likeliest items were a repeat of Tunis: bully beef, tinned sardines, canned hash called 'donkey dung' along with hard-tack biscuits known as 'armour plating', and the eternal K-rations: pork and beef compress, fruit compress, 'energy biscuits', soluble coffee, three lumps of sugar, a stick of chewing gum and four Camel ciga-rettes.

They had long been hardened to the dead. They might avow,

as Moorehead did outside Tunis, 'I will never, even if this war goes on another ten years, grow used to the sight of the dead.' But Moorehead, like Wes Gallagher of AP accepted that the dead were not 'news'. At Souk-el-Khemis, Tunisia, Gallagher would recall one incident out of many: 'the street was strewn with dismembered bodies' following a bomb attack, but who, he thought, 'in New York's Broadway or London's Piccadilly cared that four bombs had fallen in a little Tunisian village and killed twenty or thirty men'? He had not filed a line. Carl Mydans, back on the Italian battlefield after his long internment in Japanese prison camps, was truly shocked to see the German dead near Santa Maria Infante 'gathered and tossed into a grotesque heap . . . all bereaved of their last earthly dignity'. Only Edward Ardizzone, as an Official War Artist, took some comfort from this. 'A maddening war,' he had grumbled in Sicily, 'only the dead and dying stay still for you to draw.'

In Italy, given time, they became hardened to the climate too. All too soon, the mainland campaign, launched with such high hopes in September, was to become less of a battle against the Germans under Field Marshal Albert Kesselring than against geography. The sunny autumn days in Calabria had degenerated into a soldier's purgatory: a land of knife-edged cliffs, of pelting rain that turned fields into grey quagmires, of cold so paralysing that dispatch riders had to be lifted from the saddle and massaged until circulation was restored. From January onwards there were, to be accurate, two Italian campaigns: the mainland campaign, stalled on the twenty-five-mile Gustav Line, huddled round the monastery town of Cassino, and the beachhead campaign, which saw 110,000 men landed behind the German lines at Anzio on the Tyrrhenian Sea, thirty-three tantalizing miles south of Rome.

The mainland campaign was the worst, Herbert Matthews thought. The sheer logistics of what Ernie Pyle called 'a pack-mule war' decreed that. Around the Monte Camino massif, south of Cassino, the ridges towered 3000 feet high and their attackers had to be sustained: by cases of K-rations weighing 48 pounds, by five-gallon cans of water weighing 43 pounds, by 100 rounds of heavy mortar shells. The pack mules took these one-third of the way; the GIs 'the last bitter two-thirds, because the trail was too steep even for mules'. Sometimes the mules were carrying letters for dead men.

Despite themselves, the warcos could not forsake the field. 'I hate to go back to the front,' Pyle wrote, before leaving for Italy in November 1943. 'I dread it and I am afraid of it. But what can a guy do?' Once there, he wrote of the homesick GIs, to whom '"forward"', no matter what direction, is toward home': hardly ten minutes ever goes by, Pyle noted, 'without some nostalgic reference to home'. Yet, as A. J. Liebling would stress, Pyle himself was never homesick. From 1939 onwards, Geraldine Siebolds Pyle had been drinking heavily; by the time of Pearl Harbor she had become a psychopathic alcoholic. In April 1942, reluctantly and against her will, Pyle had divorced her: by April 1943, following 'Jerry's' six months in a sanatorium, he had remarried her by proxy at her own request. In Italy, in the winter of 1943, Pyle himself was now drinking heavily.

But for most correspondents even a happy marriage was a secondary consideration in time of war. Come peace, Moorehead looked forward to a sedentary writing career with Lucy and the family in a house they were purchasing near Regent's Park, London, but of his return to the Tunisian desert he wrote in ecstasy, 'It was like coming home.' Like every warco, he relished 'being able to travel out into the distance far beyond the range of money, of bosses and jobs, and of responsibilities'. It was this divine irresponsibility, a freedom from the reality faced by countless million householders – the starchy bank manager, the problem child – that all of them cherished. Once, hating the mists and squalor of Monte Cassino, Christopher Buckley returned to the 'excessively gay ... spurious brightness' of liberated Naples, with its dances and baccarat parties, then 'quite suddenly ... realized that I couldn't stand it a day longer' and fled back to the miseries of Monte Cassino with the Eighth Army. It was a reaction that Quentin Reynolds, although recently married to the Broadway actress Virginia Peine, understood perfectly. 'It might be Sardinia or Corsica or Crete,' he had mused, pondering on the next invasion after Sicily. 'We didn't care as long as we went along.'

The Hungarian-born photographer, *Life*'s Robert Capa, caught the same footloose mood: 'For a war correspondent to miss an invasion is like refusing a date with Lana Turner after ... a five-year stretch in Sing Sing.'

Martha Gellhorn agreed fervently – the more so since her three-year marriage was on the rocks. At San Francisco de Paula, Cuba, the Ernest Hemingway she had long admired, the author of spare taut masterpieces like *A Farewell To Arms* and *The Sun Also Rises*, had by degrees become 'Papa' Hemingway, a macho insensitive braggart, beset by hangers-on, whose drinking routine ran the gamut from absinthe through red and white table wines, champagne and

Scotch highballs. Averse to dressing up, Hemingway often went barefoot even to smart bars in downtown Havana, dressed only in faded blue bathing trunks and a sweaty shirt, and the fastidious Martha resented it. 'Ernest,' she once challenged him aboard his 28-foot cruiser *Pilar*, 'you're dirty. Why don't you take a bath more often?' But Martha's refusal to become one more sycophant enraged Hemingway. On another occasion, as she drove him home after one of his drinking bouts, he slapped her face with the back of his hand. Martha's reaction was to brake his cherished Lincoln to a cautious ten miles an hour then plough it through a ditch and into a tree. Then, leaving him to sober up, she walked home.

Martha's logical solution was thus to go where the war was calling, and where it called from early in 1944 was that section of the Cassino front besieged by the Free French Expeditionary Corps of General Alphonse-Pierre Juin.

On the right of this sector, Martha recounted, were the Poles of Lieutenant General Wladyslaw Anders, few of whom would ever see their homeland again, and on the left were the Americans. Looming above them all were the skull-and-crossbones signs cautioning in French: THE ENEMY SEES YOU. It was cold as Martha Gellhorn's jeep approached the front, past the 'endless camps – tents pitched in the mud lakes that formed under olive groves,' a part of the 'steady stream of khaki-coloured traffic' coming north from Naples, so cold that she used her tin hat to shield her face against the driving hail.

Her destination was San Elia, across the valley from the Rapido river, where a French first-aid post staffed by a doctor and a transport officer was sited in a partly ruined building five miles from the Cassino front. That night she and the two Frenchmen were joined for dinner by an American AMG (Allied Military Government) major and his aide; dinner was warmed-over K-rations, with a bottle of Italian cognac which tasted of 'perfume and gasoline'. The rigours of life in the field emerged matter-of-factly: in the mountains it was 'not unusual for a wounded man to be carried for ten hours before he reached a road and a waiting ambulance'. Each day they learned by trial and error: one threw a rope to a wounded man now, after seven men had been killed trying to drag one of their number from a minefield. They ate at an old marble-topped table lit by two kerosene lamps, in a basement smelling of mice and damp walls, and it was a world away from the drunken false bonhomie of San Francisco de Paula.

Next morning, she watched the Italian refugees coming by 'with the usual bundles, the usual blank eyes and the usual slow, weary walk'. There was a lesson to be learned from war, Martha Gellhorn thought, in the faces of the French soldiers who stood watching them. There was everything in those faces but kindness. 'There were refugees on all the roads in France,' one man said quietly. 'Each one in his turn.'

In the mountains of the American sector, Ernie Pyle dreamed a wonderful dream: how could 'any survivor of war ... ever be cruel to anything, ever again'?

Iris Carpenter was a correspondent as shrewd as they came. As a representative of the London *Daily Herald*, she had hit on the one sure way to view the shape of southern England in the weeks preceding the second front, otherwise D-Day: an in-line-of-duty tour with the doughnut girls of the American Red Cross.

On any such tour, she found the plans for the greatest seaborne and airborne invasion in history were there for all to see. For ten miles inland along a 550-mile coastal strip, only those with special identity cards might now go. The grass verges of the roadside had vanished, swallowed up beneath vast stands of ammunition. Wayside signs loomed large on aluminium tanks – 'DO NOT DRINK THIS WATER WITHOUT HALOGEN TABLETS' – or cautioned truck drivers: 'KNOW YOUR DISTANCES. THIS IS SIXTY YARDS FROM THE LAST SIGN.' Red crosses shimmered through woods of misty bluebells: hundreds of tents, hundreds of ambulances, waiting to bring the first wounded back.

Parachutes blossomed in the spring sky, as airborne men rehearsed the last desperate act. Endless convoys – tanks, jeeps, bren-gun carriers – lurched through the pale green countryside. On countless stony beaches in the west country, assault troops splashed wearily ashore.

This was the time when selected warcos stayed close to the generals as they took to the open road, to sell themselves to the troops like US politicians in the primaries. In Hampshire and points west, GIs took a long cool look at the First Army Group's newly promoted Lieutenant-General Omar Bradley and saw, in the words of *Time*'s London Bureau Chief, the handsome hell-raising Charles Christian Wertenbaker, a man 'as unruffled as an Ozark lake on a dead-calm day'. As the senior US ground-forces commander in

Britain, Bradley was reassuring: 'This stuff about tremendous losses is tommyrot ... Some of you won't come back but it will be very few.'

Alan Moorehead thought that soldiers surveying General Sir Bernard Montgomery, as he now was, took away a different picture. Following a half-mile walk between troops drawn up in hollow square, grey eyes peering intently at each man, Montgomery would mount a jeep with a loudspeaker, to tell them: 'Break ranks and gather round me.' Then, noted Moorehead, who watched this process up to five times a day, came an astonishing moment: 5000 men in heavy boots would stampede towards the jeep 'like charging buffaloes'. The address, which was repeated until a million men had heard it, never varied: 'I have come out here to see you today so that I can get a look at you and you get a look at me.' A calculated pause – 'Not that I'm much to look at' – followed by an easy ripple of laughter. 'We have got to go off and do a job together very soon now, you and I ... and now that I have seen you I have complete confidence ... absolutely complete confidence ... and you must have confidence in me.'

Politicians, and even warcos like Alaric Jacob, might look askance at Montgomery, but among Tommies and dogface GIs, Moorehead recorded that Montgomery never lacked the common touch. 'Seen the paper? Here, take my copy.' 'Have some cigarettes. My lady friends send them to me.'

At Broadcasting House, Portland Place, London, Richard Dimbleby was in his element. After almost five years, the advent of D-Day was vindicating his every belief. One year earlier, the BBC's War Reporting Unit had been formed, and with its formation, as Dimbleby's son Jonathan recounted later, 'a fistful of shibboleths were to be discarded'. Of the twenty-nine warcos covering the D-Day front, each man was to be, as an internal document put it, 'the BBC's observer'. For the first time, reporters were to 'move with the microphone', bridging the gap that had divided combatant and civilian in older wars. For the first time, too, armed with forty-pound recording units known as 'midgets', they were to give their listeners, all 15 million of them, 'the broad canvas' – their own personal view of how events were shaping. All Dimbleby's Middle Eastern footwork had at last paid off, and soon after D-Day dawned he himself was to head up the War Reporting Unit.

The one question unresolved was: when would those twenty-nine observers take up their microphones?

One BBC correspondent already knew. As one of a four-man pool assigned to the new Supreme Allied Commander, Europe, General Dwight D. Eisenhower, Robert Barr, a plucky and tenacious Scot, had for weeks been installed in a tented camp at Southwick House, the advance D-Day HQ near Portsmouth. Along with his colleagues, 'Red' Mueller of NBC, Stanley Birch of Reuters and AP's Ned Roberts, Barr's job was to dog Eisenhower's footsteps throughout the day – breakfasting with him, making one of the group on official inspections, climbing the aluminium steps to his trailer for a final nightcap and a lighthearted discussion of Eisenhower's bedtime reading, usually a paperback western.

Ever since arriving in Europe, 'Ike' Eisenhower had relied on the trust system to ensure that the Machine turned over smoothly; warcos like Christopher Buckley had been briefed on the Sicilian landing one month earlier in Algiers. The Patton slapping incident had more than proved the point. Thus, weeks before D-Day, Barr and his colleagues along with a few hundred key personnel code-named 'Bigots' knew that on Monday, 5 June, if all went well, 250,000 men backed up by almost 5000 ships would land on five beaches, codenamed Utah, Omaha, Gold, Juno and Sword, along the Normandy coastline.

This disclosure, Barr recalls now, enraged Eisenhower's Chief of Staff, the cantankerous ulcer-racked Major-General Walter Bedell Smith. In Barr's words: 'Beetle tore us off a strip as if we were schoolboys and insisted we should be confined to camp.' At times like this, though 'the almost Christlike wisdom of Eisenhower' – Barr's words again – asserted itself. 'But,' he told Bedell Smith, almost guilelessly, 'I've made all four of them staff officers. And if they tell what they know, then they'll be shot. Now what else can happen to *you*?'

In those weeks of waiting, 'Ike's' four-man pool came to know him very well. Among the myriad of troops whose hands he shook daily, they knew that he sought – but never found – a man from his home town, Abilene, Kansas. They knew that at other times his temper could flare like a blowtorch – most especially in the days leading up to 5 June when worsening weather over the Channel would not only ground aircraft but render naval gunfire ineffective. 'By God,' he exploded, more than once, 'where I was born, when the summer started the summer stayed! Here you can't bet on the weather for two hours at a time.'

But on Sunday, 4 June, such news as came from the weather

men was all bad. Reluctantly, Eisenhower and his commanders postponed D-Day for twenty-four hours.

In a tented camp near Southampton, Alan Moorehead was one of 150 warcos scheduled for the first wave of the assault, but almost all, like himself, were travelling as individuals, assigned to separate LCIs or mother ships. There was no press camp, no camaraderie. Moorehead was thankful on just two counts: months earlier, he and Alex Clifford had turned down a chance to land at Anzio, certain that no second front would open there. Secondly, he knew his approximate destination; at the paymaster's tent his proferred £10 had been changed into French francs. But now that his jeep was stored aboard an LST, along with kit, petrol cans and blankets, there was only the aching boredom of waiting. 'The invasion was already like an over-rehearsed play.'

For the men forming the invasion spearhead – more than 1000 glider pilots, 13,000 American paratroopers and 4255 British – boredom was at a premium. On the night of 5 June, these last hours were among the longest they had ever known. On a score of airfields pivoting on Newbury, Berkshire, 'the four most privileged war correspondents in the world,' in Robert Barr's recollection, were accompanying Eisenhower on his last visit to those paratroopers before H-Hour. 'They were smearing their faces with cocoa and burnt cork,' Barr remembers, 'and throwing letters and snaps of their wives and girlfriends onto a fire.' He was close enough to Eisenhower to hear the Supreme Commander's tribute to Brigadier-General James M. 'Jumpin' Jim' Gavin, commanding the 82nd US Airborne parachute assault: 'It's no longer anything to do with me. The war is yours.'

At the 101st Airborne Division's headquarters at Newbury, Eisenhower and the warcos later watched the tow-planes take off, trundling slowly down the runway, lifting painfully into the night. 'At Control Tower level,' Barr recalls, 'we could no longer see the riding lights of the gliders. We could see the tow-planes circling but hear nothing.'

At this moment, 'Red' Mueller glanced at Eisenhower. The Supreme Commander's eyes were filled with tears.

In Italy, the Normandy beaches seemed a world away. Rome was the prize now, and all the warcos knew it.

All through the week of 25 May, the week that the Allies broke free from the Anzio beachhead, they were rolling on unimpeded up the shin of the Italian boot. On the fifteen-mile Cassino front – whose monastery had been needlessly destroyed by Allied bombing as far back as 15 February – the Poles and the Free French had stormed the monastery's ruins. Two roads to Rome now lay open – Highway No. 6, the Via Casalina, plus Highway No. 7, the Via Appia – and General Mark Clark wanted Rome.

To the Allied C-in-C, General Sir Harold Alexander, Rome was not itself of first priority. What he wanted, above all, was to see one wing of the retreating German Tenth Army entrapped at Valmontone, thirty-four miles northeast of Rome. But in the absence of specific written orders, Mark Clark trusted to his own judgement. ROME FALLS! was an international headline, but whoever had heard of Valmontone?

'A rangy hawk-featured man,' as Cyrus L. Sulzberger of the *New York Times* remembered him, 'who looked much like the sheriff in a Wild West movie', the Fifth Army's commander made no secret of that ambition. 'Cy,' he had told Sulzberger on one occasion, a comradely arm round the journalist's shoulder, 'When we make our breakthrough I want you to ride in a jeep with me. I'll see to it when we get there that you can tell the world just how Mark Clark took Rome.'

In fact, when the day came, Sulzberger was in Cairo interviewing King George II of the Hellenes, but Mark Clark did the next best thing: a prominent passenger in his jeep was Paul Wyand, the chubby chief cameraman of British Movietone News.

Ahead of Clark and his entourage streamed the entire Fifth Army with Brigadier-General Robert T. Frederick's 1st Special Service Force, the 'Devil's Brigade', forming the spearhead, their mission to secure the city's nineteen Tiber bridges before the Germans blew them. But in advance even of these troops weaved the jeeps of 'Dangerous Dan' DeLuce, AP, and Reynolds Packard, UP, each agency man intent on scooping the other, until they reversed hastily at the sight of a German armoured car with a black cross on its turret. Both men now returned to berate General Frederick: a fine state of affairs if two accredited warcos had gone 'in the bag' because the 'Devil's Brigade' was slow off the mark.

By now, more warcos were following in their wake, and along the white dusty roads leading to the capital, Denis Johnston was one of a three-man BBC team watching the scarred milestones tell the story: Roma, 20 km. Roma 18 km, Roma, 15 km. At the eight-kilometre mark, *Life*'s Carl Mydans was stopped short by a bizarre sight: an Italian wedding procession, eight strong, the bride with a bouquet of roses and green leaves, the groom holding a pair of yellow gloves, quite oblivious both to a GI sighting along a bazooka atop a gate pillar and to a heap of dead Germans strewn across the road by a shell explosion. Quite undeterred, still holding hands, the couple led each other 'on tiptoe around the carnage'.

It was the free world's first liberation of 1944, and appropriately, on Trinity Sunday, 4 June, church bells were pealing. As the first main body of troops, borne in grimy jeeps and tanks, nosed through the Porta Pia, dusk was falling but still the crowd went wild, surging forward to press wine and flowers on the bearded, mud-stained GIs – who responded with whole cornucopias of chocolates, cigarettes and biscuits.

This was a day – the Germans having declared Rome an open city and withdrawn beyond the perimeter – that no correspondent would ever forget, and every man treasured his own vignette. Carl Mydans, checking into the Hotel Majestic, was flummoxed by the porter's Fascist salute until the man apologized hastily, 'A habit of twenty years.' Herbert Matthews, after almost three years' residence in Rome, had never thought to see GIs buying flowers in the Piazza di Spagna, or jeeps, among them General Mark Clark's who had arrived to confer with his corps commanders, on the Campidoglio.

Next day, in the great piazza before St Peter's, Eric Sevareid of CBS remembered the fountains sparkling in the sunlight and a crowd of almost 100,000 pouring in, summoned by the largest of all the Cathedral's bells, the eleven-ton Campanone. Denis Johnston, with wicked relish, nurtured the spectacle of Pope Pius XII giving thanks for Rome's deliverance before the gigantic tapestry of the crossed keys, then submitting with a helpless frozen smile to his first Allied press conference, bemused by the photographers' raucous cries of 'Hold it, Pope – we gotcha in focus.'

In the dining room of the Albergo Città, the newly established British press camp in the city centre, all of them recalled how the BBC's Godfrey Talbot brought them back to earth with a jolt.

'Boys, we're on the back page now. They've landed in Normandy.'

VIII

I Think I See The End
Of Germany Here

6 JUNE – 16 DECEMBER 1944

By 10 pm on 5 June there was no turning back. The great armada was underway, ploughing inexorably towards Hitler's Fortress Europe – what *Time*'s Charles Christian Wertenbaker saw as 'a floating island of men and metal'.

A young Irishman, twenty-four-year-old Cornelius Ryan of the *Daily Telegraph*, later the historian of D-Day, caught something of the majesty of that fantastic cavalcade: 'They came, rank after relentless rank, ten lanes wide, twenty miles across, five thousand ships of every description,' while ahead of them were processions of 'Coast Guard cutters, buoy-layers and motor launches' plus 'a formidable array of 702 warships'.

There had never been an armada like it: mighty command ships bristling with antennae, shallow-draught landing ships, 350 feet long, rusty decrepit little minesweepers, sleek whippet-like destroyers, heavy cruisers. Some, after four years of war, were already a part of history: the USS *Augusta*, flagship of Rear Admiral Alan Kirk, which had carried Roosevelt to Placentia Bay, Newfoundland, for his 'Atlantic Charter' meeting with Churchill, the USS *Nevada*, sunk at Pearl Harbor but now raised to fight again. All of them wallowed and plunged through the same grey choppy waters, along with Channel steamers, coasters, self-important little tugs fussing like ducklings on a pond, and bone-white hospital ships such as the one which carried Martha Gellhorn, with their scalloped green lines and the stacked cans marked 'Whole Blood'.

Impressions of that night would remain inescapably vivid.

Aboard the 3rd (Canadian) Division ship, HMS *Hilary* heading for the British beaches, Ross Munro, that veteran of Dieppe, recalled how 'the wind howled through the wireless masts', 'a sky ... black as the inside of a gun barrel' and 'the spray and rain that dashed the decks'. Aboard LCT 947 Lieutenant Lambton Burn, of Naval Public Relations, listened with fascination as a colonel briefed his Royal Engineers under the single light of an electric lamp: 'Look at your maps. Caen is Poland, Hermanville is Mexico ... All bogus names to be destroyed tonight ... 0430 all troops to be issued tea or hot soup.'

Conditions varied markedly from ship to ship. Aboard the USS *Chase*, a solidly built mother ship ferrying many assault barges, *Life* photographer Robert Capa marvelled at the nonchalant way the mess boys at 3 am served hot cakes, sausages, eggs and coffee, wearing neat white jackets and white gloves. Aboard LST 302, Flight Lieutenant Alan Caverhill, RAF Public Relations, better known as the playwright Alan Melville, browsed through his D-Day phrasebook – everything from '*Encore une verre du vin rouge, s'il vous plaît, mademoiselle*' to '*Hande hoch*'. On other transports men chatted aimlessly, played cards, wrote eleventh-hour letters – or vomited helplessly as heaving waves smashed from one end of the landing craft to the other.

Aboard LST 816 Alan Moorehead took comfort that this American ship was a veteran of three assault landings, but the troops aboard knew nothing of this and 'were oppressed by a sense of strangeness and insecurity. In the darkness the dangers of the voyage became magnified and unbearable, and the rising sea alone seemed a sufficient terror.' Ernie Pyle, aboard LST 353, was sufficiently content to be voyaging anonymously despite an invitation from General Bradley to cross the Channel on the *Augusta*. 'My men always fought better when Ernie was around,' Bradley had noted in Tunisia, but Pyle, weary of contact with the top brass, had opted to go it alone, dosing himself with seasick pills and drifting off to sleep.

From the air, as the first bombardment began, the Channel was an unbelievable spectacle. Facing the assault troops along the Normandy coastline was the Atlantic Wall: a hitherto undreamed-of barrier of minefields six miles wide, which Rommel who had taken charge of coastal defences in March, had patterned after the 'Devil's Gardens' of El Alamein. From a Marauder called the *Dottie Dee* Roelif Loveland, of the *Cleveland Plain Dealer*, saw his plane's bombardier drop sixteen 250-pound bombs on one section of the

Wall alone, and although this was 'the greatest drama in the history of the world', he did not fail to mention that his pilot was a Cleveland boy, First Lieutenant Howard C. Quiggle, of 17118 Lipton Avenue, SE. Overhead other planes thundered like a vast steel umbrella, and the roar of their engines filled even the ears of Ed Murrow, 100 miles away in London. 'It was the sound of a giant factory in the sky,' he strove to enthuse his listeners, as early as 10.07 am, although the mien of Londoners walking the streets was so stoic he wanted to shout at them, 'Don't you know that history is being made today?'

From the sea, the impact was as awe-inspiring. At 5.40 am Murrow's colleague, George Hicks, in a tower above the USS *Ancon*'s signal bridge, kept up a nonstop running commentary like a sportscaster: 'The steel bridge on which we stand vibrates from the concussion of the heavy guns ... the Germans are replying from the land with flashes and then the battleship lets go with its entire broadside again ... The first Allied forces are reaching the beaches in France ... If you'll excuse me, I'll just take a deep breath for a moment.' Aboard a destroyer off the British beaches, Reuters' Desmond Tighe, who had so narrowly escaped the Germans in Oslo four years earlier, took up the narrative: '5.37 am. the night bombing has ceased and the great naval bombardment begins ... 5.45 am. The big assault ships start lowering the boats ... 6.30 am. The whole invasion fleet is now waiting just seven miles offshore ... 7.23 am ... I could see the first wave of assault troops touching down ... and fanning up the beach ...'

Now his commentary became staccato: 'Red tracers from close-range enemy weapons are searing across the beach. Men leap out of the craft and move forward. Tanks follow them. By now everything is an inferno.'

To Ross Munro, aboard *Hilary*, 'the barrage sounded like the rhythmic beating of a gigantic drum as it boomed along the coast'. An ominous message, flashing to *Hilary*'s bridge, signalled that the Germans were now fully alerted: 'Under fire on all beaches.'

Aboard an American landing craft, the skipper, a veteran of Guadalcanal, assured the BBC's Robin Duff whose reports, like all his colleagues', were routed to 725 US radio stations: 'Not even a rabbit could be left alive on those beaches.'

The one correspondent who should have reported on this scene, Quentin Reynolds, was at this moment 3000 miles away on an electoral campaign for Franklin Roosevelt, who now sought – and was duly accorded – a fourth term of office. For the first time,

Reynolds's high-level connections had let him down: neither the President nor Reynolds's good friend Harry Hopkins had so much as hinted that invasion was imminent. Thus Reynolds saw none of the hard-learned lessons of Dieppe put into practice: the capital ships, the rocket ships, the fearsome naval bombardment, the saturation bombing that vindicated the slaughter. Even the portable harbour, code-named 'Mulberry', was towed into position at Arromanches in the British sector on 13 June – sketched in advance by the Official War Artist, Richard Eurich, who complained: 'They wouldn't tell me what it was for ... it was like a lot of factories standing out of the water.'

Off the British beaches – Juno, Gold and Sword – the battleships *Warspite* and *Ramillies* had lobbed tons of steel from their 15-inch guns towards the powerful German batteries covering the mouth of the river Orne: in the wake of this a strange élan prevailed. Off Sword Beach, Lambton Burn, on LCT 947, watched the green-bereted commandos of Lord Lovat's 1st Special Service Brigade, who had proved their worth at Dieppe, striding through the surf 'with shoulders hunched like boxers ready for in-fighting'. Off Gold Beach, Alan Moorehead found the invasion 'lacked the element of danger or excitement, even of movement'. Aside from the landing barges, beached, awash or rapidly sinking, this was no more than a sunlit French beach, the kind to which one took the children for the summer holidays. It was harder going for the troops the *Daily Mail*'s Noel Monks accompanied, also off Sword. As they plunged from the LCI, with 60-pound packs on their backs and weapons raised aloft, they 'disappeared like plummets at the bottom of the ramp'. Struggling ashore, the six-foot Monks, despite himself, was treading on an invisible carpet of squirming men. 'Some managed to rid themselves of their heavy packs and come up. Some didn't' – but this unpalatable detail was summarily blue-pencilled from Monks's dispatch.

Even so, the British beaches were strangely tranquil by noon. From a bomber flying low over enemy-occupied France, Richard Dimbleby was gratified to see 'only long stretches of empty roads, shining with rain, deserted, dripping woods and ... much nearer the battle area ... a solitary peasant harrowing his field, up and down behind the horses, looking nowhere but before him and at the soil'.

In the American sector – off the beaches called Omaha and Utah – chaos reigned from the first.

From the USS *Chase*, *Life*'s Robert Capa, boarding an invasion barge that descended from its crane 'like a slow-moving elevator', had the uneasy feeling that 'this would develop into the father and mother of all D-Days'. Nor did his instincts play him false: the air cover on which General Bradley had pinned so much hope had hopelessly overshot their target, dropping 13,000 bombs up to three miles inland. Dominating the 7000 yards of Omaha Beach was Rommel's finest fortress, still intact, and as the first American troops hit the pounding surf eighty-five machine guns and four field artillery batteries opened up. Everywhere landing craft were foundering and capsizing; all through the shallows men fell dying. As they lay pinned down by withering fire, an army lieutenant whispered to Robert Capa: 'Do you know what I see? I see my ma on the front porch, waving my insurance policy.'

What Capa saw through the viewfinder of his Contax camera over the next six hours was a 'foreground ... filled with wet boots and green faces': above those boots and faces, 'the picture frame was filled with shrapnel smoke; burnt tanks and sinking barges formed my background'. Then the camera jammed, the roll was finished, but as Capa reached in his musette bag for a new roll, his 'wet shaking hands' ruined the roll before he could insert it. Then, as he later admitted, his nerve broke. A Red Cross LCI was rolling with the waves, and he ran for it. By sheer chance it delivered him, along with many wounded men, back to the USS *Chase*. The white jackets of the mess boys who had served coffee at 3 am were now smeared with blood, and they were busy sewing the dead into white sacks.

Seven days later, Capa learned from *Time*'s London office that his pictures were the best of the invasion. But an excited darkroom assistant, drying the negatives, had turned on too much heat; the emulsions had melted and run down. Out of 106 pictures, only eight were salvaged.

Other correspondents knew the same black frustration. Try as he might, Ernest Hemingway, who returned to the battlefield after seven years, never even set foot on Omaha Beach; from the attack transport *Dorothea M. Dix* he was transferred to another transport, the *Empire Anvil*, but although it did put troops ashore, Hemingway, handicapped by an injured knee, did not make it. (Martha Gellhorn did, and this made for much bitterness at the Dorchester Hotel, where the Hemingways were pointedly occupying separate rooms on different floors.) Another sorely tried man was the 190-pound Jack Thompson of the *Chicago Tribune*. After his first unschooled paradrop in Tunisia, Thompson had developed a taste for the life, dropped again in Sicily, hit an olive tree and broken two ribs. A peremptory cable from his proprietor – 'JUMP NO MORE MCCORMICK' – quashed his third attempt, and all that remained for Thompson was a landing with the infantry on the same section of Omaha Beach as Robert Capa. Still a paratrooper at heart, Thompson never ceased to curse his fate.

Yet those who made it with the airborne troops were equally out of luck. the task of the 82nd and 101st Airborne Divisions, landing some six hours before the seaborne forces, was to carve out an 'airhead' twelve miles long by seven miles wide, securing the five narrow causeways dominating Utah Beach. But thanks to low cloud and heavy flak, scores of pathfinder aircraft failed to find their drop zones: the hapless Americans were scattered all over the Cotentin Peninsula. Along with them trudged *Time*'s William Walton, who began his night by landing in a pear tree and ended it wading with the paratroopers through chest-deep water, his typewriter hoisted high above his head in lieu of a rifle.

Walton was unaware – nor would the censors have passed the story – that 4000 men of the 82nd Airborne were then unaccounted for, and that 60 per cent of their equipment had been lost.

The British had at least secured their prime objectives: two vital bridges over the Orne river and the Caen Canal, north of the city, and the silencing of the coastal battery at Merville, which menaced Sword Beach. Along with the 9th Battalion of the 5th Parachute Brigade dropped Leonard Mosley, now a *Daily Telegraph* man, who five years earlier had heard Hitler's strident pronouncement in Bayreuth: 'You will not go to war!' Now Mosley, his face thickly camouflaged with cocoa and linseed oil, was draining a glass of cider and listening to more hospitable words from the Mayor of Merville: 'Thank God you've come now, Monsieur. We have waited a long time for the hour of liberation.'

Good news like Mosley's was swift to reach the outside world: the Machine was seeing to that. Among the 700,000 items required by D-Day, from Trousers, Wool, Protective, to Bags, Vomit, Soldiers, For the Use Of, scores were geared to a mighty public relations exercise: sponge-rubber cases to protect portable typewriters, white canvas duck bags striped with red or orange bars imprinted PRESS, vivid yellow labels to attach to tins of film warning USELESS IF DELAYED, even eight gross of condoms, guaranteed to render photographers' negatives watertight if closed with a rubber band. And backstopping this masterly organization was a speedboat courier system, guaranteed shore to shore, teletypes installed at every southern coastal port, a Press Wireless radio installation attached to the US First Army, and motorcyclists standing by to roar to London with every dispatch and photo cleared by the censor.

Among fifteen Reuters men assigned to cover D-Day, two felt that even the Machine at its most streamlined was too sluggish: why not hark back to the example of their founder, Paul Julius Reuter, who in 1849 had spanned the telegraph gap between Aix-la-Chappelle and Verviers, Belgium, by using pigeons? It was less than a success. The pigeons dispatched by Robert Reuben, an enterprising Nebraskan, finally did reach a police station at Ryde on the Isle of Wight, but fifty-six hours after D-Day. Those launched from Juno Beach by Charles Lynch, an excitable Canadian, flew instead towards the German lines, pursued by frenzied cries of 'Traitors! Damned traitors!' Only four pigeons released by Lynch's rival, Joseph Willicombe of INS, proved 'loyal', arriving at the Ministry of Information within hours.

With some newsmen, the urgency to secure a D-Day 'beat' amounted to an obsession. Aboard HMS *Hilary*, Ross Munro felt that his day was made the moment he stepped ashore: off Bernières-sur-Mer, a Canadian public relations officer, Captain Jack Wilson of Halifax, Nova Scotia, was already wading out to returning landing craft to hand the canvas press bags to the skippers. 'Once it was [in London],' Munro exulted, 'it was practically in the papers at home.' On Sword Beach, Noel Monks witnessed a dedication above and beyond the call of duty: a sergeant of the Army Film Unit, his right arm hanging in ribbons from his shoulder, beseeched him, 'Hey, War Correspondent ... Could you see they get back for me? I've copped one.'

'He was far more worried about his films than his terrible wound,' Monks remembered. 'He actually lost his arm.'

Ironically, at 6 am that day, as the naval bombardment began off Normandy, scores of men and women had assembled in the 300-seater conference room off the Ministry of Information's marble entrance hall. All had one thing in common; although they were officially accredited correspondents they had failed to secure a winning ticket in the D-Day draw. Now, as a succession of Eisenhower's staff officers rose to brief them, the doors to the conference room were locked.

At 7.30 am Colonel Ernest Dupuy, 'Ike's' press officer, passed the word to Rear Admiral George Thomson, the Chief Censor. The landings had gone ahead more quickly than expected. All were now free to release the communiqués they had received on arrival.

FLASH UNDER THE COMMAND OF
GENERAL EISENHOWER ALLIED NAVAL
FORCES SUPPORTED BY STRONG AIR
FORCES BEGAN LANDING ALLIED
ARMIES THIS MORNING ON THE
NORTHERN COAST OF FRANCE

Now they were fully as wise as the warcos on the spot.

In the British sector, scenting victory, the long khaki-clad files were already moving inland towards Caen, Bayeux and Périers. On bloody Omaha, too, men were awakening slowly, as if from an anaesthetic. Rallying by degrees, they were coming to realize they must fight their way inland or perish. An infantry colonel voiced the basic truth: 'Two kinds of people are staying on this beach – the dead and those who are going to die. Now let's get the hell out of here!'

All along the beach, officers and noncoms took this as a cue – raging, swearing, urging shell-stunned men to struggle to their feet. And gradually, as morning gave way to afternoon, barbed wire was cut, beach exits opened up and the first men reached Saint-Laurent, three-quarters of a mile inland. Even on Omaha, at a cost of 2500 casualties, the Atlantic Wall was irreparably breached.

Now, along the Bay of the Seine, a thin line like a high-water mark stretched for fully sixty-five miles, and Ernie Pyle took stock of the aftermath of D-Day: soldiers' packs and shoe polish, diaries, socks, hand grenades and Bibles, many Bibles. All these he noted, along with snapshots of families who would never grow older, and the last letters from home, each address razored out for reasons of security – together with torn pistol belts and pocket books, bloody abandoned shoes, metal mirrors and thousands of waterlogged cigarettes.

'If I had the courage I'd chuck the whole business,' Pyle wrote in a letter home. 'I'm so sick of living in misery and fright.'

It was the strange weakness of the opposition that puzzled some warcos – among them Charles Christian Wertenbaker and Martha Gellhorn. Granted that the timing of D-Day had been impeccable – with Rommel, as at El Alamein, once more absent from the front – the first German prisoners seemed to have little heart for fighting.

Were they all conscripts of a labour battalion? Martha Gellhorn wondered. 'There was no sense in imagining that the entire Wehrmacht would turn out to be five foot four and hangdog.'

'Fatigue, as thick as dust, marked everyone's face,' Martha Gellhorn noted, and this was understandable, but not the fact that some were waiting with suitcases already packed, like children eager for the end of term.

Near Cherbourg, which was to fall on 26 June, Wertenbaker put it to one prisoner man to man: were he and his fellows the best the German Army could offer?

The reply was an epitaph for Adolf Hitler's dreams in the east: 'The best of the German Army is dead in Russia.'

For exactly twenty weeks before D-Day, the Red Army had been underscoring that truth. A formidable quintet of Soviet commanders had monopolized the free world's headlines: Marshal Ivan Konev, General Rodion Malinovsky and Marshal Georgi Zhukov in the south, General Konstantin Rokossovsky and General Ivan Bagramian farther north.

Against all odds, their progress had been phenomenal. By February they were 800 miles west of Stalingrad, only 500 miles from Berlin. Harrying their foes with white-painted Stormovik pursuit planes, pounding them with multi-barrelled Katyusha rocket guns, they had marked the 1002nd day of their war by swooping across the Dniester river in one night. Seven days later the Wehrmacht had retreated fully 850 miles from the Volga – back to the line of the Prut river, from which the Russian invasion had been launched on 22 June 1941.

In one short week they had wrested back the Crimea and all but a tiny corner of the blazing Ukraine peninsula, moving at fifty miles a day, besieging Odessa, relieving Sevastopol after seventy-two hours of bombardment. Nothing, it seemed, could stop their advance to the west.

As a 'confirmed Marxist', no man watched the advance with keener interest than Alaric Jacob. From January 1944, Jacob had been appointed *Daily Express* representative in Russia, accompanied by his wife, Iris Morley, covering for the *Observer* and the *Yorkshire Post*, and before even reaching Moscow he was convinced that all Churchill's 1940 rhetoric concerning Britain's 'finest hour' was meaningless alongside the suffering of the Russians. In Archangel, disembarking from the SS *Aert van der Neer*, he had seen war cripples crawling on their stumps across the narrow planks that spanned the Dvina river – and learned that in Russia there were no wheechairs at all, and that some of the artificial limbs were 'so painful that the cripples prefer to go around with the stub'. A longtime Red Army *aficionado*, following a visit to the Caucasus in 1942, Jacob never ceased to stress the sterling quality of their troops: 'We must throw out of the window the absurd notion the Soviet troops ... are somehow rough-and-readier than Western armies ... a sturdier, more vital body of men no army can boast.'

Not that Jacob's pro-Russian bias won him any concessions from Nicolai Palgunov or Solomon Abramovich Lozovsky. From his small three-room suite in Moscow's Metropole – where he ran the *Daily Express* office for 10,000 roubles (aproximately £200) a month – he underwent the same protracted runaround as Quentin Reynolds had done: a month to arrange a visit to a collective farm, six weeks to get inside a factory. 'I have read more graphic reports about a cricket match at Lord's in peacetime,' Jacob groused, 'than about some of the great battles in Russia.' Yet like a fond lover bowled over by a coquette, Jacob would always count it 'a privilege to live in the Soviet Union'.

And for a diligent Russophile with time and an expense account, there were still scoops to be found. One such was at the Suvorov Academy at Kalinin, northwest of Moscow, where youthful partisans who had served in the field were ultimately rewarded with higher education – youngsters like Vassili Malinovsky, fourteen, who had killed two Germans with a grenade, 'and three more with a tommy-gun'. Nicolai Mischenko, thirteen, had actually served as a Red Army scout, like Lazar Bernstein, of the same age, who had helped derail a German troop train. 'I killed several Germans. I saw them fall,' he told Jacob, who could only reflect in bafflement, 'I wonder what Doctor Arnold of Rugby would say.'

The biggest bonus, though, came with the fall of Odessa. That was on 15 April, just seven weeks before D-Day, and five days after General Rodion Malinovsky's troops had freed the Black Sea port. 'Ploughing through mud at the head of a troupe of wallowing correspondents,' General Alexander Rogov of Malinovsky's staff quartered them all for the night in peasant cottages.

On that bitterly cold April Saturday, kitted out in fur coat and gloves with boots and a fur cap, Jacob was 100 feet below ground in the catacombs of Odessa, along with the guerrilla leader Anatole Loschenko and his deputy, Dmitri Gaschin. It was here, even under

German occupation, that 10,000 partisans had lived unmolested, secure in a warren of 100 miles of passages, stealing out by night to terrorize the street patrols.

This was a world, Jacob reflected, that the Allies could never comprehend. Gaschin seemed to divine his thoughts. 'By God,' he burst out, 'if you people in the West had learned to hate as we have you'd have finished your war long ago!'

For Alan Moorehead, hatred was a quality conspicuously lacking in the British sector of Normandy. So, too, was speed. Marooned aboard LST 816 all through D-Day, fifty yards offshore, listening to swing music that jarred his nerves and eating grilled steaks he didn't want, Moorehead felt 'nothing but a confused sense of anti-climax'. On D plus one it was much the same. When a ferry he had boarded grounded in the shallows, a six-foot soldier hoisted the bantamweight Moorehead onto his shoulders and set him down, typewriter dry and intact, on the sand of Gold Beach.

His jeep retrieved, Moorehead made for the cathedral town of Bayeux, seven miles inland, along with Christopher Buckley, another warco in the first wave. They lunched at the Lion d'Or, 'a bright little provincial hotel, set back from the road around a courtyard', to the sound of Vichy collaborators running a gauntlet of blows in the main square. Days later, with the tacit complicity of Montgomery, General Charles de Gaulle, 'a stiff lugubrious figure', appeared on Bayeux's main street before moving on to Isigny and other towns in the bridgehead – firing collaborationists, appointing his own men, organizing housing for refugees. He who had stood for Free France while Pétain, Laval and Darlan sought accommodation with 'the hated Boche' was accepted as a *fait accompli*. 'There was ... no possibility of de Gaulle being disowned,' Moorehead recognized.

Now, after the first fine fury of activity, the Normandy front was *the* place for a correspondent to be seen – replacing once-fashionable venues like Cairo, Moscow and Algiers. As a true connoisseur of war, Ernie Pyle saw it first as a sniper's war – 'snipers everywhere ... in trees, in buildings, in piles of wreckage, in the grass'. It was likewise a hedgerow war – 'a series of skirmishes'. This was what the Normans called *bocage* country – small fields bounded by mounds of earth topped with thick bushes that emphasized the small farmers' proud sense of personal property. These would help the crack German troops rushed into the breach to ensure that Normandy was a slow war, a war of attrition.

For six weeks, in a pastoral parody of the Anzio–Cassino stale-mate, the British and Canadians remained stalled before Caen, ten miles inland – although this had been Montgomery's objective on the first day. But now, in the tradition of Alamein, Caen was to become a 'set-piece' battle, planned by a general the *Montreal Gazette*'s Lionel Shapiro dubbed 'as methodical as a railway dispatcher, coldly practical as a moneylender' – careful, precise, using armour as a parry, with murderous assaults from the air as part of the strategy. For the warcos, what the BBC's Frank Gillard called a 'game of musical chairs from slit trench to slit trench' was now infinitely less dangerous than holding down a desk in Fleet Street. From 13 June, the first of Hitler's pilotless V–1 reprisal weapons, their warheads packed with a ton of Amatol, had been turned against London, an eighty-day ordeal that was to destroy 500 houses a day and claim 6000 lives.

Even London blitz veterans like the *New Yorker*'s Molly Panter-Downes felt 'a certain, illogical Wellsian creepiness at the phen-omenon', and though Normandy might be the fashion, London was once again the frontline. When the war artist John Groth, of *Parade* magazine, departed for the beachhead late in June, the press camp at London's Senate House saluted him with a scornful farewell chorus of 'Sissy!'

For the first time in months the Allies faced a setback, and from the warco's viewpoint this was reflected in a captious niggling censorship alien to the Eisenhower regime. The NBC reporter William W. Chaplin found all the cards stacked against him: the story that 'leaflets had been showered on the town of Montebourg, warning them in advance of a bombing raid, was nipped in the bud. High winds had scattered the leaflets miles distant and the people of Montebourg had died in the ruins. When the US Seventh Corps' Major-General J. Lawton Collins issued an ultimatum to the German garrison of Cherbourg calling for their surrender, this, too, was blocked by a technicality. Since Collins had failed to clear it with the First Army's General Courtney Hodges, the irregularity must be kept in the dark.

The breakthrough did not come until early in August – pri-marily because of Hitler's stubborn insistence that every yard of French soil must be held whatever the cost. For months, the phrase 'promoted to Fortress' had been a standing joke with both Rommel and his superior, the aging Field Marshal Gerd von Rundstedt, the Commander-in-Chief, West: all told, some sixteen strongpoints were accorded fortress status, among them Dunkirk and Dieppe, tying up 200,000 men. It was this last-ditch mentality that on 7 August sealed the fate of the German Seventh Army, boxed in a rectangle between the Norman market towns of Falaise, Vire, Argentan and Mortain. Although an escape route ten miles wide remained between Argentan and Falaise, Field Marshal Hans von Kluge, who had taken over from Rommel, was ordered to counter-attack at Mortain.

Now the Seventh Army was trapped inside a monstrous killing ground, twenty-two miles wide by eleven miles deep: what one survivor termed 'a Stalingrad in Normandy'. For one whole day the battlefield was strafed by rocket-firing Typhoons, until almost a hundred tanks had been reduced to smoking scrap metal. 'Certainly this is the most awful sight that has come my way since the war began,' Moorehead cabled the *Daily Express*. 'I think I see the end of Germany here.'

For in the village of St Lambert he witnessed a devastation that was almost indescribable. Prisoners emerging from the battlefield moved with glassy unseeing eyes like the walking dead of Haiti. Some 300 transport horses had stampeded, dragging their carriages through farmyards, galloping for the banks of the river Dives, 'and plunged headlong with all their trappings down the twelve-foot banks into the stream below, which at once turned red with blood'. In a twentieth-century recreation of Borodino or Waterloo, at least a thousand German vehicles had been reduced to smouldering piles of black metal.

Here were scatters of dark grey blankets, loads of bread green with mould, flasks of wine, radio sets, typewriters, wallets stuffed with banknotes, dead cows 'like overturned rocking horses', everywhere corpses in shabby grey, slumped as if in sleep. In the seven kilometres between Coudehard and Tournai, villagers were unable to set foot on solid ground; handkerchiefs pressed to their noses, they trod a squelching carpet of dead soldiers and dead cattle, 'wading in blood'. The massive, ancient, evil smell of 2000 putrefying horses penetrated even to the cockpits of reconnaissance aircraft hovering overhead.

'This was their best in weapons and men, their strongest barrier before the Rhine,' Moorehead wound up. 'It has been brushed aside, shattered into bits. The beaten Wehrmacht is a pitiable thing. I say again I think I see the end of Germany here.'

*

The eyes of the warcos were now fixed firmly on a once-in-a-lifetime goal: Paris. Every correspondent in France, from young novices to fifty-seven-year-old Mark Watson of the *Baltimore Sun*, the oldest man in the field, coveted *La Ville Lumière* for a dateline. In bivouacs scattered from Caen to Falaise, marked out by the dispatch bags with the red-lettered 'PRESS' hanging in the doorway, the inhabitants eyed each other warily, suspicious that a hitherto trusted roommate had a trick up his sleeve where Paris was concerned.

When Bradley's First Army was 100 miles west of the city, a bold quartet – Ernie Pyle, Jack Thompson, UP's Hank Gorrell and Clark Lee, on the job without a break since Corregidor – asked permission to form a flying column ahead of the main troops. They were peremptorily refused.

Although few war correspondents were in his confidence aside from his four-man D-Day pool, the truth was that Eisenhower had no plans for Paris at all.

In his command caravan codenamed 'Shellburst', two miles inland from the Normandy beachhead at Granville, the Supreme Commander had in fact resolved to bypass Paris altogether. To reach the city would call for thousands of gallons of gasoline: to administer it would swallow up the equivalent of eight divisions of civil affairs officers. To feed its citizens would call for 75,000 tons of food and medicine and 1500 tons of coal daily.

But by 21 August, as the BBC's Robert Barr had cause to know, Eisenhower was wavering. One day earlier, a visit from de Gaulle – who left the caravan 'looking like thunder' – had revealed Paris as a troubled city. A Communist-inspired uprising by the FFI (French Forces of the Interior) had chimed with Hitler's decision to leave much of the city in ruins before the Germans pulled out – including the destruction of the forty-five bridges that spanned the Seine. Although Lieutenant-General Dietrich von Choltitz, newly appointed fortress commander of Paris, was resisting this, the Communists' hunting down of lone German soldiers might yet force his hand. That same evening, an envoy from the city had pleaded with Bradley's intelligence chief that American intervention was crucial – 'or there is going to be a terrible slaughter'.

At his morning conference of 23 August, Eisenhower's brow wore the familiar frown that had preceded the decisions for D-Day. 'Well, what the hell, Brad,' he sighed finally. 'I guess we'll have to go in.'

Within hours the word was passing: the French 2nd Armoured

Division, under General Jacques Philippe Leclerc, soon to be back-stopped by Major-General Raymond O. Barton's 4th US Infantry Division, was ready to roll. And at 9.22 pm on Thursday, 24 August – 1532 days after Quentin Reynolds, as the last war correspondent had left the city – the lead tanks of Leclerc's division swept with a rush through the Porte d'Italie. For those warcos seeing Paris for the first time, these were electric hours: would her heart, they wondered, recalling the old song, still be young and gay? To war artist John Groth, who had hitched a ride with the first French column, it seemed that it would: so many girls were already astride the tank turret he thought of 'floats in a Rose Bowl parade'. Before his jeep had travelled two blocks, his hair was waxed to his scalp with lipstick as if with pomade.

'Everybody was eighteen years old, free of shackles, bursting with joy,' remembered *Time* magazine's Mary Welsh, and even Alan Moorehead, his emotions almost deadened after four years, felt six years slip away as his jeep zoomed through the Porte d'Orléans: the young Moorehead, in the Paris bureau of the *Daily Express*, was once again endeavouring to find his feet in a seventh-floor studio, looking 'like a struggling doctor's waiting room', in the suburb of St Cloud. His impressions reached the London office in a vivid montage or words: 'Nothing has changed, nothing really altered. The cobblestones, the flapping signs in red and gold over the pavement cafés ... Three golden horse heads over the horse butcher ... The *flics* with their flat blue képis ... Had we ever been away?'

All that night, and throughout the next day, Moorehead noted, Paris was a strange city – 'like separate sets at a movie studio'. From thousands of open apartment windows the strains of '*La Marseillaise*' from radios and tinny gramophones mingled with the crack and splatter of snipers' bullets as Germans in field grey and FFI in dirty sweaters and Basque shirts battled each other from the roof tops – sounds at times overwhelmed by the joyous pealing of bells from 146 churches. Many correspondents, after months in the field, were content to take time out from war. At pavement cafés as far apart as Montmartre and the Rue Royale, John Groth and the Swedish warco Sven Auren noted the astonishing chic of the women after the dowdiness of London: the Mode Martiale of Lucien Lelong and Jacques Fath featuring broad shoulders, wide belts and short skirts. Yet privation lurked not far below the surface. 'My stomach is empty,' an elderly Frenchwoman told Maurice 'Bud' Kane of the army newspaper, *Stars and Stripes*, 'but my heart is full of happiness.'

For all those with stories to file, the Machine was already geared for action. Almost three months after D-Day 500 correspondents were converging on Paris, and all of them were packed into the Hotel Scribe, on the Rue Scribe, for the best of logistical reasons: it stood midway between the fashionable Madeleine church and the Café de la Paix, with the Eiffel Tower, the Arc de Triomphe, the Champs Élysées and Notre Dame within easy reach. Soon the new arrivals were filing more than three million words a week, as well as submitting 35,000 still pictures and 100,000 feet of newsreel film, for around those landmarks, Colonel Barney Oldfield predicted, 'actions, emotion, picture opportunities were sure to swirl'.

And swirl they did. More and more liberators swarmed into the city: Tuaregs from the French Sudan, Africans from the jungles of Cameroun, even Ernest Hemingway, checking in at the Ritz with two truckloads of grimy FFI, to demand of the bartender: 'How about seventy-three dry martinis?' There was the same fire brigade captain who had brought the tricolour down from the Eiffel Tower on 13 June 1940, climbing the 1750 steps to the summit to hoist it once again. There was General von Choltitz in the billiard room of the Prefecture, signing a surrender document tapped out on a typewriter borrowed from Harold Denny, a machine which Public Relations promptly lost. Lastly on Saturday 26 August, there was de Gaulle, moving in stately file from the Arc de Triomphe down the Champs-Élysées for a Te Deum service in Notre Dame, narrowly escaping a crossfire of guerrilla bullets as he entered the nave.

It took a correspondent of the old school like John D'Arcy Dawson to proceed decorously to the British Embassy amd sign the visitors' book: his employer, Lord Kemsley, would have expected no less. More were as emotionally overcome as an Australian colleague of Iris Carpenter, who cabled his editor: BURP BURP THAT IS PRESENT PARIS STORY STOP WERE DRUNK WITH JOY AND GETTING DRUNKER BURP BURP.

It was Ernie Pyle who summed up the mood of the city to his old friend, Clark Lee: 'Anybody who doesn't sleep with a woman tonight is just an exhibitionist.'

For Japan – on paper at least – the war was already lost. The problem, as the warcos reported from the immensity of the southwest Pacific, was that the Japanese did not know it.

On 15 June – when Montgomery was still stalled before Caen – 127,000 fighting men, among them 8000 US Marines, splashed ashore on Saipan, the largest of the island group called the Marianas. It was the turning point. 'The war was lost when the Marianas were taken away from Japan,' Prince Higashikuni, C-in-C, Home Defence headquarters, was to avow, and with reason: from Saipan to Tokyo was 1125 miles, and the new American bomber, the B–29, capable of carrying four tons of bombs, had a range of 3500 miles. The fall of Saipan would secure one more 'unsinkable aircraft carrier' for the United States.

When Saipan did fall on 9 July, Premier Hideki 'The Razor' Tojo, who had prosecuted the war incisively since 1941, resigned with his entire Cabinet. But Saipan caused no tremor in the Japanese fighting man.

On all fronts, the warcos reported the Japanese as indomitable – essentially the same message that Richard Tregaskis and his colleagues had relayed from Guadalcanal back in August 1942. In the fourth battle for the Solomon Islands, which raged for five days and nights over an area of 250,000 square miles, Vice-Admiral William 'Bull' Halsey, US Naval Commander in the South Pacific, had stressed unequivocally: 'There is no shortcut to victory over Japan.' World War One veterans saw the fighting as more desperate than in the Argonne Forest, and NANA's correspondent, Ira Wolfert, came up with a verdict calculated to diminish naval recruiting lines: 'There can be no question of our being better fighters than the Japs. The best anybody can possibly do is to be as good . . .'

Each contested island became, in Wolfert's words, 'a desperate terrain filled with more desperate men,' and the warcos, living alongside the combatants, Ernie Pyle fashion, strove to live up to that example. One such contender was the *Christian Science Monitor*'s Gordon Walker, described as a 'Hollywood typecast . . . of a war correspondent', who, in New Georgia in June 1943, embarked on a Hollywood-type newsbeat; chartering a native war canoe, he was paddled for ten hours under cover of darkness before his copy could be delivered to a troop lighter.

It was the same with AP's Richard Johnston on 23 November 1943, when the bloody landing on Tarawa atoll, in the Gilbert Islands, cost 1000 marine lives and almost 4700 Japanese for possession of a three-strip landing field. Like the marines, Johnston struggled 500 yards through the shallows under a hail of machine-gun crossfire. After sixty hours he reported, 'The sweet, sickening smell of death literally permeates the blasted shell-torn beaches,' yet, despite all, 'most surrenders, which probably total no more than 200, were by labourers. The soldiers prefer *hara-kiri*.'

Whatever the terrain, it was the same story. The mountainous Aleutian Islands, extending westward from Alaska, were no tropical paradise, but cold, damp and shrouded with fog, yet the battle for Attu island, testified *Time*'s Robert Sherrod, was one of 'cold, hungry little men in little black rubber boots and muddy khaki uniforms, waiting for death in their foxholes'. On the spot translations of their last letters read with a strange monotony: 'I await death with a smile' or 'I shall smile when the enemy arrives'.

'It was a war without chivalry, without honour,' Ian Morrison cabled the London *Times* from Papua, New Guinea. 'It was a bloody fight to the death, an elemental struggle with only one password – kill or be killed.' That was on 7 April 1943; sixteen months later, when the British Fourteenth Army gained impetus down Burma's Khabaw Valley from Manipur, Gerald Hanley was reporting in the same vein to the London *Spectator*: 'How are we to defeat these people, not in Burma, but in the whole of the East? when they regard death as the answer to both victory and failure.' The only Japanese to give up, as Hanley witnessed, were men who 'had come back, starving and dying, struggling along with sticks or crutches'. One man's 'ears were filled with maggots and he was about to die', and he only shook his head and grinned idiotically, unable any longer to hear or to understand. Six months after that, as a twenty-one-year-old war correspondent for Lord Mountbatten's *Phoenix* magazine, I was reporting the words of a British CO in Burma, from Milestone 19.4 on the Toungoo–Mawchi Road: 'We have to clear out all the bunkers. The Japs fight to die there; those are their orders. They won't get out – you have to kill them where they lie.'

In July 1944 – one month before the carnage of the Falaise Gap that opened the road to Paris – that scourge of the Japanese, General Douglas MacArthur, was already making his plans. 'I have come through and I shall return,' he had vowed after reaching Australia from Corregidor on 17 March 1942, and from that time on his entire war had been dedicated to this end. His successive headquarters, in Melbourne and at Port Moresby, New Guinea, had both been codenamed, like his private plane, 'Bataan', in memory of the 70,000 troops who had surrendered on the peninsula, and all his press conferences emphasized his determination to return. Frank Legg, of the Australian Broadcasting Corporation, frequently had the press camp in stitches with his imitation of MacArthur's silent perambulation, corncob pipe clenched grimly in teeth, and the sudden explosion that followed: 'Gentlemen! With Gahd's help, I shall conquer the little yellow man! Here I shall throw in my right! Here my left! With Gahd's help, I shall crush him in a vice!'

And true to his word, on 20 October MacArthur did return, exactly two years, seven months and three days after his promise: a voyage aboard the light cruiser *Nashville* to the glassy green waters of Leyte Gulf, still 250 miles from his primary goal, Manila. Thanks to a crotchety beachmaster, the world knew of his arrival; the *Nashville*'s landing barge had grounded in shallow water fifty yards from the shore and the beachmaster had growled 'Let 'em walk.' Angrily descending to his midriff in the surf, MacArthur had splashed forty wet strides to the beach, a historic picture caught by UP's William B. Dickinson. As appreciative of a 'good press' as Mark Clark, Montgomery and my own boss, Lord Louis Mountbatten, MacArthur at once sensed the dramatic impact; next day, with more photographers in tow, he waded ashore all over again.

What the world did not know until 28 May 1945, when NANA correspondent Phelps Adams was allowed to break the story, was that five days after MacArthur's arrival the first of the Japanese *kamikaze* suicide attacks heralded the Battle of Leyte Gulf. Three Zero fighters, guns blazing, dived for the carriers *Santee*, the *St. Lo* and the *Kalinin Bay*, severely damaging flight decks, blasting elevators and entire aeroplanes high into the air. The shape of the resistance still to come was clear to the navy, but not to the world at large.

But as Moorehead had said long ago, from another theatre of war, 'You must always give the public good news.'

In those first heady days of September the daily surfeit of good news from Europe was breathtaking and the names of the falling towns told the story: Rouen, Meaux, Soissons, Amiens, Arras, Verdun. From 15 August, the 286,000 men of Major-General Alexander Patch's allied Seventh Army, which included the Frenchmen of the impeccable General Jean de Lattre de Tassigny, had poured ashore in southern France to add new names to the register: Cannes, Toulon, Marseilles. Everywhere the speed of the Allied advance was astounding, and so, too, was the reception from the liberated. 'Even today, you daren't stop your jeep in a main street without it getting almost buried with people,' reported the BBC's Wynford Vaughan-Thomas from Lyons. 'Our jeep was almost festooned with humanity – with FFI fighters and small boys, businessmen, everybody who could hang on.'

A dizzying euphoria prevailed. One day earlier, as dusk fell on 3 September, Major-General Allan Adair's Guards Armoured Division rolled into Brussels beneath the line of masked streetlights that hung above the centre of the Chaussée Ninove, 'like a green necklace suspended in the sky', a street bathed in the smell of cheap perfume and cigars, with the great dome of the Palais de Justice burning like a flambeau in the night. 'The joy of Paris was a pallid thing compared to this extravagance,' Alan Moorehead marvelled, for 'Brussels continued with this madhouse atmosphere for ten long days and nights on end.' Citizens scrambled for soldiers' autographs in the streets as if they were visiting royalty. One girl unearthed a bottle of hoarded champagne to pour it over the head of the first British soldier she saw, as if she was launching a battleship. Well aware that the warcos had good tidings to spread, Major Geoffrey Keating, of Army Public Relations, took a tiny Piper Cub aircraft low over the German lines to collect their dispatches from the Hotel Metropole, then roof-hopped back over the suburbs to the British lines, harassed by German ack-ack all the way.

Antwerp, which fell on 4 September, was like Tunis all over again: an advance so precipitate that the first Germans glimpsed by the 11th (UK) Armoured Division were peaceably sipping beer in pavement cafés. Moorehead, arriving in their wake, was at first astonished by a scene resembling 'the Coliseum in Rome about the time of the Emperor Caligula'. Since the hard-pressed population had long ago consumed the animals in the zoo, the entire complex had been taken over to house the 6000-strong Axis garrison – officers in the lion cages, other ranks in the monkey house, Belgian Fascists in the tiger pens.

'These,' explained a Belgian officer, indicating the Germans, 'we will turn over to the British authorities.' 'These,' indicating the collaborationists, 'will be shot this evening after a fair trial.'

Yet Antwerp was a useless prize without the fifty-four-mile Scheldt Estuary and its strongpoint, Walcheren Island, which the Germans still commanded. That, remembered Reginald Thompson of Kemsley Newspapers, was a lonely battle, when a howling wind brought the endless gossip of machine guns: a land of sheep grazing on the fields of rich black polder land, and Dutch peasant women in their white winged lace bonnets spreading salvaged onions to dry on the roadsides. Not until 28 November would Antwerp function again as a port, but it was a campaign which correspondents like Ross Munro relished, for when night fell he could take a streetcar back from the front to Antwerp's Century Hotel for dinner served by waiters in white tie and tails. Not so the Regina Rifles of Canada, whose exploits he recorded by day: unable to leave their slit trenches to eat, they existed on rations heated in a central dugout and lobbed into space like grenades, so that one isolated rifleman was heard to yell: 'Why the hell do I keep getting marmalade?'

By degrees, as the combat grew more cut-and-dried, veteran warcos rationed their contact with the fighting men. 'We tended to be more sickened by ruins than stimulated by danger,' Moorehead admitted, 'and skirmishes at the front which once would have filled our day's horizon now often seemed to us repetitive and useless folly.' Yet the remorseless flow of news continued unabated; from October onwards, when the press camp of Lieutenant-General William Simpson's Ninth (US) Army moved from the Paris Scribe to the Hotel du Lévrier, at Maastricht in the Netherlands, 150 correspondents, British and American, were filing stories to 278 million readers on six continents, like the scriptwriters of a long-running soap opera. '[They] bore the simulated rank of captain, in case they were captured,' recalled the press camp CO, Colonel Barney Oldfield 'however, they assumed the rank of field marshal . . . and recognized no conventions.'

It was a truth that Moorehead and his colleagues freely acknowledged. 'Like the children of very wealthy parents,' he confessed, 'it seemed quite natural to us that we should occupy the best houses and hotels, that we should have at our command cars, motor launches, servants and the best food.' And food was only the tip of the iceberg, as the war artist Edward Ardizzone, a gourmet of stature, appreciated after the short commons of Italy. 'Much of the best gone,' he noted of one visit to an abandoned wine cellar with Moorehead, Clifford and Buckley, 'but chose some young château-bottled claret and a 1929 burgundy for the Mess.' Conceivably, 'much of the best' had already gone to the cellar Moorehead and Clifford were establishing – 'incredibly fine,' Ardizzone purred. 'Haut Brion 1895 and 1911. Lafitte '24, all in jeroboams.'

It was, briefly, a world away from 'the long cold nightmare of the war in Nothern Europe' that Moorehead had anticipated. 'History now was old K-ration boxes, empty foxholes, the drying leaves on branches that were cut for camouflage,' Ernest Hemingway wrote nostalgically, but as the Germans abandoned town after town, retreating towards the sanctuary of their West Wall (the Siegfried Line to the Allies), history was increasingly an endless parade of small-town boys seeking out other small-town boys. Robert Barr, attached to the Ninth Army for the BBC, was at first bewildered by press jeeps whose drivers demanded peremptorily: 'Anyone here from Iowa?' But all too soon, Colonel Oldfield recorded, this became routine, with ever-more specialized requests from 'short-timers' in the field: 'Can you line up about ten men from northern Ohio in a tank outfit?' or 'Find me four men from Brooklyn who are in foxholes along the front.'

A conspicuous failure in this quest for home-town copy was Victor O. Jones of the *Boston Globe*, who found GIs from Massachusetts, the Bay State, hard to come by. Following the example of Gordon Gamack, of the *Des Moines Register Tribune*, who simply inscribed his windshield 'Iowa', Jones painted his own with an abbreviated 'Mass' – only to be besieged by penitent Catholics pining to confess.

The one cloud on this clear horizon was Operation Market Garden, Montgomery's audacious but disastrous plan to bring the war to a speedy conclusion by surrounding the 4000-square-mile industrial area of the Ruhr – thus forcing Germany to sue for peace. The fulcrum of this plan was a 60-mile-long airborne carpet of 9000 paratroops and 1100 glider pilots, dropping and crash-landing to secure five major bridges. The northernmost tip of this carpet was the bridge that spanned the Rhine at Arnhem, Holland.

Few more garbled accounts emerged from any theatre of war than came out of Arnhem between the assault on Sunday, 17 September and the withdrawal on Monday, 25 September, a time-span that encompassed a total or more than 17,000 Allied casualties. There were manifold reasons for this. Of the five British warcos who dropped closest to the bridge at Arnhem, all were limited to a few hundred words a day. Strict censorship, an uncritical cheerleader spirit among the Allied commanders and faulty communications only added to the muddle. The BBC's Cyril Ray, who dropped with other warcos eleven miles from Arnhem at Nijmegen, where another key bridge was sited, never filed a word. A featherwitted public relations officer, stuffing the correspondents' messages into his battledress blouse, completely forgot to send them.

Worse, charged Colonel Barney Oldfield, some correspondents, who had pursued the war chariots no farther than the glossy Canterbury Hotel, Brussels, were also filing 'Arnhem' stories – a deception known to the trade as 'magic-carpeting'. The confusion was compounded. Thus the BBC's hailing of Arnhem as 'one of the outstanding operations of the war' was swiftly amended to 'a valuable stand' by 'a depleted, gallant and undaunted force'. One of the few messages that went straight to the point was dispatched from an Arnhem foxhole by Alan Wood, a lean, contentious Australian warco, to the *Daily Express* editor in London. It read: 'How about a rise now, Mister Christiansen?'

'For the Allied army now no hopeful alternative remained,' Moorehead summed up cogently. 'Thre was only one way – the hard way ... all hope of a quick end of the war in 1944 had gone.' For the British and Canadians the hard way would now lead through the Reichswald Forest, which encompassed the northern end of the West Wall: a battle that would drag on into early March, as 20,000 German paratroops contested some thirty square miles of ground. In November, the American way centred on the Hürtgen Forest, where *Time*'s William Walton reported that the close-ranked firs towered 100 feet high, and even the brightness of noon was muted to an eerie twilight, filtering onto spongy brown pine needles and rotting logs. The battle raged for ten weeks in a fathomless sea of darkness: the forest changed hands eighteen times, the forest village of Vossenack twenty-eight times.

From September on, the bombing of German industrial centres had been another facet of the way ahead, and this, too, had become a fashionable assignment for hand-picked warcos. One early contender had been Richard Dimbleby, who had glimpsed Berlin from a Lancaster bomber piloted by Guy Gibson of 'Dam Busters' fame, as far back as January 1943: paralysed with nerves and excitement he 'achieved immortality in the ranks of the RAF,' he told Wynford Vaughan-Thomas later, 'by being the only man to be violently sick *after* a raid was over' – narrowly missing the bomb aimer beneath him. But after twenty missions with the RAF, Dimbleby – like Ed Murrow, who himself went on twenty-five – had become virtually blasé. On later flights, an eerie silence enveloped the Ruhr valley: the vast Krupp works at Essen, 'the biggest armament works in the world, is incapable of producing a hairpin,' one observer reported.

'This morning, in broad daylight,' Dimbleby told his listeners triumphantly on 14 October, 'the RAF has delivered its greatest single attack against a German industrial target since the start of the war – more than a thousand heavy bombers, more than 4500 tons of bombs.' A year ago, he reminded them, 'it would have been near-suicidal to appear over the Ruhr in daylight,' but as 'great broad streams of Lancasters and Halifaxes crossed the frontier of Germany there was not an aircraft of the Luftwaffe to be seen in the sky'.

Undetected by generals, intelligence officers and warcos alike, the danger to the Allies lay not in the overcast skies but in the densely wooded Ardennes Forest through which the Germans, four and a half years earlier, had bypassed the Maginot Line.

From early in December, along a fifty-mile 'ghost front' between Monschau and Echternach, Luxembourg, 250,000 Germans of the Fifth, Sixth and Seventh Panzer Armies were silently assembling under the C-in-C, West, Field Marshal Gerd von Rundstedt, backed by 900 guns and 970 tanks. Their ultimate objectives were Antwerp and Brussels, for, as Moorehead rationalized it later, 'the Americans . . . were braced for offensive, they were not expecting a German counter-attack.'

Certainly the troops bedding down at 10 pm on Friday, 15 December, in the high patrician houses of Echternach and Monschau saw no cause for alarm. Ahead lay the coldest Christmas Europe had known for fifty-four years; most of them had retired early to thick feather beds. At 4 am on 16 December surprise was thus total along a front held by only six divisions – three of them grass-green, three of them suffering from battle fatigue. From hundreds of cannon (including 14-inch railroad guns), launching platforms and mortars, a storm of shell and rocket fire that wrecked telephone communications from one end of the sector to the other caught the American positions totally unawares.

Flames seared through the splintered trees, bathing the snow-bound woods in leaping light. Closely in their wake came searchlights, a drenching blue-white glow through which ghostly figures seemed to stumble. By degrees, the wraiths on the 'ghost front' grew substantial: hundreds and hundreds of white-clad bucket-helmeted German soldiers, advancing with ominous steadiness, twelve or fourteen abreast. Behind them lumbered 60-ton tanks, their tracks debauching the powdered snow to black icy slush.

Along and behind a crumbling front, all was confusion. 'The order that everyone hoped would never come, came,' reported the BBC's Robert Barr, with the US Ninth Army at St Vith. 'We had to move out quickly . . . There was handshaking and many questions. How near were the Germans? Did we think they'd come at their town again? ... There were awkward silences. The GIs couldn't answer that question.'

Already some American units had been cut off and surrounded. Others were fighting desperate rearguard actions. Many were in headlong flight, clogging the narrow winding roads, their vehicles bumper to bumper. At one HQ Richard Hottelet of CBS watched an officer besieged by telephone calls put down the receiver with weary disbelief. 'It sounds like the stock market crash in 1929,' he mumbled.

Robert Barr had his own yardstick of just how disorganized things were. On the road near Malmédy he flagged down the jeep of Major-General Matthew B. Ridgway, the tough incisive commander of the US 82nd Airborne. Unusually, aside from an aide, Ridgway was alone. 'Where's your command post, General?' Barr asked him.

For answer Ridgway tapped his steel helmet. 'Inside here, boy.'

IX

Goebbels Never Told Us It Would Be Like This

17 DECEMBER 1944 – 8 MAY 1945

Historians would call it the Battle of the Bulge – those forty-two days when the Germans drove a forty-mile wedge deep into the Allied lines between Aachen and the Luxembourg border, cutting off whole corps of Americans. But the warcos would remember the human above the strategic aspects. For Kemsley's Reginald Thompson, it was the battle in which Montgomery, given temporary command of the American First and Ninth Armies by Eisenhower, toured the freezing front handing out cases of Oxo to the tank crews. It was a battle when bulldozers fought, yard by yard, mile by mile, to clear the hard-packed ice and when cheeky children peppered the military policemen doing twenty-four hour point duty at the crossroads with snowballs. Noel Monks remembered it as the coldest war ever. After ten hours on the road in sub-zero temperatures, warcos returning to Maastricht had to be hauled bodily from their jeeps.

Petrol froze in the tanks, recalled Alan Moorehead – and this was unusual – while the antifreeze mixture in the radiators froze as well – which was unheard-of.

For Cyril Ray, it was the battle when 11,000 men of the 101st Airborne Division, beleaguered for nine days in the junction town of Bastogne, greeted their liberators: 'Christmas? Splendid – that was the day we got twenty-eight German tanks.' Martha Gellhorn singled it out as a landscape of other-worldly beauty – 'scenery for a Christmas card: smooth white snow hills and bands of dark forest and villages that actually nestled'. It was in Bastogne, on New Year's Eve, that she thought up a 1945 resolution for the men who ran the world: to get to know the people who had to live in it.

Colonel Barney Oldfield claimed it was the one battle of World War Two in which the correspondents had reason to be grateful to the censors – a debt which they freely acknowledged. 'Sheer hysteria characterized many of the first press offerings from the Bulge,' he recorded, and Captain Ed Lavelle, the press censor for both the Ninth and First Armies, 'told his staff to be generous with the blue pencil'. In tribute Wes Gallagher cabled AP Headquarters in New York: WHAT COULD HAVE BEEN UNHOLY MESS WAS SAVED BY GOOD SENSE OF FRONT LINE FIELD CENSORS. This won Lavelle a Christmas greetings telegram from AP's general manager, Kent Cooper.

In truth the panic had been premature, as both Montgomery and Patton, though far from being twin souls, had agreed – 'What the hell is all the mourning about?' Patton had challenged Larry Newman of INS when Bastogne was surrounded. 'This is the end of the beginning.' And Moorehead, a Montgomery rather than a Patton man, felt the same. Although the battle was to cost Eisenhower some 80,000 casualties, 'it probably expedited the end ... the morale of the Americans and British ... rose sharply ... the Germans now knew at last that their cause was hopeless.'

For finally the fog had lifted. Allied aircraft 5000 strong swept down to batter the German supply columns in a repetition of Falaise. Despite the hard-won gains, with advance units within fifteen miles of Liège, the German position was no longer tenable.

Now all the warcos saw all the days ahead as red letter days, for at last the names of the falling towns were German names: München-Gladbach, Krefeld, Trier, Rheydt and triumphantly, on 7 March, Cologne.

In Cologne, almost all of them succumbed to dateline fever, which meant penetrating inside the city limits to make the dateline valid. 'The military forces,' Colonel Oldfield reminisced, 'were treated to the strange sight of this motley collection of grown men sprinting into the Cologne city limit a few feet, spinning on their heels and running back.' Since the Germans were hotly contesting Cologne, the besieging GIs were mostly laconic. 'Hi,' AP's Ken Dixon greeted one soldier crouched behind a tree. 'What are you doin' here?' In true Tennessean vernacular, the man gave what Dixon took to be a classic definition of war: 'Why, suh, there ain't really nothin' to do up heah 'cept shoot folks.'

Eleven days later, at Venlo, on the river Maas near the German frontier of the Netherlands, Lieutenant-General Sir Miles Dempsey, commanding the British Second Army, perched a map on a wooden bench, expounding on the movements of four corps under his command to an attentive group of correspondents. Major roles had also been allotted to the 18th (US) Airborne – the 6th (British) Airborne, and the US Ninth Army. The gist of the briefing came in his opening sentence: 'We will cross the Rhine on the night of the 23rd.'

When it came to questions, Moorehead was succinct: 'This well might be the last battle?' Dempsey was equally succinct: 'Yes.'

March 23rd was a black night along the Rhine. From the second-storey room of an abandoned villa Moorehead, Clifford and Buckley had the town of Wesel in murky focus at the moment that a pathfinder aircraft, 'a single hurrying black moth in the air', showered clusters of red flares which signalled that Wesel had approximately ten minutes to live. Then the Lancasters brought with them 'the cataclysmic unbelievable shock of the strike', when buildings, trees and acres of parkland 'simply detached themselves from the earth' and arced upward like a fountain.

Simultaneously the commandos had launched their armoured boats and were landing on the opposite shore. All that night along the river the reports were coming in of near-bloodless landings.

On 24 March the doyen of living correspondents, Winston Churchill, was there on a hilltop at Xanten to revel in the grand spectacle: a mass assault by 6000 Allied aircraft, dwarfing the mightiest fly-pasts of peacetime. 'I should have liked,' he told Moorehead roundly, 'to have deployed my men in red coats on the plain down there and ordered them to charge.' As an afterthought, he added with zest, 'But now my armies are too vast.'

Suddenly, springing to his feet, Churchill went careering down the hill. 'They're coming,' he shouted, like an excited child. 'They're coming!'

In one of the thousands of planes aloft, a Mitchell bomber, Richard Dimbleby, a microphone clamped tight to his mouth, was shouting above the noise of the engines: 'We are off – full boost now, as fast as we can go ... we are climbing gently into the air, the glider floating steadily behind us ... we are in the air and on our way.' The glider behind him held the BBC's Stanley Maxted, a Canadian veteran of Arnhem, plus a truly precious consignment, a £40,000 miniature transmitting station, designed to give listeners the actual sounds of battle, although Dimbleby was too discreet to say so.

Instead he apologized to his audience: 'I'm sorry if I'm shouting – it is a very tremendous sight.'

'Overhead a thousand express trains went screaming heedlessly by,' Moorehead related, and Dimbleby's was one of them.

Inevitably, with gliders crash-diving through space and the sky blossoming white with parachutes, there were mishaps. One of them involved Dimbleby's own glider, which plunged flaming into an orchard, leaving Maxted with the broken rib that was fast becoming obligatory and a shell splinter over one eye. The £40,000 transmitting station was a write-off. Another involved the *Daily Express*'s Geoffrey Bocca, who was shot five times after a glider landing, largely through trying to rescue a typewriter entrusted to him by UP's Robert Vermillion. (Two years later, in New York, Bocca rang Vermillion out of the blue to apologize profusely.) A third casualty was the accident-prone Robert Capa, who hit the ground as entwined in his own parachute as a trussed turkey. As he cursed furiously in his native Hungarian, a paratrooper nearby was mindful that they had landed on German soil. 'Hey, bud,' he advised Capa, 'them Jewish prayers ain't gonna do you no good here.'

Despite the chaos, the warcos had their own yardstick of a milestone passed. John D'Arcy Dawson realized that General Dempsey had broken all precedent: for the first time in World War Two correspondents had been given freedom to mention individual regiments, though not, of course, names. (The British soldier, by War Office edict, remained 'Tommy Atkins' to the bitter end.) Paul Wyand saw signs that the Germans were acknowledging defeat; an embittered citizen of Wesel spluttered into British Movietone's microphone a line that might have been scripted by the Ministry of Information: 'Goebbels never told us it would be like this.' Cameras were lowered and notebooks put aside as Churchill made his own comment on the situation: unbuttoning his fly he urinated copiously on a bastion of the Siegfried Line.

The last stages of the campaign had moved to German soil, 'and Germany now,' the London *Observer* noted, 'is Heartbreak House.' Towns burned like torches for a night, smouldering for a day, then lay blackened and dead. Great centres like Frankfurt and Mannheim were becoming ghost cities, stark in their architectural wreckage. Yet the advancing warcos, billeting themselves mostly in farmhouses and small hotels, looked in vain for convinced Nazis. Among 62 million Germans, no one could be found who had wholeheartedly supported Adolf Hitler, his plans for world conquest, his mass extermination of ethnic minorities. 'No one is a Nazi,' Martha Gellhorn reported, after scouring the villages around Cologne. 'No one ever was,' and her dispatch mimicked the refrain that had met her on all sides. '"I hid a Jew for six weeks." "I hid a Jew for eight weeks." All God's chillun hid Jews.'

Richard Dimbleby found the same lack of involvement. In the hotel kitchen of one small town, he had called in to hear the BBC's nine o'clock news: his old friend Freddy Grisewood was reading out a long list of captured German towns. As he spelled them out, to a background of tanks rumbling by in the main street, the old hotel-keeper and his family clustered round a map, carefully and without comment marking off each fallen town as it was mentioned. 'There was not one sound or sign of regret on their faces,' Dimbleby told his listeners later. 'No shock, no despair, no alarm ... just as if they were a bunch of neutrals hearing all about somebody else. And indeed, I believe that's what many of these front-line German people are: neutrals in their own country.'

It was Dimbleby, on Sunday, 15 April, who formed the van-guard of the world's press in viewing the greatest horror of all.

Word had reached the press camp at Second Army's advance headquarters that the commander of a German camp a few miles away had offered his surrender: typhus had broken out. 'I couldn't see anything newsworthy in it,' Wynford Vaughan-Thomas con-fessed later, 'but Richard said, "I have a feeling this one's different," and took off in his jeep'.

His way took him on the road from Winsen to Celle, in Lower Saxony, where the blue smoke from many fires hung thickly in the pine woods and the young corn was green in the clearings. 'Speed Five Miles an Hour', warned the signs. 'Dust Spreads Typhus', and suddenly the warm wind brought what the war artist John Groth called 'the honey-on-herring stench of death'.

Although Dimbleby was the first to report on the 60,000 pris-oners in the six-square-mile barbed wire compound called Bergen-Belsen, his heart-cry was no more than an overture. 'You can't tell that on the air,' Vaughan-Thomas expostulated, for Dimbleby, recording his dispatch with the BBC's engineer, Harvey Sarney, had broken down for the first time in his career. 'I must,' Dimbleby had answered. 'I must tell the exact truth, every detail of it, even if the people don't believe me, even if they feel these things should not be told.' But at first, as Vaughan-Thomas had foreseen, an impasse arose. It was the BBC who refused to believe it, or to broadcast it, insisting on confirmation from other sources, so that Dimbleby, in rage and anguish, telephoned the newsroom with an ultimatum: unless his report went through, he would never again broadcast in his life.

But the confirmations, in dispatches charged with what Vaughan-Thomas called 'the controlled fury of an acetylene torch', *were* coming through: dispatches that told of compounds piled with mountainous heaps of putrefying corpses, of ditches choked with bodies, some of them still breathing but without the strength to struggle out from beneath the dead. Tales of the living tearing ragged clothes from the dead to build fires to boil pine needles and roots for soup. Staccato accounts of naked bodies with gaping wounds in their backs and chests where their kidneys, liver and hearts had been hacked away by those who still had strength to use a knife.

'If the heavens were paper and all the water in the world were ink,' a Jewish rabbi told UP's Richard McMillan, 'and all the trees were turned into pens, you could not even then record the sufferings and horrors.' But McMillan, a Western Desert veteran, admitted later that during much of his visit to Belsen he had been forced to peep through his fingers like a frightened child.

'They lie down and they die,' recorded Kemsley's Reginald Thompson dazedly, one of many warcos ushering in the age of the holocaust. 'Now deep into the camp the dead lie in bundles, neat bundles, grotesque limbs in terrible positions ... in truth they are dead before they die.'

'I have seen many terrible sights in the last five years,' Dimbleby was now permitted to tell his listeners, 'but *nothing*, *nothing*, approaching the dreadful interior ... of Belsen.' Alan Moorehead was perhaps the most affected of them all. In the brilliant spring sunshine, under the impassive lizard eyes of the commandant, Joseph Kramer, he found himself 'having no stomach for this sort of thing' – most 'especially when it was not always possible to distinguish men from women, or indeed to determine whether they were human at all'. Handerkerchief to nose, fighting off the stench of ordure, averting his eyes from 'livid straining faces and emaciated arms and legs under the filthy bedclothes', he finally told the Conducting Officer, 'I've had enough of this.' But the captain was pitiless. 'You've got to go through one of the men's huts yet. That's what you're here for.'

In that moment the world of the good war correspondent Moorehead was falling apart. He was telling himself frantically: 'This is not war ... This is timeless and the whole world and all mankind is involved in it ... Why has it happened? How did it happen?'

Yet in truth, as Moorehead acknowledged, Belsen was no more than proof of the total breakdown of the Third Reich: a dumping ground for prisoners from all over Germany as the country approached its death throes, a camp whose pumping plant had been destroyed by bombs and whose food supplies had been strafed by Allied fighters. The true enormities had been perpetuated in Buchenwald, near Weimar, the hometown of Goethe – which Ed Murrow entered with Patton's Third Army on 11 April – and at Dachau, outside Munich – which Martha Gellhorn entered, in the wake of the US Seventh Army, on 30 April.

'He felt inadequate, defeated by his inability to handle what he saw,' Charles Collingwood, a CBS colleague, related of Murrow's reaction to Buchenwald: 'the torture chambers; lampshades of human skin; the piles of clothes, gold teeth, human hair, children's shoes in the thousand'. On 15 April, the Sunday that Dimbleby entered Belsen, Murrow, broadcasting from London, warned his CBS listeners: 'If you are at lunch or if you have no appetite to hear what the Germans have done, now is a good time to switch off the radio.' Those who stayed tuned in did not know how Murrow, giddy with incomprehension, had wandered through Buchenwald pressing a small fortune in dollar bills – the winnings from a poker game – on the living skeletons around him. Nor did they hear how Margaret Bourke-White, a warco of sterner mettle, had leaped into an open grave at a funeral to photograph the minister from her favourite worm's eye view.

Dachau came close to ending the war for Martha Gellhorn. A Polish doctor, five years a prisoner, had talked at length yet with detachment about the experiments he had watched in the hospital. No sooner pose a medical conundrum than a medical experiment followed. How high in the sky could an aviator go without oxygen? The solution: place a man in a closed car and pump it free of oxygen. It took only 800 deaths to prove that no one could survive without oxygen above 36,000 feet.

How long could an aviator survive in water like the English Channel? To solve this problem, 600 prisoners were immersed at varying times, in vats of water chilled to eight degrees below zero. It was proved conclusively that no one could survive more than two and a half hours.

The instructions of PM to their roving correspondent,

Raymond Davies, JEWISH ATROCITY STORIES NOT ACCEPTABLE NEWS MATERIAL, seemed strangely irrelevant now.

Some of Dachau's victims had joined their fellow sufferers at the crematorium – people who had died more easily, in the gas chamber, because they were too weak to work, or more slowly, of sheer starvation. 'There, suddenly, but never to be believed, were the bodies of the dead,' Martha Gellhorn recounted of her first sight of the crematorium. 'They were everywhere ... the bodies were dumped like garbage, rotting in the sun, yellow and nothing but bone, bones grown huge because there was no flesh to cover them, hideous, terrible, agonizing bones and the unendurable smell of death.'

Even as 1945 dawned her faith had been sorely tested. 'Oh, what a world!' she had written to Henry La Cossitt, her editor at *Collier's*. 'To think that Our Lord bothered to die for it!' But Dachau put paid even to that tenuous persuasion. Was she still a believer? she was asked many years later.

'In God? After Dachau?' The question somehow emerged as a monstrous obscenity.

More than ever, in this era, the warcos were existing from day to day. They lived enclosed in their own private worlds. ('Why is it that the story ahead,' wondered Marguerite Higgins of the *New York Herald Tribune*, 'always seems so much more potentially exciting than the story you have just covered?') Events taking pride of place in the world's headlines seemed things that were happening to other people. On 12 April, three days before Belsen, President Roosevelt died of a massive cerebral haemorrhage at Warm Springs, Georgia, and the nation mourned. That same day, the thirty-fourth Vice-President, Harry S. Truman, a dapper ex-haberdasher, became the thirty-third president of the United States. The President was dead: long live the President.

In the light of reality, the post-war world for which Roosevelt had striven seemed largely irrelevant. February had seen him, a sorely ailing man, at the Yalta Conference in the Crimea, together with Churchill and Stalin – just as November 1943 had seen him in the same company at Tehran and January of that year at Casablanca. Some seventy correspondents had covered Casablanca, which had laid down the doctrine of 'unconditional surrender' – 'portentous and hollow,' was Moorehead's verdict – but Tehran and Yalta had been no-go areas, Tehran had preempted Stalin's right to dictate the course of the war; Yalta had produced a fuzzy Declaration on Liberated Europe, which the Russians reneged on within weeks.

As the warcos had long seen it, the politicians laboured to write the scenario but the Red Army was acting out the script. In the process they were also redrawing the map of Europe.

All the old stamping grounds where Clare Hollingworth, Walter Duranty, David Walker and others had watched so sedulously for Axis affiliations – King Carol's Bucharest, King Boris's Sofia, Horthy's Budapest – were already or were soon to become Communist fiefs. Even Prince Paul's Belgrade was under the suzerainty of the Communist guerrilla Josip Broz, better known as Tito, who enjoyed an accommodation with Stalin until 1948.

The halting point of the Red Army would be the eastern bank of the Elbe River, forty-eight miles from Berlin, and it was there that the correspondents attached to General William O. Simpson's Ninth Army met them on Wednesday, 25 April.

Understandably, reactions were mixed. At Yalta, Stalin had emphasized the loss of four million Soviet soldiers – and every Western warco, conscious of the Red Army's sacrifice, was initially primed with goodwill. At the medieval town of Torgau, the meeting point, the *Christian Science Monitor*'s Falstaffian Ronald Maillard Stead succumbed unreservedly to their charms; recognizing a *tovarich* when they saw one, two husky Russian officers commandeered a clinker-built shell from the Torgau Rowing Club, sculling Stead perilously across the Elbe to a picnic of fried eggs, sardines, tinned salmon and spaghetti. British Movietone's Paul Wyand struck even luckier; once he had photographed 'a fat, merry, unshaven major-general' with his men, they produced 'a beautiful blonde silk-stockinged wireless operator with the sort of figure one dreams about'. In the orgy of vodka toasts which followed, with tumblers smashed ritually on the floor following each bumper, a hysterical exchange of cap and uniform badges and wristwatches wound up the session.

Edward Ward, no sooner released from prison camp than he seized up his BBC microphone, reported the same convivial atmosphere; at Torgau, a burly Ukrainian soldier hugged him and kissed him on both cheeks, while other Russians 'fired off mortars and rifles out of sheer joy'. Yet there was another side to the medal. Barely a mile from the scene of his own party, Paul Wyand saw a barrier of barbed wire had sprung up and the cheerful bearded sentry who had waved him on earlier had been replaced by 'a sinister Asiatic', whose rifle was trained menacingly on a fuming party of warcos. Martha Gellhorn, whose politics were well left of centre following the Spanish Civil War, found all her attempts to cross the Elbe and socialize with the Russians were in vain. 'There was no nonsense,' she reported, 'about walking across a few hundred yards of pontoon bridge and fraternizing with your allies.' The only word she knew in Russian was *nyet* – 'but you hear it a lot and afterwards there is no more arguing'.

What the Red Army had they held, and by 1 May it was plain that after a two-day battle they held Berlin, so that all over Germany surrender was in the air. Hitler, it was rumoured, had committed suicide in the *Führerbunker* of the Reichschancellory on 30 April together with his mistress, Eva Braun, although not until July did the former Berlin stalwarts, Pierre Huss of INS and Sigrid Schultz of the *Chicago Tribune* penetrate the capital to confirm the truth of this. But for both of them, at best, it was an unsatisfactory story: too many of their sources feared the Russians and thus could not be named.

Only at Lüneberg Heath, southeast of Hamburg, on 4 May, was the Russian presence an insubstantial shadow. It was here that Montgomery had come to accept the surrender of all German forces in Holland, northeast Germany and Denmark, and it was Montgomery, Moorehead noted, who dominated the proceedings all through, 'rather like a schoolmaster taking an oral examination'. There were to be no frills over the ceremony – ordinary unpainted Post Office pens were used for the signatures – but Montgomery had worked in with Movietone's Paul Wyand until the cramped stuffy tent was 'lighted like a Hollywood film set'. Like any good cameraman, Wyand exulted in the unrehearsed performance of Admiral Hans von Friedeburg, the principal signatory – 'absolute misery and abysmal despair ... superb picture material' – an effect dispelled when a photoflood bulb slipped from its socket and exploded with a bang on the Admiral's bald head.

At Reims, one day later, the situation was more confused – again due, as Charles Christian Wertenbaker and his fellows knew, to the looming Russian presence. It was plain that the hands of Friedeburg and General Alfred Jodl were securely tied: from his headquarters at Flensburg, in Schleswig-Holstein, Grand Admiral Karl Doenitz, to whom Hitler had passed on the torch, would authorize no surrender to the hated Bolsheviks. All that Saturday, as rain bathed northwest Europe and smoke from the railway shunting yards hung motionless over Eisenhower's headquarters, a red-brick technical school, the wrangling continued. Although Major-General Walter Bedell Smith, whose stomach ulcer was paining him, tried the soldier-to-soldier approach, the Germans would not budge.

Finally, towards midnight on the Sunday, Eisenhower lost patience. Either the Germans signed now or he would order his armies to close their ranks and accept no more surrenders. They would be left to the mercy of the Russians. Jodl, for one, saw the light. At 2.39 am on 7 May, the Germans, as Wertenbaker reported, 'gave up to an American general with a pain in his stomach', and Bedell Smith, holding himself stiffly as if to counter that pain, was the first to break the news. He was swinging his swagger stick and as he got into his car he said, aptly if ungrammatically, '*Fini la guerre.*'

Even now, thanks to Josef Stalin's obduracy, the surrender was not official until the Germans had formally yielded to the Russians in Berlin on 8 May. Until that time, all correspondents were bound to secrecy. It was a ban which struck the AP's Edward Kennedy as ludicrous: no security was in question, merely Stalin's *amour-propre*. From his room at the Paris Scribe, Kennedy at once phoned the story to his London office, where a Ministry of Information censor, unconscious of the ban, passed it for transmission to New York. It was the last 'unofficial' scoop of the war in Europe, but since the Machine was still all-powerful, it cost Kennedy dearly: not only the censure of fifty-three colleagues but his accreditation in Europe and his job with AP. To flout the wishes of Josef Stalin was still the worst kind of *lèse majesté*.

Thousands were now willing to surrender – to anyone save the Communists. The lesson of Benito Mussolini in Italy underscored that. Hunted by Communist partisans as he fled north from Salò, he and his mistress, Claretta Petacci, were apprehended, shot out of hand, then hoisted by their feet to the girders of a bombed-out garage in Milan along with fifteen Fascist adherents. The warcos who witnessed this grisly spectacle were puzzled by only one aspect: why had *Il Duce* and Claretta been granted a last night in a cottage with a lakeside view before the execution? When the UP's James Roper put this to one partisan, the man spread his hands in a classic Italian gesture: 'We're all Italians, after all.'

The warcos were now as involved in accepting surrenders as any combatant – 'it was a manhunt with notebooks and cameras,' recalled the *New York Times*'s Richard Johnston. In the forefront of this bloodless battle was Ernest Hemingway, armed, in defiance of the Geneva Convention, with a brace of pistols, but other warcos soon followed suit. Evelyn Irons of the London *Evening Standard* found that when travelling with the Free French Army, revolvers were obligatory; arriving in a small Bavarian village ahead of the Allies, she and three other correspondents forced its surrender at gunpoint.

The *New York Herald Tribune*'s Marguerite Higgins, along with Sergeant Peter Furst of *Stars and Stripes*, whose German was fluent, negotiated the surrender of Augsburg to the 3rd (US) Division after a long-distance telephone call guaranteed: 'You can tell *Herr General* that there will be no resistance.' With most the telling 'quote' came first, the surrender second. Noel Monks who broke off sunbathing on the banks of the Elbe to accept the surrender of Lieutenant-General Kurt Dittmar, the Army High Command's radio spokesman, was swift to ask him: 'When did you realize Germany had lost the war?' Dittmar, who seemingly believed his own propaganda, replied: 'About two days after the landing in Normandy, when Eisenhower had nearly half a million men ashore.' At Flensburg, granted a 'background interview' with Grand Admiral Doenitz, Edward Ward pressed him on the iniquity of camps like Buchenwald. Perhaps truthfully, Doenitz claimed to know nothing about it, but if true, '*dann ist das eine Schweinerei!*'

The greatest coup was when Richard Johnston and Reuters' Arthur Oakshott, a dignified World War One veteran resembling Lord Kitchener, tracked down Field Marshal Albert Kesselring in his five-car train near Rosenheim, Bavaria. Throughout World War Two Kesselring, chunky and scar-faced, had been at the forefront of at least two key campaigns: Chief of the Luftwaffe's Air Fleet Two during the Battle of Britain, and C-in-C, Southern Command, Italy.

It was a meeting that began as a comedy of errors: while Johnston and Oakshott knew they had come to interview Kesselring, the Field Marshal took them for Eisenhower's staff officers, there to negotiate his personal surrender.

The misunderstanding clarified, Kesselring chuckled. He muttered an aside in German. ('The Field Marshal says he is amused,' an aide translated, but Oakshott rendered it as 'Well, bugger me!') For their cheek, the warcos were invited to lunch: ham, cabbage, potatoes, beer and reminiscences.

'Allied air power,' Kesselring mused, that had been the heart of the matter and, thoughtfully, he reached down to pick up his field marshal's baton. 'Six of these I have left behind in the ruins of command posts, thanks to your air forces,' he admitted.

Things being as they were, Johnston suggested, would he yield it up as a souvenir? Kesselring shook his head.

'Sorry,' he replied, 'but I think this is the last I shall ever have. I shall keep it.'

It seemed as civilized a way as any, both men thought, of winding up a war.

X

For The Rest Of My Life, Peace Will Be Unnatural

8 MAY–12 SEPTEMBER 1945

It was the Other War that Ernie Pyle found hard to grasp: Mac-Arthur's war, the war in the southwest Pacific. In retrospect, Eisenhower's war had been easy: French towns with names like Ste Mère-Église and St Lo had resisted then toppled, and that was the way it had been until September 1944, when Pyle returned to the States. By contrast, the Pacific war was like a combat on another planet. It was, Pyle tried to explain, a 'war of vast water distances', which involved 'making gigantic bases of each group of islands we take, in order to build up supplies and preparations for future invasions farther on'.

Friends had sought to dissuade him from the venture. 'Go home and stay home,' Omar Bradley had advised him when Paris fell; he saw Pyle's chances as 'about used up'. Even so the Pacific was akin to a duty, for no one boosted the fighting man's morale like Ernie Pyle. At his urging, from May 1944 Congress had granted all US soldiers 50 per cent extra pay for combat service, and this would always be known as 'The Ernie Pyle Bill'. And to his dismay the reclusive Pyle had found himself a living American legend. Two secretaries were needed to cope with the influx of mail. Hollywood was filming his life, *The Story of GI Joe*, with Burgess Meredith cast as Ernie. His house in Albuquerque, New Mexico, had become a shrine, with tourists arriving to gawk as early as 6.30 am.

All this had reacted badly on Geraldine, clinging to a marriage that she realized was beyond repair. She sensed, David Nichols wrote, that 'Ernie had abandoned her years before to marry his

196

audience,' and her answer was to lock herself in the bathroom and hack at her throat with a pair of scissors, slicing at her left breast and wrist with a razorblade. It was a cry for help to which Pyle could only respond negatively: while 'Jerry' was undergoing thirty days shock therapy, he was receiving honorary doctorates in New Mexico and Indiana. Their last night together was spent at Ciro's, the Hollywood nightclub, after which a nurse escorted 'Jerry' back to Albuquerque. Pyle was leaving for the Marianas, to answer other heartcries: from readers in Peoria, Illinois, and Keokuk, Iowa.

There was much for him to explain. The Mariana Islands, as he discovered, were fully 1500 miles away from the Philippines, China and Japan. The climate was good, the native Chamorros were 'nice people', the troops were healthy, living in Quonset huts, and it was all a world away from the fetid savagery of Guadalcanal. The war was so monotonous that men sometimes went 'pineapple crazy'. Yet the geography was mind-boggling, for as MacArthur's biographer, William Manchester, admitted, 'Egypt and Algiers evoked memories of schooldays, but who had heard of Yap? Or of Ioribaiwa? What was the difference between New Caledonia, New Guinea ... and the New Hebrides?'

'You plan something for months,' Pyle told his public, following a briefing from an anonymous admiral, 'and then finally the great day comes when you launch your plans, and then it is days or weeks before the attack happens, because it takes that long to get there.'

One operation planned long before Pyle arrived in the Pacific theatre was Iwo Jima, which lay 750 miles from the Marianas but only 750 miles from Tokyo. Following a seventy-two-hour bombardment by the US Fifth Fleet, a task force headed by the Marines went ashore on Monday, 9 February: the first stage of a thirty-six day assault against an island only eight miles square – 'the most densely populated slice of real estate in the world,' one warco noted. But Iwo had to be secured, as one more unsinkable aircraft carrier, an awesome snail-paced advance in which the first men ashore sank to their calves in black volcanic ash. 'Tanks were clustered,' remembers *Times*'s Robert Sherrod, 'like so many black beetles struggling to move on tar paper,' and over all hung the pungent sulphurous odour of rotting eggs.

For four days, the bitter bone of contention was an extinct volcano, Mount Suribachi, 556 feet high, which the marines dubbed 'Son-a-bitchie', for Suribachi alone, following Japanese habit, had 1000 fixed defence points. At dawn on 23 February, forty marines, knifing their way into pillboxes and underground galleries, reached the summit; at 10.30 am, an American flag secured to a long piece of iron pipe was hoisted by a lieutenant and five men. At noon, when a larger flag was secured from an LST, Joe Rosenthal, the plump little AP photographer, duly ascended the summit, using another group of marines as stand-ins, and shot a picture that went round the world.

Elsewhere events had moved as swiftly as an unravelling spool of film. Before dawn on 10 January, a thousand anchors had churned the waters of Lingayen Gulf, on the main Philippine island of Luzon, to white froth: with one giant step, 100,000 men of MacArthur's troops, to be followed by a backup force of a further 100,000, had been transported 2000 miles from Leyte, where MacArthur had returned in October. Then on 1 February, MacArthur had instructed the First Cavalry Division: 'Get to Manila! Go around the Japs, bounce off the Japs, but get to Manila!' The climax to this 120-mile hell-for-leather dash across Japanese-held rice paddies and ploughed fields was a thirty-day battle for the city, which *Life*'s Carl Mydans photographed from his old internment camp, Santo Tomás. 'The US Marines were burdened with few prison cages,' was his predictable report.

There had equally been little need for stockades on Iwo Jima, which by 27 March, the day the island yielded, had cost the Americans 28,648 killed, missing and wounded. 'I hope to God that we don't have to go on any more of these screwy islands,' one wounded marine was heard to gripe, but that hope was unfounded. There was one more 'screwy island' yet; its name was Okinawa, and it marked the end of Ernie Pyle's war.

That was on Easter Sunday, 1 April, and it also marked the last and greatest land battle of the Pacific war: an eighty-three-day conflict which cost the Americans 49,000 casualties, and a yardstick by which all future Japanese resistance potential would be measured. Yet oddly, this was not an aspect of the invasion that featured much in Pyle's dispatches. Put ashore with the seventh wave – no correspondents were permitted to land before the fifth – he reported: 'Never before had I seen an invasion beach like Okinawa ... There wasn't a dead or wounded man in our sector ... There wasn't a single burning vehicle. Not a single boat lying wrecked on the reef or shoreline.'

Instead he wrote glowingly of the pre-invasion turkey dinner, of a first lunch ashore of turkey wings and oranges. 'Brother, I've had all the excitement I need for a lifetime,' he told the marines he landed with. 'This kind of invasion suits me fine.' One of his columns featured PFC Ben Glover, of Baird, Texas, who had adopted a white nanny goat as a pet. Soon scores of marines had followed suit. The Japanese were thought to be in the far hills of the island, but even on 16 April, moving inland, Pyle's idyllic picture remained constant: 'There wasn't a shot nor a warlike sound within hearing.'

On 18 April, Pyle went ashore on tiny Ie Shima, an island west of Okinawa which the marines had secured two days earlier. He was travelling in a jeep with four soldiers, scouting out a command-post site for the 77th Division. Suddenly a sniper opened up and all five men dived for cover in the roadside ditches. After a moment Pyle raised his head, solicitous, as always, for the GI's wellbeing. The sniper's bullet hit him in the right temple.

He was one of the thirty-seven American correspondents killed, together with 112 wounded, in the course of World War Two, but unlike the others Pyle had kept a testament. It was his last column, still folded in his pocket, and perhaps 'Jerry', who was to die of uremia in November, had been in his mind, as he wrote it, the wife whose heart-cry he could never assuage. 'The companionship of two and a half years of war and misery is a spouse that tolerates no divorce. Such companionship finally becomes a part of one's soul, and it cannot be obliterated.'

If he had never filed another line, that would have said it all.

The Other War was marking time in Burma, too. It had come alive to a degree after months of stagnation as 1945 dawned; in January Akyab fell, and farther to the north Lieutenant-General Sir William Slim's 'forgotten' Fourteenth Army crossed the Irrawaddy River in February. Before the end of March, they had reached Mandalay, seizing Meiktila en route. On 3 May Rangoon fell, and along with other correspondents I recorded bomb damage, civilian morale, black-market rates: the small change of war.

In the havens frequented by Calcutta warcos, Spence's Bar and the *Phoenix* mess, where I then lived, on Chittaranjan Avenue, the talk reverted time and again to the question posed by the *Spectator*'s Gerald Hanley, a year earlier: 'How are we to defeat these people?'

Unknown to any of us, one correspondent already had an inkling. In April, William Leonard Laurence, a fifty-seven-year-old Science Editor on the *New York Times*, had been called aside by his managing editor, the cocky little Edwin L. James; a General Leslie

R. Groves was on his way to see Laurence. Groves was plainly aware
that on 5 May, 1940, Laurence's exclusive story, covering seven
Times columns, had disclosed how German and American physicists
were engaged in a race against time to develop atomic energy from
an isotope of uranium. On 7 September Laurence had followed up
with a *Saturday Evening Post* article, 'The Atom Gives Up' – all
copies of which had been impounded, late in 1942, by the FBI.

What General Groves now sought from Edwin James was permission to 'borrow' Laurence for work on a top-secret job. The
permission being granted, what Laurence in turn sought was the
freest of hands. 'If you want me to do any writing,' he bargained, 'I
must be given access to first-hand sources.'

A tense, scholarly little man, who rarely found time to visit the
barber, Laurence now vanished from the *Times*'s city room. To fool
both his wife and his colleagues, a London byline was arranged.
In reality, Laurence had been plucked without trace into General
Groves's top-secret empire, the two-billion-dollar Manhattan
Project, whose focal points, Oak Ridge, Tennessee, Richland, Washington, and Los Alamos, New Mexico, were geared to the construction of the atomic bomb.

'It was Buck Rogers stuff,' was Laurence's later comment on
the enterprise which might have annihilated every physicist at work.
'I got a tremendous kick out of it.'

On 13 July, while correspondents in Calcutta, Rangoon and
New Delhi were still cooling their heels, Laurence had been two
months with the Manhattan Project. On that day he wrote a letter
to Edwin James, which read in part: 'The story is much bigger than
I could imagine, fantastic, bizarre, fascinating and terrifying . . . The
world will not be the same after the day of the Big Event. A new era
in civilization will have started.' The letter was passed to the *Times*
publisher, Arthur Hays Sulzberger, uncle of the war correspondent
Cyrus T., who annotated it tersely: 'This looks like IT.'

Four days later, as the only war correspondent behind the scenes
of this apocalyptic pilot scheme, Laurence, his eyes shielded by
welder's goggles, was waiting in a control tower five miles from
Ground Zero at Alamagordo, New Mexico, where the bomb, code-
named 'Fat Man' in Winston Churchill's honour, was encased in a
steel cage. 'From the east,' ran Laurence's report, 'came the first
faint sight of dawn. And just at that instant there rose as if from the
bowels of the earth a light not of this world, the light of many suns
in one . . . On that moment hung eternity. Time stood still . . .'

From Albuquerque, the AP Bureau shortly afterward released an anodyne cover-up story: 'An ammunition base exploded early today in a remote area of the Alamagordo Air Base reservation, producing a brilliant flash and blast, which was reported to have been observed as far away as Gallup, 235 miles northwest.'

Laurence all unwittingly now measured up to the classic definition of a scoop-winner by the veteran Alistair Cooke: 'Only by the wildest freak is a reporter ... actually present at a single convulsion of history.' Armed with sealed orders, he arrived on Tinian Island in the Marianas, confident that he would be the sole reporter aboard the first atomic bomber, the *Enola Gay*. The target, dependent on the weather, was to be Hiroshima, Kokura or Nagasaki. He was too late. The *Enola Gay* – with a full crew, but no press observer – was scheduled to take off on its 3000-mile round trip at 2.45 am on 6 August.

President Truman's call for surrender, issued to Japan on 26 July, had thus far been met with silence – and the decision to drop the bomb, Laurence learned, was prompted by the example of Okinawa. Any assault on Japan, it was estimated, would be resisted by an army five million strong backed by perhaps 5000 *kamikaze* planes. Such an assault, dragging on until late in 1946, could result in a million American casualties. Thus at 8.16 am on 6 August, the atom bomb called 'Little Boy' blew Hiroshima apart.

But Laurence's moment was still to come. On the evening of 8 August, over a beer in the Officers' Club on Tinian, he learned that he was to fly at 3.50 am next day as the chronicler of the second atomic bombing mission. (In event of capture, an embossed card stated, he ranked as a full colonel.) In one of two B–29s accompanying a bomber called *The Great Artiste*, he was over Nagasaki at 12.01 pm when a 'tremendous blast wave struck our ship and made it tremble from nose to tail ...' followed by 'a giant pillar of purple fire, ten thousand feet high, shooting skyward with enormous speed ...' To his colleagues, from that time onward, Laurence would always be 'Atomic Bill'.

In Calcutta, where I was one of fifty correspondents assigned to the invasion of Singapore, the reaction in the *Phoenix* mess was dismissive. 'But they've just dropped a couple of bloody great bombs. The war's over!'

That much was conjecture, but six days later at noon on 15 August, 100 million Japanese heard for the first time in their lives the voice of the godlike emperor Hirohito addressing his 'good and loyal subjects' in a broadcast recorded the previous day: 'We have decided to effect a settlement of the present situation by resorting to an extraordinary measure ...' Already on 10 August a Foreign Ministry telegram accepting Truman's ultimatum – provided that the Emperor's status was not affected – had winged its way to the capitals of the Allied powers.

But despite the Emperor's declaration, what weight would it carry with the Japanese fighting man? None of them, from general to private, had ever heard his voice, but all of them knew that they were not defeated. In the Rangoon press camp, a broken-down merchant's house on Golden Valley Road, there was much speculation when we reassembled on the night of Sunday, 26 August. As an unpromising augury, the Japanese surrender envoy, Lieutenant General Takazo Numata, Chief of Staff, Southern Army, along with his aides, travelling in 'Topsy' transports marked with green crosses, had arrived two hours late at Mingaladon airfield. At best Numata was empowered to surrender only the 262,000 square miles of Burma.

No American saw this corner of the British Empire as newsworthy, but Fleet Street had sent top talent. Ian Morrison of *The Times*, was preeminent, slight, blue-eyed, a chain smoker of cheroots, together with his friend, the *Daily Telegraph*'s Christopher 'The Bishop' Buckley, eyes twinkling through gold-rimmed spectacles, a true Trollopean. (Both men were killed when their jeep hit a land-mine in Korea on 12 August 1950.) Tom Driberg, until recently the gossip columnist 'William Hickey', had flown in for the *Daily Express*; George Edinger, uncomplaining though handicapped by a crippled foot, was there for Reuters; Ronnie Noble, still grumbling about the film footage he had lost at Tobruk, covered for Universal News. The *Daily Mail*'s Noel Monks, plump, pink and alert as a pointer, was looking in reasonable shape for a man who had just lost his wife, Mary Welsh of *Time*, to Ernest Hemingway; laying heavy siege to Mary after the liberation of Paris, Hemingway had compounded the injury by setting up Noel's portrait photograph on a lavatory bowl at the Paris Ritz and blasting both to smithereens with a German machine pistol.

Some of these men had been intermittently in the field since the Abyssinian war of 1935, but no one was prepared to venture more than intelligent speculation on Burma and the Japanese. Bats were whirling eerily in the rafters of the Durbar Hall at Government House at 1 am on 28 August when the Japanese, under blazing arc lights 'as unreal as a pantomime glade', finally did surrender to Lieutenant-General Frederick 'Boy' Browning, Mountbatten's Chief of Staff, in a ceremony of almost total silence. But in the thirty-six hours of tension that had passed awaiting the Japanese decision, none of us had showered, shaved or removed our clothes.

If Burma had been in doubt, so too was Singapore. As our convoy wound its way down the Strait of Malacca, and the little clusters of black balls marked with a yellow flag showed that we followed the path of the minesweepers, All-India Radio, from Calcutta, told us that General Itagaki, the area commander, was determined to defend Singapore to the end. The brigadier who briefed us in the wardroom on the evening of 4 September stressed much the same point. It had not yet been possible to evacuate all the Japanese troops over the Johore Causeway. 'At the moment there are still 60,000 unbeaten troops on Singapore Island. Whether there'll be trouble or not we don't know. For the time being you will move nowhere without the escort of armed troops. That is all, gentlemen.'

No warco, of course, failed to notice that All-India Radio signed off that evening with 'Good Night, Sweet Dreams, Good Night'.

The end, as so often, was pure anticlimax. Next morning, as Punjabis and Dogra troops sprang from the landing barges, deploying in quick snaking movements across the quayside at Keppel Harbour, with the East Indies Fleet standing by, there was no hint of opposition. The Japanese, lined up in solid phalanxes along the docks, watched with stolid disapproval, like servants at a party thrown by *nouveau-riche* hosts. What followed was an orgy of 'liberation', Singapore-style: the only connotations were emotional. The Cathay Building, the city's only skyscraper, was liberated and the fourth floor became the press camp, just as in 1942. All of us liberated Changi Gaol, where the male POWs were housed. Together with the urbane Marquess of Donegall, of the *Sunday Dispatch*, I helped to liberate Sime Road Camp, the women's prison. Noel Monks disappeared over the Causeway to liberate the Sultan of Johore. With memories of Hemingway at the Paris Ritz, I and my cameraman, Joe Waddell, a laconic Texan formerly with the Scripps-Howard chain, 'liberated' Raffles Hotel, with its echoes of Maugham and Kipling. Our reward was a suite apiece, by courtesy of the management, for as long as we cared to stay. But after side trips to Hong Kong, Shanghai, Saigon and Bangkok, I was off to cover the Indonesian war of independence.

A fine irreverence prevailed. At Mountbatten's Government House press conference, following the official surrender on 12 September, cocktails flowed as freely as questions. Asked what he planned to do with the ceremonial pen, Mountbatten replied, 'Hang it on the lavatory wall at Broadlands.' Waddell, who had formerly been Mountbatten's personal photographer, adjudged that 'Photogenic Lou' was in top form.

Word came from Tokyo that the mood there, although controlled, was tense. As Russell Brines of AP emphasized, it was the first time in history that a defeated country had surrendered by radio and aeroplane. It was also the first time that the victors flew in to occupy an enemy terrain without having fought for it. Millions of Japanese citizens, who had been ready to repel the invaders with bamboo spears or to form 'Sherman Carpets' over which the tanks would roll, must now accept that an era was ending. Some could not accept it. On 11 September the former Premier Hideki Tojo attempted *hara-kiri* on his living room sofa in the Setagaya district of Tokyo. Inevitably a press gang of warcos, including Clark Lee and Graham Stanford of the *Daily Mail*, were on tap to stay his hand; Tojo survived to face both trial and execution.

The true surrender, as both Lee and Brines reported, had come on Sunday 2 September, aboard the 45,000-ton battleship USS *Missouri*, eighteen miles offshore in Tokyo Bay. It was a vessel bristling with scaffolding erected for warcos and cameramen – fittingly, in a ritual that MacArthur ensured lasted a full eighteen minutes. In contrast to the tall silk hats and morning coats worn by the Japanese delegates, Brines reported that the General wore no tie, no decorations, no sword. The ceremony over, a vast armada of 1900 Allied planes, B–29s and carriers, swept over the warship from the south, and MacArthur, facing a battery of microphones, proclaimed: 'The entire world is quietly at peace.'

Back in Singapore, it was becoming plain that this peace had been purchased at a price. For more than a year Wilfred Burchett, whose byline identified him as 'Peter', had been Arthur Christiansen's *Daily Express* stalwart in the Pacific, accredited to Admiral Chester Nimitz of the Pacific fleet, island-hopping from the Carolines to Leyte Gulf. On 6 August, queueing in a Marine chow-line for lunch on Okinawa, Burchett, a radically minded Australian, heard the radio crackle out the first news of Hiroshima. '[That] would be my priority objective should I ever get to Japan,' he noted, and exactly one month later, a *Daily Express* headline, carrying Burchett's byline, proclaimed:

THE ATOMIC PLAGUE
I Write This As a Warning To The World

From Okinawa to Hiroshima had been no easy transit. MacArthur had placed all southern Japan off limits, to concentrate press coverage on the prison camps of the north, and what one jaded source called the 'Look-Mom-I'm-free' stories. From Tokyo to Hiroshima was a twenty-four-hour train journey, which Burchett undertook in a compartment crammed with hostile Japanese officers. But once at Hiroshima, a letter of introduction to the Domei news agency representative, Mr Nakamura, plus a gift of US Navy rations, brought results. Across a devastated city, 'as if a giant rake had scarified the soil', Burchett was driven to the Communications Hospital, the only one surviving. Along with the hospital chief Dr Gen Katsube, he saw ward after ward of patients 'terribly emaciated' who 'gave off a nauseating odour which almost halted me at the first door'. Others had large, suppurating third-degree burns. 'We know that something is killing off the white corpuscles,' Dr Katsube explained, which was Burchett's first intimation of radiation sickness. 'And there is nothing we can do about it ... Every patient carried in here as a patient is carried out as a corpse.' He told Burchett passionately: 'I was trained in the United States. I believed in civilization ... But how can Christians do what you have done here?'

Despite vehement denials by MacArthur's headquarters, Burchett with the aid of the local *Express* man, Henry Keys, who contrived to bypass the censor, had secured the war's last scoop. It was a story to dumbfound not only his editor but his proprietor as well. Should the bomb, Beaverbrook asked Christiansen, ever have been dropped at all?

'The first casualty when war comes,' Senator Hiram Johnson, Governor of California, had warned when America entered World War One in 1917, 'is truth.' Had that condemnation applied equally to World War Two?

In retrospect, few correspondents thought that it had. True, scores of stories deemed likely to cause what the British Home Office called 'alarm and despondency' did not reach the front pages at the time. Yet over the years almost all the great unpalatable truths *did* emerge – slowly enough to secure reputations now safe in retirement. And all along warcos like Moorehead, Reynolds, Pyle and Martha Gellhorn had kept faith with the infantryman and the hapless civilian, recording their sufferings theatre by theatre, year by year. In the vernacular of a later day, the most reported war in history had been 'told like it was'.

From Berlin, the war's youngest correspondent, twenty-year-old Tom Pocock, of *The Leader* magazine reported frankly on a degraded city, where most undernourished German soldiers lacked teeth, yet where Allied officers, by contrast, cleaned their teeth with hock rather than with polluted water; where sex could be had for five cigarettes, though the sewers were ruptured beyond repair and thousands of corpses rotted under the rubble. It was also a deeply divided city, as Richard Dimbleby reported forthrightly after a Red Army patrol in the Russian sector had marched him into their command post at gunpoint and held him for twenty minutes. 'Without cooperation and some degree of trust,' he maintained in a broadcast that then caused a storm of outrage, 'we can hope for nothing for the future. At the moment, that trust is lacking ... there is a barrier of suspicion and reserve. It is rather like trying to make friends with a fellow you can't see on the other side of a high wall.'

At Fulton, Missouri, on 5 March 1946 Winston Churchill, too, remarked on that 'high wall': to Churchill it was the Iron Curtain. Those 'splendid fellows' Dimbleby had met in Tehran four years earlier had assumed a different guise.

Few correspondents in the autumn of 1945 felt nostalgia for the past. At heart they had been romantics, and the cost in illusions had been too great. As far back as April 1940, disillusion had been apparent. 'Earlier wars were like boxing,' Ed Murrow had complained on the eve of the invasion of Norway, 'hitting only with the fists and above the belt. This one is rapidly reaching the point where nothing is barred – teeth, feet, heads, toes and fingers will be used by all belligerents; anything to get at a vulnerable part of the opponents' anatomy.' Five years later the disillusion had become total. 'There are white crosses and scrap iron scattered round the world,' Murrow reflected, 'and already some of the place names that will appear in the history books are fading from memory.'

Six years of anguish had trespassed too largely on human hope. Young men had been struck down, boundaries had been swept aside, loyalties had faltered. The whole world, from the Arctic to the southern Pacific, had learned to fear, to suspect and to hate. Everywhere there had been symptoms of insanity. Saxons had fought against Anglo-Saxons and destroyed their monuments; Orientals had fought against Orientals; ally had turned against ally. Trust had died.

More than six million souls – Jews, Russians, political 'criminals' – had perished, in the slave labour camps, the extermination camps, the 'guinea-pig' camps. Many lessons had been learned, and most of them were negative. An age of innocence had ended: there was no choice for mankind but to grope ahead into the atomic age.

The warcos, who had seen more than most, felt too keenly to share in the worldwide jubilation of VE Day and VJ Day. 'I just want to go and sit in a corner and thank God it's all ending,' was Dimbleby's reaction. Moorehead and Clifford, offered a trip with the Seventh Armoured Division into the streets of defeated Berlin, knew not a second's hesitation: they turned it down. Four years back they would have rejoiced in the breakneck race for the Brandenburger Tor, the scoops, the plaudits from The Desk. But now? 'We could not bear to see another ruined city. We no longer possessed the necessary emotions for a victory parade.'

Cecil Brown, perhaps, had summarized it best, within a year of the sinking of HMS *Repulse* and his escape from the South China Sea. 'For the rest of my life,' he predicted, 'peace will be unnatural. Forever in my nostrils will be the smell of death. Always there will be in my ears the scream of Stukas and always in my eyes the crash of bombs ... Forever there will be in my heart the lust to kill evil men, the consuming desire for vengeance against men who had sown misery in this world.'

And yet, and yet ...

By November 1946, the war seemed light years away. I was editing *Town and Country*, a magazine which had briefly been the dreamchild of Lord Beaverbrook, from an office at the Temple Bar end of Fleet Street. It was next-door to the office, in the Kardomah Café, that I met up by chance over coffee with two old colleagues, Noel Monks and Graham Stanford, both still with the *Daily Mail*.

Our talk was all of another freebooter, O'Dowd Gallagher. He, we marvelled, had the luck that warcos need: on 22 July ninety Arabs, Jews and Britons had been killed when the Stern gang blew up a wing of the King David Hotel, Jerusalem. But not O'Dowd: although hurled across his room, he had survived to make the front page of next morning's *Mail*.

That was his style, we said. Hadn't he, when Pembroke Stephens, the *Daily Telegraph*'s correspondent, was shot in the head and killed in 1937 during the last day of the Chinese stand outside Shanghai, written the story and sent it not to his own paper, then the *Express*, but to the *Telegraph*? 'I couldn't,' he had explained, 'scoop him on his own obituary.'

And not knowing that Korea and Vietnam were yet to come we were silent and wistful, thinking how splendid those days had been.

'The trouble is,' Noel said soberly, 'Nobody's killing anybody anywhere any more.'

Bibliography

Ardizzone, Edward, *Baggage To The Enemy*, London: John Murray, 1940.
Diary of a War Artist, London: Jonathan Cape, 1974.
Arenstam, Arved, *Tapestry of a Débâcle*, (trans. E. Neville Hart), London: Constable, 1942.
Auren, Sven, *Signature Tune*, London: Hammond and Hammond, 1943.
The Tricolour Flies Again, London: Hammond and Hammond, 1946.
Austin, A. B., *We Landed At Dawn*, London: Victor Gollancz, 1943.
Bach, Julian, Jr., 'De Gaulle', in *Life* Magazine, New York, July 28, 1941.
Baillie, Hugh, *High Tension*, London: Werner Laurie, 1960.
Baker, Carlos, *Ernest Hemingway: A Life Story*, London: William Collins, 1969.
Balfour, Michael, *Propaganda In War, 1939–45*, London: Routledge Kegan Paul, 1979.
Baume, Eric, *I've Lived Another Year*, London: George G. Harrap, 1942.
Bayles, William D., 'Wartime Germany', in *Life* Magazine, New York, January 7, 1940.
'Lisbon: Europe's Bottleneck', in *Life* Magazine, April 28, 1941.
Postmarked Berlin, London: Jarrolds, 1942.
Beattie, Edward W, *Passport To War*, London: Peter Davies, 1943.
Belden, Jack, *Retreat with Stilwell*, London: Cassell, 1943.
Bennett, Lowell, *Assignment To Nowhere: the Battle for Tunisia*, New York: The Vanguard Press, 1943.
Berger, Meyer, *The Story of The New York Times*, New York: Simon and Schuster, 1951.
Bess, Demaree, 'Our Frontier On The Danube', in the *Saturday Evening Post*, Philadelphia, May 24, 1941.

'And After Hitler ...?', in the *Saturday Evening Post*, September 13, 1941.

'Our Underground War in France', in the *Saturday Evening Post*, January 3, 1942.

Bessie, Simon Michael, *Jazz Journalism*, New York: E. P. Dutton, 1938.

Blundy, David, 'The Scotsman Who Became The Voice of America', in the *Sunday Telegraph*, London, August 9, 1987.

Boothe, Clare, 'Der Tag in Brussels', in *Life* Magazine, New York, May 19, 1940.

'Europe In The Spring', in *Life*, July 29, 1940.

European Spring, London: Hamish Hamilton, 1941.

'MacArthur of the Far East', in *Life*, December 8, 1941.

Bourdan, Pierre, *Carnet des Jours d'Attente*, Paris: P. Trémois, 1945.

Carnet de Retour avec la Division Leclerc, Paris: Plon, edn of 1965.

Bourke-White, Margaret, *Shooting the Russian War*, New York: Simon and Schuster, 1943.

Brant, Irving, *New Life in Poland*, London: Dennis Dobson, 1946.

Brendon, Piers, *The Life And Death of the Press Barons*, London: Secker and Warburg, 1982.

Brines, Russell, *MacArthur's Japan*, Philadelphia: J. B. Lippincott, 1948.

Bridson, D. G., *Prospero and Ariel: The Rise and Fall of Radio*, London: Victor Gollancz, 1971.

Brock, Ray, *Nor Any Victory*, New York: Reynal and Hitchcock, 1942.

Brome, Vincent, *Confessions Of A Writer*, London: Hutchinson, 1970.

Brown, Cecil, *Suez To Singapore*, New York: Random House, 1942.

'The Germans Are Coming', in the *Saturday Evening Post*, Philadelphia, August 23, 1941.

Brown, David, (with Bruner, W. Richard) *I Can Tell It Now*, New York: E. P. Dutton, 1964.

How I Got That Story, New York: E. P. Dutton, 1967.

Buckley, Christopher, *The Road To Rome*, London: Hodder and Stoughton, 1945.

Greece and Crete, London: HMSO, 1952.

Five Ventures, London: HMSO, 1954.

Burchett, Wilfred, *At The Barricades*, London: Quartet Books, 1980.

Burman, Ben Lucien, 'Free France On The Congo', in the *Reader's Digest*, Pleasantville, New York, August, 1941.

Burns, Eugene, *Then There Was One*, New York: Harcourt, Brace, 1944.

Busch, Noel, 'England At War', in *Life*, New York: January 1, 1940.

Busvine, Richard, *Gullible's Travels*, London: Constable, 1945.

Byford-Jones, Wilfrid, *The Greek Trilogy*, London: Hutchinson, 1946.

Caldwell, Erskine, *Moscow Under Fire*, London: Hutchinson, 1942.

Canham, Erwin D., *Commitment to Freedom: The Story of the Christian Science Monitor*, Boston: Houghton Mifflin, 1958.

Capa, Robert, *Slightly Out Of Focus*, New York: Henry Holt, 1947.

Capell, Richard, *Simiomata*, London: Macdonald, 1946.

Carey, John (ed.), *The Faber Book of Reportage*, London: Faber and Faber, 1987.

Carlson, Oliver (with Ernest Sutherland Bates), *Hearst, Lord of San Simeon*, New York: The Viking Press, 1936.

Carpenter, Iris, *No Woman's World*, Boston: Houghton Mifflin, 1946.

Carroll, Wallace, *We're in This With Russia*, Boston: Houghton Mifflin, 1942.

Casey, Robert J., *Torpedo Junction*, London: Jarrolds, 1944.

Cassidy, Henry C. *Moscow Dateline, 1941–1943*, London: Cassell, 1943.

Childs, Marquis W., 'The President's Best Friend', in the *Saturday Evening Post*, Philadelphia, April 19 – April 26, 1941.

Christiansen, Arthur, *Headlines All My Life*, London: William Heinemann, 1961.

Clark, Russell S., *An End To Tears*, Sydney, NSW: Peter Huston, 1946.

Clifford, Alexander, *Crusader*, London: George G. Harrap, 1942.

Three Against Rommel, London: George G. Harrap, 1943.

Collier, Richard, 'Six Years Was Too Long', in the *Morning Standard*, Bombay: August 29, 1945.

'Back To Singapore', in *Phoenix*, Calcutta: September 8, 1945.

'Journey To Surrender', in the *Sunday Standard*, Bombay: September 30 – November 25, 1945.

'Bloodshed In Sourabaya', in *Phoenix*, Calcutta: December 1, 1945.

'I.N.A.: Are These Guilty Men?', in the *Morning Standard*, Bombay: November 12, 1945.

'Goodbye Kaladan', in *Phoenix*, January 19, 1946.

Collins, Larry (with Dominique Lapierre), *Is Paris Burning?*, London: Victor Gollancz, 1965.

Congdon, Don (ed.), *Combat: War In The Pacific*, London: Mayflower Books, 1965.

Cooper, Kent, *Barriers Down*, New York: Farrar and Rinehart, 1942.

Kent Cooper and The Associated Press, New York: Random House, 1959.

Courtney, W. B., 'Panzer Diary', in *Collier's* Magazine, New York, July 19 – July 26, 1941.

Cowles, Virginia, *Looking For Trouble*, London: Hamilton Hamilton, 1941.

Cox, Geoffrey. *The Red Army Moves*, London: Victor Gollancz, 1941.

Cudlipp, Hugh, *Publish and Be Damned! The Astonishing Story of The Daily Mirror*, London: Andrew Dakers, 1953.

Curie, Eve *Journey Among Warriors*, London: William Heinemann, 1943.

Daniell, Raymond, *Civilians Must Fight*, New York: Doubleday, Doran, 1941.

Davies, Raymond Arthur, *Odyssey Through Hell*, New York: L. B. Fischer, 1946.

Dawson, John D'Arcy, *Tunisian Battle*, London: Macdonald, 1943.

European Victory, London: Macdonald, 1946.

Delmer, Sefton, *Trail Sinister: An Autobiography, Vol. I*, London: Secker and Warburg, 1961.

Denny, Harold, *Behind Both Lines*, London: Michael Joseph, 1943.

De Rochemont, Richard, 'France Takes Her Stand', in *Life*, New York, June 17, 1940.

Deuel, Wallace, *People Under Hitler*, London: Lindsay Drummond, 1942.

Dew, Gwen, *Prisoner of the Japs*, London: Hutchinson, 1944.

Dimbleby, Jonathan, *Richard Dimbleby*, London: Hodder and Stoughton, 1975.

Dimbleby, Richard, *The Frontiers Are Green*, London: Hodder and Stoughton, 1943.

Dos Passos, John, *Tour of Duty*, Boston: Houghton Mifflin, 1946.

Downing, Rupert, *If I Laugh*, London: George G. Harrap, 1940.

Driberg, Tom, *Beaverbrook*, London: Weidenfeld and Nicolson, 1956.

Duranty, Walter, *The Kremlin And The People*, London: Hamish Hamilton, 1942.

Elson, Robert T., *Time, Inc.*, New York: Atheneum, 1968.

Fabricius, Johan, *Java Revisited*, London: William Heinemann, 1947.

Fisher, John, 'I First Saw The Ruins of Dunkerque', in *Life*, New York, June 27, 1940.

Flannery, Harry W. 'Germany Faces A Five-Year War', in the *Saturday Evening Post*, Philadelphia, December 27, 1941.

Assignment To Berlin, London: Michael Joseph, 1942.

Fleet Street: The Inside Story of Journalism, London: Macdonald, 1966. Anonymous.

Foster, Reginald, *Dover Front*, London: Secker and Warburg, 1941.

Fredborg, Arvid, *Behind The Steel Wall*, London: George G. Harrap, 1944.

Friedrich, Otto, *Decline And Fall*, London: Michael Joseph, 1972.

Gallagher, O'Dowd, *Retreat In The East*, London: George G. Harrap, 1942.

Gallagher, Wes, *Back Door To Berlin*, New York: Doubleday, Doran, 1943.

Gander, Marsland, *After These Many Quests,* London: Macdonald, 1949.

Gellhorn, Martha, *The Face of War*, London: Rupert Hart-Davis, 1959.

Travels With Myself And Another, London: Allen Lane, 1978.

Gervasi, Frank, 'Hell's Corner', in *Collier's* Magazine, New York: May 3, 1941.

'Hell From On High', in *Collier's* Magazine, July 26, 1941.

'Turkish Toss-Up', in *Collier's* Magazine, August 23, 1941.

'Around A World At War', in *Collier's* Magazine, November 22, 1941.

'Thunder Over The Pacific', in *Collier's* Magazine, January 3, 1942.

Goldberg, Vicki, *Margaret Bourke-White*, New York: Harper and Row, 1986.

Goodman, Jack, *While You Were Gone*, New York: Simon and Schuster, 1946.

Graebner, Walter, 'One Year of War In Britain', in *Life*, New York, September 30, 1940.

'A Bad Bombing In Bloomsbury' (with Allan Michie), in *Life*, New York, September 30, 1940.

Gramling, Oliver, *A.P: The Story of Associated Press*, New York: Farrar and Rinehart, 1940.

Free Men Are Fighting, New York: Farrar and Rinehart, 1942.

Gray, Bernard, *War Reporter*, London: Robert Hale, 1942.

Greene, Sir Hugh (with Thomas Barman), 'Warsaw, September, 1939', in *The Listener*, London: July 24, 1969.

Groth, John, *Studio: Europe*, New York: Vanguard Press, 1945.

Gudme, Sten, *Denmark: Hitler's Model Protectorate*, London: Victor Gollancz, 1942.

Gunther, John, *D-Day*, London: Hamish Hamilton, 1944.

Haldane, Charlotte, *Russian Newsreel*, London: Secker and Warburg, 1942.

Hanley, Gerald, *Monsoon Victory*, London: William Collins, 1946.

Hawkins, Desmond (with Donald Boyd) (ed.), *B.B.C. War Report*, London: Oxford University Press, 1946.

Heiskell, Andrew, 'Attempt To Photograph Paris', in *Life* Magazine, New York, July 15, 1940.

Hemingway, Ernest, *By-Line: Ernest Hemingway*, (ed. William White), New York: Bantam Books, 1968.

Hemingway, Mary Welsh, *How it Was*, London: Weidenfeld and Nicolson, 1977.

Hersey, John, *Men on Bataan*, New York: Alfred A. Knopf, 1943.

Higgins, Marguerite, *News Is A Singular Thing*, New York: Doubleday, Doran, 1955.

Hill, Russell, *Desert War, 1941–1942*, London: Jarrolds, 1943.

Desert Conquest, London: Jarrolds, 1944.

Struggle for Germany, London: Victor Gollanz, 1947.

History In The Writing, New York: Duell, Sloan and Pearce, 1945. Anonymous.

Hobson, Harold (with Phillip Knightley and Leonard Russell), *The Pearl of Days: An Intimate Memoir of The Sunday Times*, London: Hamish Hamilton, 1972.

Hohenburg, John, *Foreign Correspondence*, New York: Columbia University Press, 1964.

Hollingworth, Clare, *The Three-Weeks War in Poland*, London: Duckworth, 1940.

There's a German Just Behind Me, London: The Right Book Club, 1943.

Huss, Pierre J., *Heil! And Farewell*, London: Herbert Jenkins, 1943.

Ingersoll, Ralph, *Covering All Fronts*, London: John Lane, The Bodley Head, 1942.

Report on England, London: John Lane, The Bodley Head, 1941.

Jacob, Alaric, *A Traveller's War*, London: William Collins, 1944.

A Window in Moscow, London: William Collins, 1946.

Jenkins, Simon, *The Market For Glory: Fleet Street Ownership in the 20th Century*, London: Faber and Faber, 1986.

Johnston, Denis, *Nine Rivers From Jordan*, London: Derek Verschoyle, 1953.

Jones, Sir Roderick, *A Life in Reuters*, London: Hodder and Stoughton, 1951.

Jordan, Philip, *Russian Glory*, London: Cresset Press, 1942.

Jordan's Tunis Diary, London: William Collins, 1943.

Kendrick, Alexander, *Prime Time*, London: J. M. Dent, 1970.

Kerr, Walter, *The Russian Army*, London: Victor Gollancz, 1944.

Keun, Odette, *And Hell Followed*, London: Constable, 1942.

Kirkpatrick, Helen P., *Under The British Umbrella*, New York: Charles Scribner, 1939.

Kluger, Richard, *The Paper: The Life and Death of The New York Herald Tribune*, New York: Alfred A. Knopf, 1986.

Knickerbocker, H. R., *Is Tomorrow Hitler's?*, New York: Reynal and Hitchcock, 1941.

Knightley, Phillip, *The First Casualty*, London: André Deutsch, 1975.

Koop, Theodore A., *Weapon of Silence*, Chicago: University of Chicago Press, 1946.

Lang, Will, 'Lucian King Truscott Jr', in *Life* Magazine, New York, October 2, 1944.

'Colonel Abe', in *Life* Magazine, New York, April 23, 1945.

Laurence, William L., *Dawn Over Zero*, London: The Museum Press, 1947.

Lee, Clark, *They Call It Pacific*, London: John Long, 1943.

One Last Look Around, New York: Duell, Sloan and Pearce, 1947.

Legg, Frank, *War Correspondent*, London: Angus and Robertson, 1965.

Lesueur, Larry, *Twelve Months That Changed The World*, London: George G. Harrap, 1944.

'Unforgettable Ed Murrow', in the *Reader's Digest*, London, September 1970.

Liebling, A. J., *The Road Back To Paris*, London: Michael Joseph, 1944.

'Pyle Set The Style', in the *New Yorker*, September 2, 1950.

Lochner, Louis P., 'Germans Marched Into a Dead Paris', in *Life* Magazine, New York, July 8, 1940.

What About Germany?, London: Hodder and Stoughton, 1943.

Always The Unexpected, New York: The Macmillan Co., 1956.

Lundberg, Ferdinand, *Imperial Hearst*, New York: The Modern Library, 1937.

McDonald, Iverach, *The History of The Times, Vol V, Struggles In War And Peace, 1939 – 1966*, London: Times Books, 1984.

McLaine, Ian, *Ministry of Morale*, London: George Allen and Unwin, 1979.

McMillan, Richard, *Mediterranean Assignment*, New York: Doubleday, Doran, 1943.

Rendezvous With Rommel, London: Jarrolds, 1943.

Twenty Angels Over Rome, London: Jarrolds, 1945.

Miracle Before Berlin, London: Hutchinson, 1946.

Maitland, Patrick, *European Dateline*, London: The Quality Press, 1946.

Mangan, Sherry, 'Paris Under The Swastika', in *Life* Magazine, New York, September 16, 1940.

Marchant, Hilde, *Women and Children Last*, London: Victor Gollancz, 1941.

Mark, Jeffrey, 'Mr Churchill Runs the War', in *Life* Magazine, New York, December 9, 1940.

Marshall, Howard, *Over To Tunis*, London: Eyre and Spottiswoode, 1943.

Massock, Richard, *Italy From Within*, London: Macmillan, 1943.

Mathews, Joseph J., *Reporting The Wars*, Minneapolis: University of Minnesota Press, 1957.

Matthews, Herbert L., *The Education Of A Correspondent*, New York: Harcourt, Brace, 1946.

The Britain We Saw, London: Victor Gollancz, 1950.

Mauldin, Bill, *Up Front*, Cleveland: The World Publishing Co., 1946.

Miall, Leonard (ed.), *Richard Dimbleby, Broadcaster*, London: British Broadcasting Corporation, 1966.

Michie, Allan A., 'Ernie Bevin, Britain's Labor Boss', in *Life* Magazine, New York, November 11, 1940.

Retreat To Victory, London: George Allen and Unwin, 1942.

Honour For All, London: George Allen and Unwin, 1946.

The Invasion of Europe, London: George Allen and Unwin, 1965.

Miller, Lee, *The Story of Ernie Pyle*, New York: The Viking Press, 1950.

Miller, Webb, *I Found No Peace*, London: Victor Gollancz, 1937.

Moats, Alice Leone, 'Russians Are Like That', in *Collier's* Magazine, New York, July 14, 1941.

'Courage To Burn', in *Collier's* Magazine, New York, September 27, 1941.

Monks, Noel, *Eyewitness*, London: Frederick Muller, 1956.

Moorehead, Alan, *African Trilogy*, London: Hamish Hamilton, 1944.

Eclipse, London: Hamish Hamilton, 1945.

A Late Education, London: Hamish Hamilton, 1970.

Morris, Joe-Alex, *Deadline Every Minute*, New York: Doubleday, Doran, 1957.

Morrison, Chester, 'Complete, Absolute Victory!', in *Collier's*, New York, January 9, 1943.

Morrison, Ian, *Malayan Postcript*, London: Faber and Faber, 1942.

This War Against Japan, London: Faber and Faber, 1943.

Mosley, Leonard, *Down Stream*, London: Michael Joseph, 1939.

Report From Germany, London: Victor Gollancz, 1945.

Muir, Hugh, *European Junction*, London: George G. Harrap, 1942.

Munro, Ross, *Gauntlet to Overlord*, Toronto: The Macmillan Company of Canada, 1945.

Murrow, Edward R., *This Is London*, London: Cassell, 1941.

In Search of Light, New York: Alfred A. Knopf, 1967.

Mydans, Carl, *More Than Meets The Eye*, New York: Harper and Bros., 1959.

Noble, Ronnie, *Shoot First!*, London: George G. Harrap, 1955.

Norris, Frank, 'Free France, Poor and Paralysed, Waits For Germany To Finish War', in *Life* Magazine, New York, September 16, 1940.

Oeschner, Fred (ed.), *This Is The Enemy*, London: William Heinemann, 1943.

Oldfield, Barney, *Never A Shot In Anger*, New York: Duell, Sloan and Pearce, 1956.

Packard, Reynolds and Eleanor, *Balcony Empire*, London: Chatto and Windus, 1943.

Padev, Michael, *Escape From The Balkans*, London: Cassell, 1943.

Page, Bruce (with David Leitch and Phillip Knightley), *Philby: The Spy Who Betrayed A Generation*, London: André Deutsch, 1968.

Paine, Ralph Delahaye, Jr. 'France Collapsed From Internal Decay', in *Life* Magazine, New York, July 8, 1940.

Panter-Downes, Molly, *London War Notes*, London: Longman's, 1972.

Parker, Ralph, *Moscow Correspondent*, London: Frederick Muller, 1949.

Parker, Robert, *H.Q. Budapest*, New York: Farrar and Rinehart, 1944.

Paul, Oscar, *Farewell France*, London: Victor Gollancz, 1941.

Penrose, Antony, *The Lives of Lee Miller*, London: Thames and Hudson, 1985.

Pocock, Tom, *1945: The Dawn Came Up Like Thunder*, London: William Collins, 1983.

Prebble, John, 'Britain's Fabulous Fleet Street', in *Holiday* Magazine, Philadelphia, June, 1957.

Pyle, Ernie, *Ernie's War: The Best of Ernie Pyle's World War Two Dispatches* (ed. David Nichols), New York: Random House, 1986.

Reyburn, Wallace, *Rehearsal For Invasion*, London: George G. Harrap, 1943.

Reynolds, Quentin, *The Wounded Don't Cry*, London: Cassell, 1941.
A London Diary, New York: Random House, 1941.
Only The Stars Are Neutral, London: Cassell, 1942,
Dress Rehearsal, Sydney, NSW: Angus and Robertson, 1943.
The Curtain Rises, London: Cassell, 1944.
By Quentin Reynolds, London: Heinemann, 1964.

Robertson, Ben, *I Saw England*, London: Jarrolds, 1941.

Robertson, Terence, *Dieppe: The Shame And The Glory*, London: Hutchinson, 1963.

Rodger, George, *Desert Journey*, London: The Cresset Press, 1944.

Ross, Allan, *Colours of War*, London: Jonathan Cape, 1983.

Ryan, Cornelius, *The Longest Day*, London: Victor Gollancz, 1960.
A Bridge Too Far, London: Hamish Hamilton, 1974.

St. John, Robert, *From The Land of Silent People*, London: George G. Harrap, 1942.
Foreign Correspondent, London: Hutchinson, 1960.

Salter, Cedric, *Flight From Poland*, London: Faber and Faber, 1940.

Schultz, Sigrid, *Germany Will Try It Again*, New York: Reynal and Hitchcock, 1944.

Sevareid, Eric, *Not So Wild A Dream*, New York: Alfred A. Knopf, 1946.

Shapiro, Lionel, *They Left The Back Door Open*, London: Jarrolds, 1945.

Sheean, Vincent, *Between The Thunder And the Sun*, London: Macmillan, 1943.
This House Against This House, London: Macmillan, 1947.

Shirer, William L. *Berlin Diary*, London: Hamish Hamilton, 1941.
End of A Berlin Diary, London: Hamish Hamilton, 1947.
20th Century Journey: A Memoir of A Life and The Times, Vol II, The Nightmare Years, Toronto: Bantam Books, 1984.

Smedley, Agnes, *The Battle Hymn of China*, New York: Alfred A. Knopf, 1943.

Smith, Howard K., *Last Train From Berlin*, London: The Cresset Press, 1942.

Smith, W. R. Franklin, *Edward R. Murrow: The War Years*, Kalamazoo, Mich: New Issues Press, 1978.

Snow, Edgar, *Battle For Asia*, New York, Random House, 1941.

Snyder, Louis Lee (with Richard Morris), *A Treasury of Great Reporting*, New York: Simon and Schuster, 1949.

Masterpieces of War Reporting (ed.), New York: Messner, 1962.

Soong, Norman, 'Flight From Hong King', in *Collier's* Magazine, New York, April 18, 1942.

Speck, Hugo, 'The Scorched Red Earth', in *Collier's* Magazine, New York, December 6, 1941.

Sperber, A. M., *Murrow: His Life and Times*, New York: Freundlich, 1986.

Stead, Ronald, 'U.S - Russian "Old Friends" Swarm Gaily About Torgau' in *The Christian Science Monitor*, Boston, April 28, 1945.

Steinbeck, John, *Once There Was A War*, London: William Heinemann, 1959.

Storey, Graham, *Reuters' Century, 1851–1951*, London: Max Parrish, 1951.

Stowe, Leland, 'A Few Thousand Nazis Seized Norway', in *Life* Magazine, New York, May 10, 1940.

No Other Road To Freedom, London: Faber and Faber, 1942.

Stursberg, Peter, *Journey Into Victory*, London: George G. Harrap, 1944.

Sulzberger, C. L., *A Long Row Of Candles*, London: Macdonald, 1969.

Swanberg, W. A., *Citizen Hearst*, London: Longman's 1962.

Luce and His Empire, New York: Scribner's, 1972.

Talbot, Godfrey, *Speaking From The Desert*, London: Hutchinson, 1944.

Talese, Gay, *The Kingdom and The Power*, London: Caldar and Boyars, 1971.

Tebbel, John, *An American Dynasty*, New York: Doubleday, Doran 1947.

The Life and Good Times of William Randolph Hearst, London: Victor Gollancz, 1953.

Thomas, Hugh, *The Spanish Civil War*, New York: Harper Bros., 1961.

Thompson, R. W., *Men Under Fire*, London: Macdonald, 1946.

Thomson, Rear-Admiral George, *Blue Pencil Admiral*, London: Sampson Low, Marston, 1947.

Tolischus, Otto D., *Tokyo Record*, London: Hamish Hamilton, 1943.

Tregaskis, Richard, *Guadalcanal Diary*, New York; Random House, 1943.

Tuchman, Barbara, *Sand Against The Wind: Stilwell and The American Experience in China*, London: Macmillan, 1970.

Vaughan-Thomas, Wynford, *Anzio*, London: Longmans, 1961.

'Richard Dimbleby: My Most Unforgettable Character', in the *Reader's Digest*, London, January, 1967.

'Vern Haugland's Adventure: Jungle, Hunger, Delirium', in *Newsweek*, New York, October 12, 1942.

Waldrop, Frank, *McCormick of Chicago*, Englewood Cliffs, N.J.: Prentice-Hall, 1966.

Walker, David, *Death At My Heels*, London: Chapman and Hall, 1942.

Walker, Gordon, 'The Art of War In The Jungle', in the *Christian Science Monitor*, Boston, June 12, 1943.

    'Jungle Man – Comrade In Arms', in the *Christian Science Monitor*, October 30, 1943.

Walker, Patrick, *The Lid Lifts*, London: Victor Gollancz, 1945.

Ward, Edward, *Dispatches From Finland*, London: John Lane, The Bodley Head, 1940.

    Give Me Air, London: John Lane, The Bodley Head, 1946.

    I've Lived Like A Lord, London: Michael Joseph, 1971.

Wason, Betty, *Miracle in Hellas*, London: Museum Press, 1943.

Waterfield, Gordon, *What Happened to France*, London: John Murray, 1940.

Wertenbaker, Charles Christian, 'Omar Nelson Bradley', in *Life* Magazine, New York, June 5, 1944.

    'The Big Days', in *Life* Magazine, June 19, 1944.

    'The Victory of the Rhine', in *Life* Magazine, April 16, 1945.

    'Surrender at Reims', in *Life* Magazine, May 21, 1945.

    Invasion!, New York: D. Appleton-Century Co., 1944.

Wertenbaker, Lael Tucker, *Death Of A Man*, London: William Heinemann, 1957.

Werth, Alexander, *The Last Days of Paris*, London: Hamish Hamilton, 1941.

    Moscow, '41, London: Hamish Hamilton, 1942.

    Russia At War, 1941–1945, London: Barrie and Rockcliff, 1964.

    France: 1940 – 1945, London: Robert Hale, 1956.

    What We Saw in Germany: With the Red Army To Berlin, by Thirteen Leading Soviet War Correspondents, London: 'Soviet News', 1945.

White, Leigh, *The Long Balkan Night*, New York: Scribner's, 1944.

White, Theodore H. (with Annalee Jacoby), *Thunder Out of China*, London: Victor Gollancz, 1947.

White, William L. 'Atlantic Crossing on U.S. Destroyer', in *Life* Magazine, New York, December 2, 1940.

Wilmot, Chester, *Tobruk*, London: Angus and Robertson, 1944.

Winkler, John, *W. R. Hearst: An American Phenomenon*, London: Jonathan Cape, 1928.

Wiskemann, Elizabeth, *A Great Swiss Newspaper: The Story of the Neue Zürcher Zeitung*, London: Oxford University Press, 1959.

Wolfert, Ira, *Battle For The Solomons*, Boston: Houghton Mifflin, 1943.

Woodhouse, Adrian, 'Luce Talk' in the *Sunday Telegraph* Magazine, London: November 9, 1986.

Woodward, David, *Front Line and Front Page*, London: Eyre and Spottiswoode, 1943.

Wyand, Paul, *Useless If Delayed*, London: George G. Harrap, 1959.

Yindrich, Jan, *Fortress Tobruk*, London: Ernest Benn, 1951.

Young, Gordon, *Outposts of War*, London: Hodder and Stoughton, 1941.
  Outposts of Victory, London: Hodder and Stoughton, 1943.
  Outposts of Peace, London: Hodder and Stoughton, 1945.

Index

Wertenbaker, Charles
Christian, 152, 158, 165–6,
192–3
Werth, Alexander: on
phoney war, 12; on Allied
defeats in West, 34, 36; on
cost of cables in France,
40; in USSR, 85–6, 91, 93;
on Lozovsky, 96
Wesel, 185–6
West Virginia, USS, 118
West Wall (Siegfried Line),
179
Western Desert: quiet in, 44,
46; Wavell's advance in,
64–7; Rommel in, 70; as
British priority, 102–3;

warfare in, 106; British
retreat, 131; *see also*
Alamein, El
Western Desert Light
Flotilla, 105
Western Front, 10
Western Union, 2
Weygand, General Maxime,
35
Wheeler, John, 124
White, Leigh, 73, 75
White, Theodore H., 110
White, William L., 19
Williams, Douglas, 33
Willicombe, Joseph, 164
Wilson, Captain Jack, 164
Winant, John Gilbert, 141

Wolfert, Ira, 126, 174
Wood, Alan, 179
Woodward, David, 34, 70–1
Wyand, Paul, 156, 186, 191–
192

Yalta Conference, 190
Yarbrough, Tom, 111
Yindrich, Jan, 104
Young, Gordon, 21
Young, Sir Mark, 119
Yugoslavia, 73, 74; *see also*
Belgrade

Zaleszczyki (Poland), 7
Zhukov, Marshal Georgi,
127, 165